On the
Commodity Trail

On the Commodity Trail

The Journey of a Bargain Store
Product from East to West

Alison Hulme

Bloomsbury Academic
An imprint of Bloomsbury Publishing Plc

B L O O M S B U R Y
LONDON • NEW DELHI • NEW YORK • SYDNEY

Bloomsbury Academic

An imprint of Bloomsbury Publishing Plc

50 Bedford Square	1385 Broadway
London	New York
WC1B 3DP	NY 10018
UK	USA

www.bloomsbury.com

BLOOMSBURY and the Diana logo are trademarks of Bloomsbury Publishing Plc

First published 2015

© Alison Hulme, 2015

Alison Hulme has asserted her right under the Copyright, Designs and Patents Act, 1988, to be identified as Author of this work.

British Library Cataloguing-in-Publication Data
A catalogue record for this book is available from the British Library.

ISBN: HB: 978-1-47257-286-8
PB: 978-1-47257-285-1
ePDF: 978-1-47257-287-5
ePub: 978-1-47257-288-2

Library of Congress Cataloging-in-Publication Data
A catalog record for this book is available from the Library of Congress.

Typeset by Deanta Global Publishing Services, Chennai, India
Printed and bound in Great Britain

In memory of my father

Ken Hulme

(1938–2014)

Writer, singer, teacher, marathon runner,
optimist and great eccentric.

Contents

4   The Bargain Store: Buying and Selling in the West's Spaces of 'Cheap'   85

Conclusion ... and Back to the Dump?   125

List of Illustrations

Glossary

CCP	Chinese Communist Party
FDI	Foreign Direct Investment
IPR	Intellectual Property Rights
LA	Los Angeles
MMM	Modern Marketing Methods
PRC	People's Republic of China
RNB	Renmenbi (the Chinese currency)
SEZ	Special Economic Zone
SOE	State-Owned Enterprise
TVE	Town and Village Enterprise
UK	United Kingdom
US	United States
USP	Unique Selling Point
YRD	Yangtze River Delta

Acknowledgements

My deep thanks go to Michael Dutton, John Hutnyk and Geir Sigurðsson, whose scholarship and advice have been a continual source of inspiration and encouragement.

My heartfelt appreciation also goes to Mark, Imrun, Sandra, Theo and my wonderful mother – June – whose friendship, love and support means everything.

Funding for much of the research carried out in this book came from the Arts and Humanities Research Council of the UK. My thanks go to them.

Thanks also to all those who agreed to share their experiences with me.

Preface

The inspiration for this book came from a casual conversation about pound stores in a pub in London's New Cross. I was, at the time, living just down the road in Catford and, surviving on a tiny income myself, was no stranger to the local bargain stores. As I recall, the conversation concerned Walter Benjamin's collected thoughts on the shopping arcades of Paris, specifically the ways in which he tended to describe the array of commodities on offer in a way that conjured a kind of chaotic dreamscape of darkened corners and half-seen glimpses of shiny curios. Totally flippantly (this was after all a social meeting over a pint), I laughingly suggested it might be an idea to do a kind of Arcades Project of pound stores, adding that 'the problem' with Benjamin's project was that it focused on the bijou objects of bourgeois Paris. 'What about an Arcades Project for the working class?' I asked, half tongue-in-cheek it should be said. It was a throwaway comment. Two hours and six beer mats of scribbled thoughts later, it was a book that had to be written.

Since Benjamin's day, thinking and writing about objects has become a micro-discipline in its own right. It is no longer the domain of the flâneur wandering through spaces of consumption and pondering on the meanings of their contents (albeit with great analytical flair); it has become an exercise in tracing the paths of things through time and space in the light of a, first colonizing, and now globalizing world. I discovered that what I would become in writing this book was a 'thing-follower', and that I would be following in the footsteps of other great thing-following studies such as Sidney Mintz's (1986) classic exploration of the journey of sugar, and more recently, Pietra Rivoli's (2006) T-shirts, Caroline Knowles' (2009) flip-flops and Ian Cook and Michelle Harrison's (2007) hot pepper sauces. My thing-following would track low-end commodities from factories in China to bargain stores in the West.

All of the above writers had taken Arjun Appadurai's call to 'follow the thing' head-on, in an attempt to understand the 'meanings inscribed in their forms, their uses, their trajectories' (Appadurai 1986: 5). Teamed with George Marcus's (1995) call to engage in multi-sited fieldwork, involving oneself in ethnographies in which commodities and their biographies are the organizing principles, this made for a vibrant new governing principle of 'doing Anthropology'. It also had the added benefit of tackling British Anthropology's age-old guilt in regard to its colonialist past, as allowing the commodity's trajectory to determine 'field sites' broke with more 'traditional' modes of anthropological enquiry in which so-called 'communities' were studied as bounded entities. It disenabled the accusation that anthropology continued to choose to go 'over there' and look at 'those exotic people' who live so differently from 'us'. Finally, the method was given a political imperative by taking on David Harvey's (1990) concern with allowing the thing to reveal everyday exploitations and reliance upon unseen others across the globe. This was part of a broad attempt on the part of Harvey to 'defetishize' the product by exposing its making. Such defetishizing projects have certainly had an impact – many keen ethical consumers quote Harvey as an influence. Personally, I felt (and still do feel) that merely shopping *differently* is a rather weak version of the outcomes Harvey's thought could potentially lead to and wanted to apply his theory in a way that did not simply berate terrible working conditions and profiteering practices, but tried to place a commodity chain within a wider vision of spaces and operations globally.

Despite the obvious common nature of our projects, the things I was following seemed to be part of commodity chains that did not display the same classic followability as my fellow thing-followers. The more I followed them, the more I found that the chains, just like the objects they produced, were somehow mutable and disposable. For example, while many of the key places along the chains were very established and historically ensconced in the chain (e.g. container ports, shipping routes, freight train lines), others seemed to be in constant flux. Areas of certain cities have suddenly and quickly become collection and sorting areas for raw materials; certain high streets have suddenly gained various bargain stores (especially since the recession hit); and new places of production are cropping up all the time. This mutability both leads to, and is a result of, the spontaneity of the players along the chain – waste pedlars who return to rural provinces, factory owners who switch production, bargain store owners who order stock from a variety of manufacturers and consumers who keep a tactical eye out for the 'genuine' bargains. In other words, constant *rupture* was playing a key part in the 'flow' of the commodity chains I was following, and the trajectory of the commodity was an unreliable and fretful journey in which breakages occurred, repositionings were *forced* and collateral damage was integral. Although, without doubt, elements of these chains had deep historical routes heading back to the days of the Silk Road, in their twenty-first-century version they were most definitely symptomatic of a fragmented and constantly shifting just-in-time globalized economy. The low-end chain's 'flow' was made up of numerous micro psycho-social, geographical and economic ruptures, and its form of globalization was far from the slowly spreading homogenous ink stain that 'flat world-ers' would have us believe. Rather, it was a phenomenon strengthened by constant rupture.

As a result, it quickly became apparent too, that many of the usual ways of talking about commodity chains simply would not do when it came to the low-end commodity. The usual rhetoric of Global Commodity Chain (GCC) analysis accepted the polarizing of production and consumption, and while I recognized that certain places along the low-end commodity chain were chiefly consuming or producing, the operations of the chain as a whole saw a blurring of the boundaries between the two. This was especially the case as domestic policies began to encourage the Chinese to consume more, in order that the amount of production required would not decrease, and economic growth in China could continue.

Furthermore, this production/consumption binary tended to sit alongside others, such as 'core' and 'periphery'. Core/peripheral to what, who, when? GCC's reliance upon the paradigms set up by World Systems Theory (Wallerstein 1974; 1993) did not sit well with me, or indeed with what I was learning about the low-end commodity chain. The assumptions regarding 'core' and 'periphery' seemed increasingly problematic as part of a skewed Western discourse, which the emergence of new non-Western hub cities – Sao Paolo, Mumbai, Shanghai – belies. But also, within the low-end commodity chain, it is not possible to map 'core' to 'consumption' and 'periphery' to 'production' in any straightforward manner. In addition, I felt that the simplistic equating of profit to power missed many of the crucial nuances and tactics of the low-end commodity chain. GCC had often been usefully utilized as a way of berating the West for scooping off excess profit along the commodity chain, creating huge disparities between 'periphery' and 'core'/'producing nation' and 'consuming nation', but it had begun to simplistically cast 'producers' as the geographically peripheral binary opposite of consumers.

GCC analysis was also caught up on tracking (financial) value, usually finding that value was added as a commodity journeyed from the place of its manufacture to the place of its consumption. It had little to say about the on-the-ground effects of these profits, however, and how they may have drastically different influences in different places irrespective of their financial value. I could not escape a nagging desire to dig into the ways in which the key places the low-end commodity passed through worked, how those who lived there survived and how the objects they made or consumed affected the ways in which they thought and behaved.

So, I began making contacts on wholesaler websites and talking to store owners and shoppers. I had nominally picked a dozen or so objects from bargain stores and thought the best way to go about following them was to trace them back to their roots in China. But the constant ruptures within the chain got in my way. The more specific my thing-following attempted to become, the less the specific elements seemed to matter. So what if I could find the actual factory that made the plastic Buddhas (incidentally, I did); by next month that factory would have shifted production to something else and a neighbouring factory would have bought their equipment, so now *they* will be making the plastic Buddhas. It became clear that not only did it not matter which factory made the product at any one time, as it did not change the story, but also a more telling story was the one which explained *why* it did not matter. In other words, what was it about the low-end commodity chain that made it so changeable, so spontaneous, (or perhaps volatile?), so fundamentally unfollowable? What were the *characteristic features* of the chain? This story had much more to say.

My thing-following became an exercise in tracing the 'typical' low-end commodity chain – the global path which sees the greatest flow of these items. I was attempting to examine the features of this chain as *paradigmatic* of certain forms of capitalism. Thing-following, for me, had suddenly got bigger, and yet had attached itself more determinedly to the micro-mechanisms of everyday life. I toyed with words to describe the chain's features and how they operated and considered how these related to everyday life in the places along the chain. I began to find real links – cultures within cultures that were creative of, and created by, this 'typical journey' chain and its paradigmatic features. I also began to realize that what these features, or characteristics, of the low-end commodity chain meant, was that players along the chain were forced to continually find new ways and means to operate. They had to be tacticians. In fact, I thought, it is these tactics of its players that make the low-end commodity chain the great survivor of capitalism. They give it a logic of its own – the logic of the bargain.

Introduction
Eight Bargain Store Commodities and their Journeys

The journey of the cheapest of commodities, from factory to front room, could almost be seen as a classic story of our times – a modern morality tale for the age of austerity. It is a strange austerity this one, and unlike other ages of austerity that have gone before it. It is not, for example, the hopeful make-do-and-mend austerity of the post-war years. Neither is it the power-cut punctuated, grey demise of the 1970s. Rather, it is an austerity in which the cheap functions not in its own right, but to facilitate the continuation of patterns from past eras – certain levels of consumption, at certain paces, maintaining a psychology of conspicuous consumption, but that now emphasizes quantity rather than quality, and the ability to waste without concern. It is an austerity that relies upon a certain speed of transaction, but which is underlaid by older, clunkier mechanisms which, were they more visible, would appear violently and perhaps ridiculously out of place in the midst of our mouse-clicking, PIN-entering, lightness of being.

The low-end commodity is the extremity of an age in which consumption is more entwined with the socio-economics of life than ever before. It represents what society now sees as the very least, achievable by all, a great democracy of consumption, whilst simultaneously implicating in the most devastating way the chasing of growth through smaller and smaller profits per item. So few pence profit – so many commodities needing to be sold – and disposed of – and re-consumed. There is a filling up of spaces with small things, a creating of ever-faster commodity chains that begin to chase their own tails becoming commodity circles. This filling up sees a kind of miniaturization of the consumption process. It becomes broken into smaller pieces (things become smaller and more plentiful), but also it becomes psychologically minimized (in part as a result of being normalized), a kind of bottom line at which everyone can join in. This is the logic of the bargain.

This book is the story of a low-end commodity's journey from its beginning as raw material on a Chinese rubbish dump to factories, international trade hubs, state-of-the-art distribution networks, business-to-business websites, overflowing high-street stores and finally to the home of the consumer. It is an actual journey, the most typical geographic trajectory of a low-end product; but it also serves as a metaphor for more overarching changes in the logic of both consumption and production. This trajectory is used to uncover the operations of the places a typical low-end commodity passes through and indeed the ways in which such places are often created *as a result of* the commodity's presence (or anticipated presence). I learnt about it through talking to those whose everyday lives were affected, sometimes governed, by it – manufacturers, wholesalers, waste pedlars, shippers, shoppers, store managers. Again and again the same place names cropped up, and the same processes.

The journey of the low-end commodity begins, and indeed often ends, in places of waste; places such as the pedlars quarters within large Chinese cities, or the so-called 'dump towns' which have emerged along the main manufacturing areas of the Pearl and Yangtze River deltas. It is here that private individuals or small recycling 'factories' collect and sort through mountains of rubbish, separating according to material and classifying according to value, in preparation for sale to manufacturers. This waste, some of it domestic, some of it shipped in from the West, is melted down and formed into small pellets, which in their turn are melted and moulded to form the basis of a new commodity.

From these sites of waste, the journey takes us into the heart of the Yangtze River delta, to the 'commodity city' of Yiwu – the place with the highest concentration of small commodities on the planet. Here, our low-end commodity is displayed alongside others in a three-metre square stall, situated on a seemingly never-ending aisle of identical stalls on the second floor of an immense wholesale market. Sometimes its virtual counterpart, like a spectral version of itself, is simultaneously displayed on alibaba.com – a business-to-business website which directly connects wholesale buyers to Chinese manufacturers. Alibaba.com is the highly successful brainchild of celebrity businessman Jack Ma – an energetic *tour de force* from rural Sichuan province who has become the Alan Sugar of China.

From the markets of Yiwu, the low-end commodity begins its long journey from East to West, heading out via the port of Shanghai, to key arrival points in Europe or the United States – Los Angeles, Rotterdam, Felixstowe. These journeys are precarious. Despite the implementation of highly sophisticated technology to plan packing and loading, navigating and arrivals, there are still many risks associated with container shipping. Storms and pirates do not only exist in romantic tales of past seafaring adventures. Spillages and blackmail are the untold side of this hyper-technological story. There are, it seems, more equivalences between the perilous journeys of the nineteenth-century tea clippers and those of the twenty-first-century commodity arks than might be expected.

Having reached its country of destination in the West, the commodity is transferred via freight train to wholesale storage units on the outskirts of major cities and, eventually, to the bargain stores on the high street. Once purchased, its life may be long, but most frequently it will find itself temporarily enjoyed, its function fulfilled, before being jettisoned. It may even find itself on a ship full of waste heading back to China to begin its process all over again. This is the life cycle of the bargain store commodity. Along its journey it has provided the manufacturer with around a tenth of its retail price in profit and the retailer with around a quarter of its retail price in profit, a squeeze which becomes all the more strangling under the conditions of global recession.

So, the journey is mapped, its key sites identified, its players introduced. Yet the stories attached to the trajectories of our bargain store commodities are multiple and contain a plurality of perspectives. There are the micro stories, laid before us in a kind of Perecquian[1] inventory; simultaneous events in distanced places, as the enactment of chaos theory par excellence:

> A peddler pushes his rickety cart, piled high with cardboard boxes, through a partially demolished quarter of Shanghai.
>
> A port employee checks the coloured rectangles on the computer screen in front of him before moving a giant crane into action to unload another container from a ship.
>
> A store owner arranges a bulk-load of plastic vases on a shelf, under a sign that says '£1 your choice'.
>
> A woman smiles as she decides upon a home for 'Gerald', the garden gnome, by the heather on her rockery.
>
> A wholesale buyer taps figures into his calculator whilst agitatedly fingering the sample mobile phone cover he has been handed.

And there are the macro stories:- China as the great manufacturing dragon, the heroic factory of the world, the impetus behind the fastest ever industrial revolution, a nation struggling with individualism whilst wholly embracing Deng's call that 'to get rich is glorious'[2]; the West heavy-handedly playing the voice of reason role, pressurizing China to 'clean up', 'behave ethically' and adopt capitalism as *we* know it, complete with 'human rights' and 'democracy', whilst proving itself desperately reliant upon 'China Price' commodities; and the mass flows of people, commodities, waste, pollution, money and ideas. By unravelling the mechanisms of the low-end commodity chain, it becomes apparent where the grounded tactics of individuals meet the strategic movements of larger systems and institutions; how the everyday politics of players involved in the bargain store product chain run contemporaneously to those of supranational and global entities in these early stages of the twenty-first century. If late modernity (to use Fredric Jameson's term) is characterized by the desire for immediate gratification, disposability, the fragmentation of old systems and the rise of China, then the commodity chain of the bargain store product is a classic trail of our times.

We begin, in Chapter 1, at the start and end point of the commodity – the waste dump – and explore the livelihoods of waste pedlars in Shanghai. Here, the attempt is to pick apart the twin paradigms of waste and profit, proving how they are intrinsically linked. The chapter explores the tactics and spaces of Shanghai's waste and the ways in which these are being utilized by various forces in the furious race for economic growth. Chapter 2 follows the waste raw materials to the 'commodity city' of Yiwu, shadowing international wholesale buyers as they try to find profitable products and make their deals. In doing so, it looks at the 'history' of Yiwu and uncovers specific practices of risk-taking and wealth-sharing which run contrary to Western logic. In Chapter 3, we journey with the products as they head out of Yiwu and set sail for the container ports of Los Angeles, United States and Felixstowe, United Kingdom. We learn of the experiences of ship captains and dock workers and consider how they are affected by 'fast capitalism' and the sheer abundance of things. Finally in Chapter 4, the low-end product reaches the bargain stores themselves. Consumers tell of their desire for 'spontaneity' and 'freedom' and the ways in which they relate to the concept of 'the bargain'. The bargain store product is considered as part of practices which serve to (re)create the inherent contradictions of the Western consumer and in the light of theories of the object and its fetishization. Throughout this journey, it becomes clearer that there is a 'logic' (illogic?) to the bargain store chain and that this is perhaps more indicative of our times than we realize – the logic of the bargain emerges as a powerful social force.

It should be noted that throughout, the term 'bargain store' is used to refer to any store that stocks 1 £/$/€ items, even if it also happens to stock slightly more expensive products. The story follows eight specific trinkets; those that appeared the most culturally poignant to me amongst the hundreds I became aware of during the course of this research. Each of these eight commodities retailed at $1/£1/€1. In some cases I met the consumer of the product first through my shopping trips and determined to trace its path. In others, I saw the commodity in the Chinese markets and recognized it as something I had seen in bargain stores. Regardless, all eight products could be traced from China to bargain stores in the West in recent years. From so many potential candidates, the eight I chose were: a pet gravestone, a pregnancy test, a garden gnome, a plastic bonsai, a model Buddha, plastic flowers, a Chinoiserie vase and a ship-in-a-bottle.

The story of the low-end trinket is the story of how the simplest and cheapest of commodities creates and changes cultures, enforces specific ways of surviving and affects geopolitical relations across the globe. Its journey uncovers places ranging from global showpieces of capitalism to the hidden raw edges of it; players ranging from global entrepreneurs to dump-dwellers. Uncovering these places and people brings to light new ways of operating and surviving through new tactical manoeuvres. We will begin at the place where our low-end commodity starts and sometimes ends its life – on the rubbish dump.

1

The Dump – Shanghai and Tianjin as Graveyards and Birthplaces of Commodities

i) The Waste Pedlars of Shanghai

The taxi driver says he will not go any closer and he cannot wait long. It would be very difficult for him to explain to any one official why he is showing a Western visitor something as tourist-unfriendly as Shanghai's municipal dump. He has told me strictly 'no photo', and he still thinks I am a journalist. He looks nervy and agitated as we get closer to the site. I stare out through the dusty car window. At first there is nothing to see but a vast expanse of half-rotting matter; a decay-scape that refuses to decay. I am reminded of the strangeness of scenes in which human-made matter takes on the appearance of 'natural' phenomena, as in Jennifer Baichwal's film *Manufactured Landscapes* (2007).[1] The seagulls are unignorable even from here; up close they must be deafening. Then, as my eyes begin to focus, a small line appears in the mid-distance; a line of carefully balanced pieces of corrugated iron, attached to wooden posts with matted bits of rope, the gaps filled by bits of crate or plastic. Assemblages of waste: homes to migrant waste collectors. I roll down the window a tiny bit, just enough to know how bad the stench would be if one were in amongst it. It would be suffocating. It would be constant and thick in the air and cloying on the skin. In the far distance, a digger moves into action, offloading another giant scoopful of debris. It sends the seagulls temporarily into the air, before they eagerly resettle to pick apart the new offerings, landing gleefully upon the remnants of a soft-drink can, a doll's arm and a perished half tyre.

The diggers tolerate the waste collectors in rather the same way a horse tolerates flies. Under China's draft 'circular economy', the dump is legally obliged to separate recyclable waste from landfill. Therefore, 'employees' from 'recycling factories' (often with uniforms and some sort of official 'front') are recognized by the official contractors as they are easily visible and aid them in reaching their quota of recycled waste. However, relations with the informal, unstructured and unmeasurable independent waste collectors are often fraught. The digger drivers often cannot see them, as they have no official uniforms, and only avoid injuring them at the last minute. Even then, injuries (and possibly deaths) have occurred. The company that runs the dump openly admits that injuries have arisen from large machinery suddenly moving into action unaware of the presence of waste collectors. In addition, these groups live on the dump itself and are frequently hostile to each other due to their differing clans and the sheer competition for survival. Yet, despite the danger, they swarm around the diggers, waiting for fresh pickings.

The taxi driver says there is nothing else to see. He has lost patience. In his eyes, I either want to expose something that in his view cannot be helped or I have a disturbing taste for the disgusting. Either way, he does not like me and he has done enough to earn his money. 'We go now,' he says, and moves off slowly, searching furtively with his eyes for any sign of officialdom that may attempt to intercept us. There is none. The desolate landscape of debris falls away behind us and the stench gradually drains from the air.

Back in central Shanghai, a small footbridge, perhaps four metres wide and no longer than ten, crosses the Suzhou river creek just before the point at which it flows into the great Huangpu river that cuts through the centre of Shanghai. On one side of it lie the famous Bund with its restored colonial grandeur, and further into town the French quarter, where international bright young things seek out European wines and bemoan the lack of 'café life'. 'How can you people-watch when everyone moves so fast?' one of them asks. On the other side lie four blocks of crumbling low-rise dwellings, some of them half-demolished and forced to display their innards with a somehow disconcerting nonchalance. This is Zhabei, home to small-time traders and waste pedlars, amongst others. Ahead, in the distance, is the iconic telecom tower, the finance building with its 'bottle opener' top-piece (created during its construction to maintain its now defunct status as the world's tallest building), and the exhibition centre with its two futuristic globes sandwiching neo-Georgian splendour. Directly ahead is the reverse side of the immense Nestlé sign, a landmark clearly visible to the tourists on their river cruises. From this angle though, it is far from the same sparkling affirmation of corporate success, but rather, a dense bedraggled mass of rusting wires, desperately and pathetically securing its letters, lest they fall to a less than graceful end. It looks outwards to the profit of Shanghai's financial district – the Pudong. It ignores the waste of the pedlars. It fails to connect the two.

It is just gone 5.30 in the evening. The weak rays of Shanghai's November sun are beginning to fade. Turning left across the small footbridge, away from the Bund, a narrow street heads into the pedlars' quarter of Zhabei. The dank smell of the river is never far away. The air is heavy with dust from houses falling down and apartment blocks going up. As the dust falls it collects in swathes

Figure 1.1 The Bund from Zhabei.

along the sides of streets and in the troughs of their uneven surfaces. Ahead, a line of construction workers, about a quarter of a mile long, wends its way along Dong Changzhi road towards the docks, to start the night shift. Now and again a street vendor cries his wares. The animated chatter of sellers and workers is momentarily silenced by a loud cracking sound, as one of the food vendor's canisters explodes. He swears and tries to rescue the blackened remains as the chatter returns.

Turning left off the main drag, the road becomes a dust path, on either side of which are numerous crumbling, half-derelict houses. Some stand, half-demolished, faded bits of paintwork revealing where a shelf or a picture once hung. There are very few cars here, only the odd bicycle, and the carts of the pedlars bringing back a day's haul to be sorted and stored: aluminium from iron, plastic from paper, wood from cardboard, dust from dust. A small man, perhaps in his mid-forties, steers his teetering cart across the potholes. Its load, although seemingly precarious, is actually ingeniously packed and perfectly balanced, so as not to risk losing even one precious piece of waste. He says today has been a good day, rich pickings and laughs when I smile and say 'hao gonzuo ma?' (Good job eh?) It is not what people would call a 'good job', but, he says, it is considered useful and respectable. How long has he been doing it? I ask. About three years. He is open to talking – he has seen me before. He explains how when he first came to Shanghai he had lived on the dump for a few weeks, but it was too dangerous for him on his own. The diggers were a constant danger and the other pedlar groups viewed him with suspicion. Without any of his own family or friends to back him up he could not look out for himself and was chased away from areas where the waste worth collecting was dumped. He explains though that working there had taught him how to sort waste very quickly and how to know how valuable it was. He says he can tell by feeling a plastic bottle between his fingers for a few seconds, whether or not it is the most valuable type – 'virgin plastic' that has not yet been recycled – or whether it is already second- or third-grade plastic. These skills are now invaluable to him in picking up waste from the streets and knowing how much he should get for it at the various informal waste markets in the suburbs. Why had he come? I ask. There's more money in this than farming, he says. 'I send it all home. I will go back in a year or so, but we wanted to save some money first.'

He heads off across the stretch of open ground that separates the derelict quarter from the main road and disappears between two crumbling buildings. A group of boys crouch in the mud and play cards. A young woman tires of attempting to ride her bicycle over such uneven terrain, lazily flicking one leg over the seat to continue on foot. Six schoolchildren chase one another up an alleyway filled with rubble and disappear. Their school uniforms are spotless despite the fact that life here is built on and around waste. I look back to see the pedlar's cart weave its way across the bumpy ground. He has a self-sufficiency about him, a man set on his task regardless of his surroundings. I cannot help but think of Walter Benjamin's description of Eugene Atget's rag and bone man. The nineteenth-century waste collector and the twenty-first-century one are perhaps too easily melded into one:

> Here we have a man whose job it is to gather the day's refuse in the capital. Everything that the big city has thrown away … he catalogues and collects. He collates the annals of intemperance, the capharnaum of waste. He sorts things out and selects judiciously: he collects like a miser guarding a treasure, refuse which will assume the shape of useful or gratifying objects between the jaws of the goddess of Industry. (Benjamin 1999: 87)

Benjamin could well have been talking about the twenty-first-century waste pedlar, whose plastic bottles and scraps of metal and rubber will be melted down to a molten state, poured into moulds whose two halves will close just like 'jaws' of 'industry', opening to reveal the form of a plate, or bowl or vase, ready to be sprayed. Our 'rag and bone man' disappears into one of the many tumbling down alleyways; a 'poacher' of the day's waste disappearing into the 'cracks' of the city – to use Michel de Certeau's terms (De Certeau 1984: 36–7).

Being a tactician is not a choice according to de Certeau; rather it is the existence of someone who has no choice but to make use of opportunities or 'cracks' and 'poach' in them, because, unlike the strategist, he does not have a

Figure 1.2 The half-derelict dwellings of Zhabei.

'proper locus' (De Certeau 1984: 36–7). This lack of locus means the tactician 'takes advantage of opportunities and depends on them' as he is without any base where he can 'stockpile winnings' and 'build up his own position' – 'what he wins he cannot keep' (De Certeau 1984: 36–7). This is true for our pedlar-tactician, who has little space or security for storage, and so is forced to sell his day's haul as quickly as possible regardless of whether the time is optimal for gaining the best price. He must purge himself of his winnings, however well he may manage to hide them momentarily in one of the unnoticed chinks of Shanghai life. He is the first tactician on our journey; there will be others. He pursues his own interests as best he can while appearing to comply with a more powerful agenda (in this case, the importance of being a 'respectable' citizen doing a 'useful' job). He wears what de Certeau calls 'la perruque' (the wig) of disguise, exhibiting a conscious will to innovate, an ability to put imagination into action and a desire to avoid pitfalls and exploit availabilities, but under the guise of one playing along with wider hegemonic forces.

Another pedlar has, in a small way, managed to push the boundaries of being a tactician without proper locus. He relates how he has secured a small, secure, hidden space in a derelict building in which to store his day's haul. He looks pleased. It means that instead of having to cycle out to the markets in the suburbs every evening to sell his waste in order to clear his cart for the next day, he can decide which market to go to and when, on the basis of what he knows is selling well that week. He is still fundamentally trapped in the tactical world, as opposed to the strategic, though. He cannot change the bigger picture and the structures at play. Despite the advantage of the storage space, it is not large enough or secure enough for him to be able to stockpile even a week's worth of waste, so he must still travel to the market every few days. I ask if I can see his store-place, but (perhaps understandably) he seems disinclined, smiling awkwardly and pointing vaguely back towards a derelict building.

The advantages of stockpiling are part of the pedlars' tactical toolkit. When spaces cannot be found, material can sometimes be used to add an element of storage to waste carts. A pedlar from Shanxi province has added side walls to his cart fashioned from thick bits of cardboard and secured by bending them under weighty objects at their base and tying them around with nylon tape. Thanks to the enclosure these walls provided, he is able to pile his findings higher than if he simply had to balance them. I comment on the effectiveness of his contraption, but he smiles and shakes his head, explaining that it will only be useful today and overnight, as tomorrow the rain will come and the cardboard will become too soggy to stand straight. 'And so I will start all over again', he says. His cart has become a daily object of bricolage for him, requiring additions and adjustments if it is to function within the limits of his tactical world. He is, in Levi-Strauss's terms, a classic bricoleur, making do with what is at hand – 'a set of tools and materials which is always finite and is also heterogeneous because what it contains bears no relation to the current project' (Levi-Strauss 1966: 17). For Levi-Strauss, the bricoleur, therefore, sits in direct contrast to the engineer whose tools and materials are specifically conceived and procured for the purpose of the project (Levi-Strauss 1966: 17).

Crucially for Levi-Strauss, what this means is that the bricoleur's projects cannot be counted by counting his 'instrumental sets' (Levi-Strauss 1966: 17). However, he also suggests that, due to his narrow set of tools, effectively a 'collection of oddments left over from human endeavours', the bricoleur is inclined to remain within the constraints imposed by his civilization; whereas the engineer 'questions the universe' and 'is always trying to … go beyond the constraints imposed by a particular state of civilisation' (Levi-Strauss 1966: 19). This is rather frustrating theorizing when applied to the pedlar's form of bricolage (and indeed many other examples of bricoleurs such as squatters or amateur inventors) as it denies the bricoleur's demonstration of how he precisely *is* attempting to 'go beyond' by engaging in bricolage in the first place. Whether he manages this within the constraints experienced, and with such limited resources, is another question, but one that should not be conflated with a perceived lack of *intention*. Our pedlar-bricoleur is certainly very aware of the difficulties involved in escaping the 'constraints imposed by his civilisation', but this does not signify a lack of desire on his part, or indeed the absence of initiative to push the boundaries of that 'civilisation'. He is not an unquestioning, accepting bricoleur – he knows what he does not know; he simply has no way of gaining that knowledge.

Pushing the boundaries is, however, getting harder and riskier for the pedlars. The cracks they poach in are coming under increasing threat from the ambitions of politicians and planners determined to display that which represents the 'new' China and hide anything reminiscent of the 'chaotic' old days. Modernity, it seems, is no place for poachers. (Modernity also, of course, promises the poachers that there will be no need for poaching.) In the run-up to the 2010 Shanghai Expo for example, cracks were papered over at tremendous speed and Zhabei found itself caught in the midst of Shanghai's fervent determination to clean up and

Figure 1.3 Eugene Atget's Rag and Bone Man, 1899.

show the world its wares. The Expo had guaranteed millions of dollars of foreign direct investment (FDI) and provoked an ambitious regeneration plan on the part of the Shanghai authorities, keen to prove themselves following the success of the Beijing Olympics. As a result, Zhabei was earmarked for razing, followed by massive regeneration. Artists' impressions of the redevelopment showed Western-style mock-Tudor family homes, surrounded by trees and green areas. This was why much of Zhabei was simply being allowed to crumble. In fact, much of the ground area had already been bought by foreign companies.

The ambitions of the Expo regeneration were two-fold and explain why the 'cracks' to be cleaned were both literal and conceptual. At first glance, the Shanghai authorities appeared to be concerned with the creation of a cleaner, greener Shanghai. They emphasized speed and efficiency – fast infrastructural links, rapid information technology – and the way in which this would aid the desired shift from manufacturing to service industries. The living spaces promoted as part of the Expo vision were spacious, open, tree-lined and suggested economic security and the presence of leisure time. They were spaces for the modern Chinese family unit who had quality of life and (of course) purchasing power. The mock-Tudor houses used a well-known architectural style that provided an immediately understandable symbol of sophistication, due to its association with the West, but also with 'history' (albeit a history that did not belong in Shanghai!). This kind of knowing nod to knowledge of Western styles and history is precisely the type of thing that enables a person to be seen as having the all-important suzhi (quality of personhood), of being well-rounded in one's knowledge and experience. Most importantly, these were spaces that were easy on the eye – neat, non-industrial and asking no questions of the viewer. Space, in the run-up to the Expo, was produced in a way that provided the images necessary for both the West and the aspirational Chinese subject. Those spaces with specific practical uses but that did not fit the agenda were forced to give way to spaces that gave out strong *impressions* of success, but had little practical use. In fact, 'use' had been given a distinctly conceptual new meaning. The spaces of 'success' precisely did have a 'use value' – that of being public relations material for the convincing of foreign and domestic subjects. They were image spaces in Shanghai's quest to gain full 'world city' status. The production of these image spaces was removed as far from actual labour as was possible. The pedlars and their 'mess' had to go.

If the regeneration campaign in the run-up to the Expo was about creating image spaces as part of a literal clean-up, it was also about the cleaning away of certain cultural aspects that were seen as part and parcel of messy places. The Expo slogan 'better city, better life' became increasingly prevalent across Shanghai's billboards, complete with cartoon mascot Haibao (derived from *si hai zhi bao* – 'treasure of the sea': *hai* = sea, as in Shang-*hai*). Haibao's message to the Shanghainese was one of promoting the quality of urban existence and improving and enhancing *wenming*[2] (civilization). He was specifically created to enhance *wenming* by teaching the Shanghainese (or perhaps more to the point, Chinese from rural provinces who had come to Shanghai) to avoid doing things the 'international community' (by which China meant Europe and the United States) may find uncouth. Haibao taught the city's population not to spit, or slurp food, and always to queue. He also provided knowledge on Western cultural traditions and could be found on screens in the back of taxis conducting a quiz with questions such as 'Which European country does spaghetti traditionally come from?' and 'What is a cream tea?' To prove how easily he sat within a variety of Western cultures, Haibao appeared in different forms – there was cowboy Haibao, Christmas Haibao, tuxedo Haibao and even bagpipe-playing Haibao. It seemed it was not only the dark cracks of the city that must be cleaned up, but also the habits and minds of certain of its inhabitants.

The pedlars, with their barrows, were seen as the image of old China – antiquated, trundling, festering and subsumed in intricate networks of allegiances based on clan and favours rather than merit. Just as the Beijing pedlars were banished to the suburbs during the Olympics, so their Shanghai counterparts underwent similar restrictions during the Expo. However, because the authorities recognized that their presence is actually crucial to the cleanliness and efficacy of the city, some pedlars were given uniforms and temporary contracts. In the longer term though, following the razing of their derelict quarters, their expulsion from central Shanghai becomes increasingly permanent. In fact, half of Zhabei has now been completely razed and fenced off with the construction hoardings of the Western hotel chain that has bought the land. The billboard reads, 'for global elites the top class living platform'; in front of it a homeless man sleeps on

Figure 1.4 A 'top class living platform for global elites.'

a bench. The neighbouring part of Zhabei is now under exactly the same process of demolition as the fenced-off area had been prior to the hoardings being put up and the construction beginning. Three men use hand-held tools to gradually cut through the beams holding the exposed first floor of a house intact. It makes for strangely compelling viewing. I watch until a great concrete beam finally falls and all three men jump away and laugh sheepishly. They have helmets, but wear jeans and trainers. The beam falls into the street a few metres away from a woman who sits cooking pot-stickers in a façade-less rubble-filled once-room. She continues to cook, impassively, amongst the wreckage, with one eye out for the next client, proof that despite determined efforts to rid Shanghai of 'cracks', one or two still exist. The image space is in the ascendancy, but is not yet king.

The sense of a 'visual' with little reality behind it can be seen as linked to the economic phenomenon known as the 'Shanghai Miracle'. Huang Yasheng (and he is not alone in this) argues that the so-called 'miracle' is largely assumed and based on the visual rather than actual living conditions and quality of life (Huang 2008: 176). He blames this mirage of a miracle on the 'Shanghai model', formulated between 1985 and 1990, and in particular the development programme of 1987, which established key mechanisms intended to leapfrog Shanghai to global city status. These were, first, the internationalization of the economy, based on advanced technology and global brands and secondly, the elimination of all features considered to be 'backward' (Huang 2008: 213–4).

Although it may not have been directly intended as such, the 1987 programme was a precursor to the anti-rural bias and small-scale entrepreneurship of the 1990s. Attempts to internationalize saw all urban planning decisions centralized and the government, as a monopoly buyer, requisition vast tracts of the Pudong area (then farm land) from rural households, compensating them at below-market prices. The land-use rights were then sold to commercial property developers at market prices, and the futuristic skyscrapers of the Pudong, representing global finance, emerged, creating Shanghai's iconic skyline and securing its place as a global player. Attempts to eliminate 'backward' elements saw the closure of small, informal market activities. Again the concern was with how such places *looked*, as opposed to how healthy they were for the economic or social life of the city:

> To the urban technocrats eager to project their city as an ultra-modern metropolis, these messy marketplaces represented not income-earning opportunities for rural merchants but rather unorganized, unlicensed, and unsightly activities to be stamped out. (Huang 2008: 214)

According to Huang, what lay behind the (in his view, false) Shanghai miracle were features a-typical of what was happening in the rest of China: a heavy-handed state intervention, a blatant anti-rural bias and a liberalization which privileged

FDI whilst discriminating against indigenous capitalists. This meant that whilst GDP per capita in Shanghai made it appear rich in comparison with other large cities and rural provinces, the wealth was siphoned off in the form of government taxes and tended to be in the hands of large foreign companies or state-owned enterprises (Huang 2008: 177–8). This said, there may be some truth in an argument which suggests that certain features of Shanghai's development, such as the privileging of FDI in the face of indigenous capitalists, is simply a legacy of the colonial relations which split Shanghai into its 'concessions', and created its present business ties. Either way, the Shanghai miracle irrevocably changed the face of Shanghai, creating of it a world city and making its image globally important and therefore domestically controlled.

Yet, despite these politics of hiding and display, 'unsightly' areas do still exist in Shanghai, making it a city of antithetical spaces, which, it likes to suggest, bear no relevance to each other, but which in reality are locked into a mutually parasitical relationship. What the foreign investment effectively does is remove the signs of both decay and surplus waste from the inner-city areas, allowing them to function as 'showcases' for profitable enterprise and attract more FDI into China-based companies. It makes the acceptable excess, in the form of profit, able to be viewed without being obscured by the unacceptable excess – waste. The Zhabei development, for example, means the waste-excess will be geographically removed; pedlars will have been evicted to the 'invisible' suburbs; and those who remain in central Shanghai will be state employees, with uniforms, hourly wages and tax receipts. Waste will officially be state property as soon as it comes into existence (i.e. the point at which something is thrown away), rather than being a free resource. Effectively, it will have been privatized in a manner not dissimilar to that which Dominique Laporte (1993) depicts as happening in seventeenth-century Paris. Laporte's intentionally provocatively titled *History of Shit* describes (amongst other things) the way in which the contents of the 'prive' (toilet room) were gradually privatized as the state began to organize the collection and purification of faeces and place fines upon those who transgressed the new laws of cleanliness (Laporte 1993: 47). Waste matter was 'turned into gold', just as the waste of the Chinese city is taken out to manufacturing areas to be sold and turned into gold as valuable raw materials.

This removal of waste, and the spaces of waste, is, of course, necessary not only in terms of imagery, but also in practical ways if Shanghai is to continue to develop at its current pace. Waste and dirt cannot be allowed to gather and overflow as Mike Davis's salutary case study of the Hyperion sewerage system in Los Angeles shows us. In *City of Quartz* (1992), Davis reveals that when the Hyperion system broke down in May 1987, causing millions of gallons of waste to flood into Santa Monica Bay, it was due to 'growth wars between homeowners and developers' being 'fought within the limits of a collapsing infrastructure' (Davis 1992: 198). Population growth brought the entire system to the brink of collapse; even the flood capacity basin could not be used as the increase in ground area covered over with tarmac had heightened the risk of flood, with the result that the facility was needed for its original purpose. Therefore, the mayor had no choice but to relinquish his usual pro-growth stance and join slow-growth activists by accepting an environmental review of all major developments. This resulted in a monthly cap being put on all new constructions due to the lack of sewer capacity. The cap applied not only to LA, but also to the other thirty municipalities contracting its sewer treatment facilities. Anyone pumping more sewerage than their quota allowed into the LA system was faced with a total growth freeze (Davis 1992: 200). Far from returning waste in the form of profit from commodities sold by reusing it as Shanghai does, LA was forced to live amongst the very waste that itself was hindering, if not curtailing completely, the flow of profit.

In Shanghai, the removal of material waste and its spaces corresponds to the desired shift from manufacturing to service and information industries. However, with the manufacturing sector being the guarantor of China's success for the middle term, and the necessity, therefore, of raw materials, the unacceptable waste-excess will remain indispensable. So too, in fact increasingly so, will the consumption that creates it. Profit will continue to be built on waste and the 'success' of the new China on the so-called 'failures' of the spaces that represent an older China. The cord that ties the two will simply have been planted over with the green turf and evergreen shrubs of an Anglo-American suburban dream. The pedlar-tactician will exist in deeper cracks.

ii) The 'Failed' Spaces of the City – The Key to Success

What can be said of Shanghai's 'cracks' above and beyond how they function for the pedlars (and others who do not fit, or rather, cannot be seen to fit, within the new China)? Theory on these types of areas has often been overshadowed by a more salacious bent towards pure description in which areas of poverty become rabelais-esque chaos, beautiful filthy mires; hellish examples of endgames. Gunter Grass's description of Calcutta as a 'crumbling, scabby, swarming city, this city which eats its own excrement' is typical (Grass 1989: 181). It is not that thick description in itself is a problem (in fact, a return to it might in some ways be welcome); it is that when this kind of description begins to dominate, the analytical element often becomes lost and the cracks are de-possessed of their economic and symbolic role – the necessary role of being places of failure.

All good 'modern', 'developed', 'successful' cities need spaces of failure. They provide a visual yardstick upon which modernity can be measured; but more crucially, they provide a sink-hole for the inevitable collateral damage 'success' causes. Through these mechanisms – the symbolic one and the economic one – they provide the important function of maintaining mainstream and normative ideas of progress. Spaces of failure then, such as the dump site and the pedlars' quarter, must be understood in terms of how their presence feeds other successes; they must be read as *escape valves* in capitalistic commodity chains. In other words, such 'failures' are crucial, precisely because they allow the fallout, to actually fallout, only to return when it has morphed into an acceptable form. The Shanghai dump, for example, is critical to the success of the city and indeed the wider manufacturing industry in the region. Pedlars' waste allows factories to gain access to cheap raw materials which they would otherwise have to buy from China's waste importers at much greater cost. The acknowledgement of the role of escape valves, then, is important in that it forces capitalism to be held accountable for the ways in which they operate and the impact they have on human lives. As Henri Lefebvre argues, 'dysfunctions … are remarkable in that they stimulate functions and functionaries alike' (Lefebvre 2008 [1961]: 65). Or as John Urry maintains, 'what is in the network [including failures] is useful and necessary for its existence' (Urry 2003: 9).

The concept of unintended consequences touches upon the idea that there is function in aberration, yet stops short of explaining how these consequences, or side effects, could be *systematic* to the network. What Urry sets out towards, through his theory of complexity, is a way of perceiving networks in which success and failure are intrinsically linked. Complexity, for Urry, is a system that is neither perpetually anarchic nor well ordered and moving towards equilibrium, but one in which the global is simply not a single centre of power (Urry 2003: x). It is a system that emphasizes diverse time-space paths, unpredictable patterns and disproportionalities between causes and effects (Urry 2003: 7–8). Viewed in this way, 'complexity can illuminate how social life is always a significant mixture of achievement and failure' (Urry 2003: 13). What is key to this understanding of failure, however, – an aspect that Urry does not mention – is the way in which this relationship between success and failure requires collateral damage to be written in to the fabric of commodity chains. In other words, not only does the capitalistic commodity chain create and require failure in order to fuel its successes and provide escape valves, but also it ignores the collateral damage caused (to people and societies) by failures.

In fact, collateral damage is seen only as damage to the smooth economic functioning of the commodity chain. It has been conceptualized as 'externalities', or overflows, and whilst sociologists have tended to see these as the norm, economists have been concerned with 'framing' and have, therefore, seen externalities as simply a rare (and expensive) outcome. The emphasis for economists is not one of moral grounds, but of efficiency and resource allocation. Therefore, for economic-oriented thinkers such as Callon, whose analysis focuses on the financial, the only issue behind externalities is that, whether positive or negative, they render the market (at least partially) inefficient because they are responsible for a gap between private marginal income and marginal social costs (Callon 1998: 247). Externalities mean the market as a whole is not able to operate at its maximum as somewhere costs must be picked up, disabling certain players. Furthermore, in order to be framed, overflows must be made measurable; thus, according to Callon, by allowing each agent to calculate interests and express them, transactions can take place, resulting in a 'robust and legitimate' reallocation of resources (Callon 1998: 256). Of course, what this assumes is that those agents express their interests honestly and/or that those in positions of decision-making make decisions fairly – one can hardly leap to the conclusion that the resulting resource allocation will be robust and legitimate!

So, whilst it is necessary to recognize how failures work to enable capitalistic chains, it is equally necessary to understand that this collateral damage is a phenomenon specific and *essential* to capitalism. In understanding the necessity of 'failures', however, we are forced to question a whole range of simplistic binary oppositions which become bound up in the same dialogue. In the case of the low-end chain (and indeed the wider discourse regarding Europe, the United States and China), along with 'success' and 'failure', comes cleanliness/dirt, visible (visitable)/hidden, organization/chaos and lastly, use/waste. These binary oppositions are held in place across a surprising range of academic thinkers from differing perspectives, and the idea of the remainder has often been imbued with a sinister, negative, edge, returning in all its horrific Freudian reality. For Georges Bataille (1991), this constant remainder, or 'accursed share', could only be successfully reinvested on a small scale and therefore on a global scale must be 'squandered' (Bataille 1991: 10). This global view required Bataille's notion of a 'general economy' within which waste-excess can only be turned to profit-excess in specific small scenarios, because systems can only grow up to a point and cannot completely absorb all the excess in that growth. So, for Bataille, excess energy, or 'wealth', must eventually be lost without profit, or as he puts it, 'spent, willingly or not, gloriously or catastrophically' (Bataille 1991: 21).

According to Bataille, therefore, it is this inability of mankind to 'increase equipment' and the impossibility of continuing growth that makes way for squander. This impossibility is related to lack of space: as pressure on space increases, extension (expansion) results, but this new space is immediately filled – 'The limit of growth being reached, life, without being in a closed container, at least enters into ebullition: without exploding, its extreme exuberance pours out in a movement always bordering on explosion' (Bataille 1991: 30). Because space-making cannot continue *ad infinitum*, it is the short-termism of space-making which results in catastrophe: 'Humanity exploits given material resources, but by restricting them as it does to a resolution of the *immediate* [my italics] difficulties it encounters ... it assigns to the forces it employs an end which they cannot have' (Bataille 1991: 21). Bataille sees waste as unavoidable, but also as part of uneven development in which the excess sees certain areas of the globe growing, while others struggle with the products of growth:

> A typical problem of the general economy emerges from this situation. On the one hand, there appears the need for an exudation; on the other hand, the need for growth. The present state of the world is defined by the unevenness of the (quantitative and qualitative) pressure exerted by human life. (Bataille 1991: 39)

Of course, Bataille's view is not that of the classical economist. While he insists that excess, finally, once at the point of ebullition, can only be squandered, the classical economic view is that we do not reach ebullition, as excess is turned into profit. Is it then a question of whether it is the profit-excess or the waste-excess that is squandered? Both accounts, in very different ways, are strangely emotional, one wallowing in the glorious filth of waste, the other in a dogmatic, zealous mission to be the hero that cleans it up and makes it useful. Both conceive of waste and non-waste as fundamentally different entities which, for the classic economists, must be linked together if efficiency is to be gained. Neither account chooses to see waste and non-waste as simply different sides of the same coin. Applied to the melted down waste of the Shanghai pedlars, remoulded into low-end products which are the driving force of China's growth, it is difficult not to feel that a reconceptualization of 'waste' and 'non-waste' is much needed.

However, the separation of waste from non-waste is written deeply not only into economic and social theory, but also into the fabric of the ways in which that theory becomes established. Academic theory has operated largely out of a concern with sifting through the 'waste' in order to find the 'truth', or the most useful bits. John Scanlon's thoughts on Western philosophy and his support of a philosophy of fragments and detritus such as that practised by Walter Benjamin are useful in further explaining this. He argues that modern philosophy from around the seventeenth century onwards is a history of the disposal and tidying away of waste, a 'sweeping away of the debris that lies on the territory of reason' (Scanlon 2005: 61). According to Scanlon, this stems from the break between Plato's order and that of the pre-Socratics, in particular, Heraclitus's ideas of flux, and the world as a beautiful heap of rubbish. This break is further sealed by Kant, for whom, according to Scanlon, it is from a kind of disposal that meaning, or value, emerged as the part retained (Scanlon 2005: 8). Following Kant's *Critique of Pure Reason*, the human is further separated from nature; therefore, knowledge is separated from garbage and decay is no longer part of existence as Heraclitus would have us believe (Scanlon 2005: 75). There are obvious parallels here with the way the waste of the pedlars is not treated as a part of China's success that can be publicly acknowledged or seen (despite being acknowledged at a state level 'on paper', as it were).

In contrast to the Kantian vision, what Scanlon advocates is a return to seeing waste as part of knowledge, or at least as providing an insight into existing knowledge, in order to follow a Benjaminian method where fragments are examined in order to reveal the detritus of knowledge – the parts thrown away (Scanlon 2005: 79). For Scanlon then, knowledge is actually recycled debris rather than the 'cleaned' part of a whole, the other half of which has been disposed of (Scanlon 2005: 69). The suggestion here is that waste has a part in the present – pure history is hell, but so is no history. Perhaps Benjamin recognized this with his concept of the historical in the present as necessary to wake us; his determination to see the 'out-moded' commodities of the Parisian arcades he wandered as having the ability to wake Europe from her 'dream sleep' (Benjamin 1999). Certainly, he was an advocate of recognizing that the discarded fragment could be useful for bringing into consciousness necessary ideas. Indeed picking through the refuse of history is exactly what he saw himself as engaged in the *Arcades Project* which, lest we forget, never was a 'book', but rather a series of fragments. Rather neatly, for our purposes, Irving Wohlfarth's essay on Benjamin – 'The Historian as Chiffonier' – depicts Benjamin as a ragpicker/pedlar salvaging unwanted bits of history to form a different story. Perhaps we could also see him as salvaging bits of 'failure' in order to recognize them as part of 'success'.

John Frow makes this link between waste and profit more concrete, arguing that waste is the 'degree zero of value, or it is the opposite of value', yet it is something from which value can still be gained, as long as the waste can be moved (Frow 2003: 21). Here, Frow is drawing upon Michael Thompson's concept of value as an effect of the circulation of objects between regimes of value, a circulation which can be driven either by wastefulness (valuable matter being turned into waste) or by the reverse process (Thompson 1979). Both agree that it is the movement, the ability to mutate, that gives a value to waste – that enable it to be transformed into profit. This transformation can be seen as only being able to arise from the privatization of waste – as in Dominique Laporte's vision of excrement in Paris. However, there are other versions of this transformation that rely not on the ability to privatize, but rather on the ability to innovate. This is Stephen Gudeman's vision. In his *Anthropology of Economy*, waste is given a kind of innate creativity, the ability to gain value through human innovation. Gudeman sees this is as an argument against classic economic accounts which, in his view, do not explain imperfect competition, monopolies or accumulation. For him, it is not simply the balancing of endowments and satisfactions, in other words, efficiency, which creates growth, but the turning of accumulated stuff, or 'waste', into profit, through innovation (Gudeman 2001: 95).

This conception of innovation is useful when considering the pedlar-tactician. Gudeman sees the innovator as part of a 'thick historical stream' through which he 'draws together traces and leavings from others … and from himself … [and] makes up an historical trajectory or personal "style"…. Through the use of traces of himself, the innovator creates a way of doing, indexed in an object or service, that becomes a model for others' (Gudeman 2001: 147). This is to perceive the pedlar not only as an innovator, but also as having more awareness of his or her position in the chain than purely economic accounts would give – of understanding the history of it and how that can be used in the present day. Certainly, we can see how this is the case for the pedlar in China, where waste peddling has a long legacy, connotations of honesty and hard work, and even some famous success stories – pedlars such as Wang Jinglian[3] who have become CEOs of large companies. As Joshua Goldstein argues, even in the Republican era, Beijing (and almost certainly, therefore, other large cities) was home to 'a growing community of the dislocated and impoverished who daily eked out a living by wandering the streets and alleys collecting the discards of the city's more prosperous residents' (Goldstein 2006: 263). These discarded objects tended to be refashioned into new ones by the pedlars themselves – more 'stewardship of objects' than a 'regime of consumption and disposal' as Goldstein puts it; it was in the Mao era that a state-managed system was brought in that began to recycle waste commodities purely for their raw materials (Goldstein 2006: 268).

This acknowledgement of the historical stream aside, Gudeman bases his argument on a Schumpetarian notion of innovation which does not seem to wholly repudiate Schumpeter's[4] classical liberal model in which *only* capitalism, and, in particular, institutions of credit, can form the backdrop for innovation (Schumpeter 1954). For Gudeman (as for Schumpeter), capitalism creates innovation, even if it is acknowledged that this innovation sometimes comes about as a result of hardship: this hardship is seen quintessentially as an opportunity rather than an injustice. Gudeman does not tackle unevenness in wealth or development; indeed for him, an uneven terrain breeds the creativity necessary for innovation. Capitalism is, therefore, inextricably linked to creativity, siphoning it off as an exclusive territory of the market, and uneven development is excused as a necessary prerequisite. Although certainly a more anthropological form of economics, Gudeman remains fundamentally concerned with the (economic) efficacy of the market; his thinking revolves entirely around understanding how people make sense of and cope with what the market throws at them, rather than how it impacts unfairly upon them. This conception of the market also follows classic economic accounts in that it posits the market as a kind of organism with its own mind, as opposed to precisely being made up of the very people who are innovating, controlling and struggling. So, while Gudeman's understanding of innovation is useful in joining waste to profit, the framework within which it sits disallows the notion of innovation to exist outside of the capitalistic marketplace, meaning waste is not seen as being enabled to turn into something valuable in any other context. This then, is a rather unsatisfying end to the attempt to put spaces of 'failure' back within cycles of 'success' – it makes of our pedlar-tactician a puppet reliant upon being within 'the market'. It ignores the possibility that he may be equally innovative (and indeed may have been so in his own lifetime in non-capitalist times) outside of the market system. This is not to say that within the low-end commodity chain he is not, painfully, reliant upon the market – of course he is, as the next section will show – but to claim his innovative capacities as capable of existing outside of capitalism should they be required to do so. In other words, the pedlar-tactician's innovation is a property of himself, not of 'the market'.

iii) The Market for Waste: From Pedlar to Factory

The recycling companies – most of them small, informal operations in backyards – mark the point at which the waste-excess, or fallout, begins its magical process of being morphed back into usefulness; of turning itself into gold and no longer being the unspeakable, the undesirable, that which must be banished from the image spaces of the world city. It is here that the contents of the 'failure' spaces of Shanghai begin to feed the success of the Chinese economy. I have come a long way from central Shanghai, forty minutes out on the number three metro line, and then a morning of haphazard wandering. I have no idea where I am, but I am at last beginning to catch glimpses of recycling yards through the half-closed gaps in battered gateways and over rough-hewn walls. This is Baoshan, Shanghai's ungleaming 'other' to the shiny Pudong. It is here that industrial Shanghai works away, collecting up the evidence of 'failure' and turning it into 'success'.

Baoshan is the location of the numerous cranes often seen rising from amongst the grey sea-mist if one looks down the Huangpu River from Shanghai's famous Bund. It is home to the container port, the manufacturing that remains in Shanghai and the recycling yards. It is, according to many of its residents, the part of Shanghai that keeps the rest afloat; the everyday miracle that enables the 'false miracle'. An elderly woman tells me that those who are from Baoshan do not consider themselves part of Shanghai, or at least not the Shanghai that has grown up since Deng Xiaoping's purchase and development of the Pudong. They are well aware of their importance to the Chinese economy, but feel overlooked in Shanghai – a city more concerned with its status as a financial centre, or 'pleasure city', and which seems unappreciative of its hard-industry quarter. This attitude is understandable. Industries in Baoshan feel a long way removed from the image spaces of central Shanghai, and indeed from its historical legacy as a playground for the decadent and corrupt.

It is here, amongst other places, that the independent Shanghai pedlars come to try to sell what they have collected to the informal recycling yards who, in their turn, sell it to the factories along China's Yangtze River Delta to be melted down and made into new products. It is getting harder since the recession hit, and many struggle to negotiate a decent rate for the plastic bottles, scraps of metal and cardboard they have collected. The downturn in export orders from the West has put pressure on Chinese manufacturers to produce at an even lower cost and therefore to acquire even cheaper raw materials from the yard owners in areas such as Baoshan. Plus, in the last decade or so, the recycling yards have been put under pressure to formalize and commercialize their operations, making them more expensive for the owners to run, without the value of materials increasing. Then, in addition, there is the fact that demand for waste materials is subject to unpredictable fluctuations depending on what manufacturers need, and yard owners have limited space so will only take what is selling. This means a pedlar has to be 'in the know' about what is in short supply and will sell for good price if he or she is not to waste time collecting things that will be rejected or paid a pittance for. Some complain that peddling is getting less viable as an alternative to the farming they would have to do for a living in their home provinces – the vast majority of Shanghai's pedlars (and indeed all pedlars) are internal migrants from rural China. I watch as one man attempts to haggle with a yard owner, but in the end seems to accept a few Yuan in return for his load and walks away despondently.

Because pedlars are so frequently internal migrants, they usually do not have any rights to employment, housing or services in Shanghai. This is due to China's Household Registration System, through which Chinese citizens are registered according to their home province and given rural or urban 'hukou'. The roots of this system stem back to Ancient China, (circa 2100BCE), when the Huji system was in place, but in its present form, was introduced by the Communist Party in 1958, as an attempt to control the movements of workers. This became especially important during the 1980s, following the opening up of the Special Economic Zones (SEZs)[5] by Deng Xiaoping and the widespread desire to seek a living in the better-off coastal provinces. As a result, it became crucial to maintain the required population mobility in order that enough, but not too much, cheap rural labour could migrate to the cities. As Michael Dutton explains, this was achieved by introducing the notion of 'legitimate' and 'illegitimate' travel, in order that the authorities could re-create the semblance of order without jeopardizing the necessary flow of labour (Dutton 2005: 274). A two-pronged policy during the early eighties saw the Household Registration system loosened to allow the resident identity card system and a contemporaneous reinvestment in shelter and Investigation Centres to crack down on transients. By the 1990s, these centres had come under scrutiny from Western human rights groups who successfully lobbied for their abolition, which occurred in 1996 (Dutton 2005: 274–89). However, a form of the Household Registration System still exists today and renders many rural migrants 'illegal', creating a tier of society with no rights to formal employment, housing or social security. (Recently there have been widespread reforms to loosen the restrictions on internal migration in order to open up the spending power of rural populations, but their impact remains largely to be seen.) This tier is often known as the 'floating population' (liudong renkou) and those who are part of it as *mangliu* (literally 'blind outflow') – a pejorative term for rural labourers who have come to the city without proper permits. The pedlar-tactician is most often part of the floating population. It is this status that makes his poaching in Shanghai's cracks so necessary for him, and that makes his presence even more of an issue for the authorities.

However, Baoshan requires *mangliu*, as does China as a whole. In fact, migrant labour is by all accounts behind the economic success of China, and the flow of workers from rural to urban areas shows little sign of abating. The massive migration of these workers back to their home provinces for the Chinese New Year has become a much talked-about phenomenon, poignantly depicted in the documentary – *Last Train Home*. Areas such as Baoshan rely almost entirely on the floating population, and China requires areas such as Baoshan to be able to provide cheap raw materials. It simply cannot afford to rely upon importing waste from the West, for which it must pay far higher prices. In fact, major port cities in China – most notably Tianjin – have become globally known as entry points for waste bought in from the West – scrap metal, plastics and paper. According to statistics from Tianjin Customs of China, from January to July 2010, Tianjin imported 402,000 tons of waste plastics (of that, 241,000 tons came from the European Union and 105,000 from the United States). But the Chinese government is well aware of the cost of these waste imports (and the illegal dumping of waste that sometimes comes alongside them), and this is one of the many reasons[6] that it is keen to encourage domestic consumption – in order that higher levels of good-quality waste can be generated. This is particularly relevant now that many Chinese consumers are able to buy better quality goods which provide waste materials of the quality needed for reuse. To encourage this, the government has implemented a series of policy changes providing more of a 'security net' for less well-off rural residents in order to encourage them to part with their savings. It is effectively harnessing the spending potential of a massive rural reserve army of consumers, and this is precisely the reason that, in the context of the low-end commodity chain, the poles of consumption and production start to become very blurred. This army of consumers are themselves indicative of the logic of the bargain. Always, in all its contexts, it is about quantity – small parts, for small amounts, an army of minor spenders keeping China on track.

I think back to a flight I had taken from Shanghai to Kunming (the provincial capital of rural Yunnan province) about two weeks earlier. As the plane was taking off, the girl next to me gently rustled the bag nestled between her feet, eager to explore its contents. She looked about twenty and wore fashionably distressed jeans and a sports top. I was the only non-Chinese face on board. The plane was full of rural Chinese heading back from their Shanghai shopping trips. Almost everyone on the flight had at least one glossy carrier bag containing clothes and presents – things that were not so readily available in Yunnan, such as Western designer labels. Once we had reached our cruising height, the girl leant down and pulled the bag onto her lap, opening it and taking out a blue Adidas zip-up top, a pale pink t-shirt with the words 'cool life' scrawled on it in glittery silver and a Hello Kitty pencil case. She held each of the things in front of her, examining them from different angles, turning them over in her hands and feeling their insides and edges. Her face was at times tense, as if fearing potential regret at her own error of judgement or taste in buying them, and at times serene. Finally, seeming pleased with her purchases, she turned to me and smiled. When we disembarked at Kunming, I watched as the long line of Chinese made their way across the tarmac, clutching their shiny bags and shielding their faces against the driving drizzle. At the terminal building, they seemed to suddenly and quietly disperse, getting into dusty, patched-up cars, strangely at odds with the glossy commercialism of their purchases – China's great reserve army of consumers, continuing their long march to soak up the overproduction China has experienced since EU and US imports fell following the financial crash.

One way of thinking about this link between consumption and production – and therefore waste (from consumption) and profit (from production) – is as a type of what I have tended to call *consumptive thrift.* When Samuel Smiles's famous book *Thrift* was published in 1875, it proved to be a liturgy on the importance of saving in order to be able to survive if times became hard in the future, even if one could only afford to save a tiny amount. It also very much emphasized that not being 'thrifty' in this manner was a 'disease' of the working classes and that they must be re-educated on the importance of saving. Smiles's thrift, then, was very much concerned with saving for hard times *in the future*. He was also a great proponent of the necessity of talking about personal finance, as opposed to state finance. What he did not reckon on was the Keynesian logic that was to emerge in the twentieth century which precisely tied personal finance to public finance through the notion of the 'paradox of thrift'.[7] Briefly, this argues that if every individual person saves, demand (consumption) will fall, economic growth will decrease, wages will, therefore, decrease too and the population as a whole will suffer. The paradox is, therefore, that while thrift is good on an individual level (as Smiles argued), it cannot be generalized, as collective thrift may have a negative impact on the economy and therefore on the population as a whole. This Keynesian thought had led to the importance of consumption being recognized at the state level and to a certain notion of the 'duty' to consumer in order to maintain a healthy economy. In fact, Keynes was quick to link the negative aspects of unemployment to the insufficiency of the propensity to consume and this idea was central to his theory of effective demand.

This is now, of course, rhetoric that sounds very familiar to us, and indeed is becoming increasingly familiar in China, but in practice it involves the consumer constantly performing a balancing act between spending and saving. In fact, whereas Smiles's thrift was all about saving for potential future need, late-twentieth- and twenty-first-century thrift is explicitly concerned with saving in order to be able to *continue spending* (even if in small amounts) *in the present.* It is thrift in the sense of being careful with money, or making savings on consumer goods, as opposed to saving (i.e. not spending) money – hence the 'thrift store'. In other words, this thrift must be *consumptive.* It is about enabling oneself to continue being part of the all-important army of consumers in order to maintain economic growth.

As Keynes admitted, Bernard Mandeville had, in fact, picked up on this idea as early as 1714 in his *Fable of the Bees*[8] in which he advocated allowing the 'private vice' of greed in view of the 'public benefits' it entailed – 'Thus every part was full of vice, Yet the whole mass a paradise.' With these lines, Mandeville had effectively outlined what Adam Smith would come to argue seventy years later. The fable describes a kingdom in which all consumption had been curtailed and as a result the kingdom had failed to survive intact, the remaining bees fleeing the hive. Keynes describes the poem as outlining 'the appalling plight of a prosperous community in which all the citizens suddenly take it into their heads to abandon luxurious living, and the State to cut down armaments, in the interests of Saving' (Keynes 1964: 360). This idea of the wealth of the few somehow enabling a better life for the many is, of course, the basis for 'trickle-down' economics, a concept adapted with ferocity in China, beginning with Deng Xiaoping and continuing to the present day. This, despite the fact that statistics reveal China is creeping up the table of countries with the greatest economic inequality based on the Gini coefficient[9] and failing to create the inclusive *xiaokang* (functionally well-off middle class) that it desires – in other words, trickle down is not working. However, the message that consumption is an important duty in continuing China's development and enabling wealth to spread is unignorable. All who can, must consume. The residents of the world's factory can no longer simply be viewed as 'producers', but must also be understood as politically defined consumers, crucial to their own survival and that of their nation. Consumptive thrift is the saviour of the chosen developmental path of not only China, but also many consumer societies in the West. It demands a combination of the propriety advocated by Smiles with the consumption posited as a duty by Keynes.

In many ways it is this combination of moralistic attitudes towards thrift that has created consumptive thrift, and in so doing, represents a change in capitalism's relationship with itself. Capitalism has proceeded down a line stemming from Augustinian thought in which avarice was seen as able to be commandeered in order to guard against other more detrimental passions (such as lust) – this avarice was what Mandeville talked of when he said that every part was full of 'vice'. This led to the Keynesian idea of benefits for all and the political rhetoric of the duty to consume. However, in travelling this path in which money is posited as capable of doing good, capitalism has also requisitioned a rather more Aristotelian notion of money as 'bad', taking the 'sin of the miser' and transforming it into something more akin to 'the sin of the saver'. Thrift in Smiles' sense is now seen as the sin of the miser on both global and individual levels, as seen by complaints about the level of China's foreign reserves (the much-maligned 'Asian thrift'). As Slavoj Žižek says, 'the capitalist is no longer the lone Miser who clings to his hidden treasure, taking a secret peek at it when he is alone, behind securely locked doors, but the subject who accepts the basic paradox that the only way to preserve and multiply one's treasure is to spend it' (Žižek 2002: 43).

Making spending available for all, however, requires the creation of cheap products, and cheap products can only be made with cheap raw materials (and cheap labour). Waste materials are, therefore, increasingly important, as is the ability of a nation's consumers to dispose of the goods they buy (as waste) relatively soon after having bought them. Only in this manner can the flow of waste materials be maintained. As Goldstein puts it, 'Today, thrift is not the goal. Wasteful behaviour is not to be avoided … and one need not try to squeeze uses out of ageing objects. Indeed, the emphasis today is to use things and dispose of them as quickly – but also as profitably – as possible' (Goldstein 2006: 297). Hannah Arendt describes this situation as follows: 'our whole economy has become a waste economy, in which things must be almost as quickly devoured and discarded as they have appeared in the world, if the process [of production and consumption] is not to come to a sudden catastrophic end' (Arendt 1998: 134).

This emphasis on waste has implications for individuals at all points on the commodity cycle – as Hawkins and Muecke point out, 'changing relations to waste mean changing relations to self' (Hawkins and Muecke 2003: xiii–xiv). In buying and disposing of and therefore creating their own waste, the Chinese subject is made a 'consumer' in the eyes of the world, which, in turn, reflect back to them the image of China as a now 'successful' nation in which thrift is no longer necessary. The emphasis here is very much on 'the eyes of the world', as, of course, being a consumer was certainly an identity position prior to 1949 as Dikotter's work on modern China and Clunas's work on earlier periods have shown.

Meanwhile, the figure of the pedlar emerges as the embodiment of the quandary between thrift and waste. He enables the transition from waste to product (and therefore profit), so is inextricably involved in capitalistic practices. Yet, simultaneously, he defies the logic of the wider commodity chain and that of capitalism in general by operating as a bricoleur who is the ultimate example of making do with what's available and being 'thrifty'. He is in many ways the 'reverse image' that Lefebvre saw as represented by Charlie Chaplin – a character who reflects the image of everyday, but who is simultaneously 'exceptional, deviant, abnormal' (Lefebvre 2008 [1947]: 12). His existence is caught up in a politics of hiding and display – the hiding of spaces of 'failure', the hiding of his own presence much of the time, yet the making visible of the products and profit that result from his labours – the hiding of waste and the making visible of non-waste, as if these two were not intrinsically linked. It is the Pudong smugly smiling across the river to Baoshan, without so much as a flicker of recognition in its eyes, as if the two had never been introduced. This separation, in turn, constitutes a tearing apart of reality and the images provided of 'reality' and thus denies the Hereclitian[10] nature of the commodity chain – the ongoing state of creation which products occupy; the plastic bottle which is a hair slide-in-waiting.

The neatly ordered piles of waste materials in Baoshan, will be melted down into small pellets of plastic, iron and aluminium and sold to factories along the Yangtze River Delta, where they will again undergo a transformation, melted and remoulded into new objects. It is in factories of these Yangtze River cities that our eight products are created, from the waste gathered from the streets of coastal cities such as Shanghai. Roland Barthes's short essay on plastic, written not long after it had been invented, remains a poignant description of this process, and is worth quoting here at some length:

> Plastic, the products of which have just been gathered in an exhibition, is in essence the stuff of alchemy. At the entrance of the stand, the public waits in a long queue in order to witness the accomplishment of the magical operation par excellence: the transmutation of matter. An ideally-shaped machine, tubulated and oblong ... effortlessly draws, out of a heap of greenish crystals, shiny and fluted dressing-room tidies. At one end, raw, telluric matter, at the other, the finished, human object; and between these two extremes, nothing; nothing but a transit, hardly watched over by an attendant in a cloth cap, half-god, half-robot. So, more than a substance, plastic is the very idea of its infinite transformation ... a miraculous substance ... transforming the original crystals into a multitude of more and more startling objects, plastic is, all told, a spectacle to be deciphered: the very spectacle of its end-products. At the sight of each terminal form (suitcase, brush, car-body, toy, fabric, tube, basin or paper), the mind does not cease from considering the original matter as an enigma. This is because the quick-change artistry of plastic is absolute: it can become buckets as well as jewels. Hence a perpetual amazement.

2

The 'Commodity City': Yiwu, the World's Factory of Bargains

i) The 'China Price' Deal: A Day in the Life of an International Wholesale Buyer

It is a Thursday afternoon in mid-November. The train is busy. Nearly every seat is taken up by a neatly dressed businessman, overnight bag in one hand, Blackberry in the other. There is a polite low rumble of business-like chatter. Phones buzz, and short, clipped phrases are uttered in sincere, efficient fashion. Such conversations are brief and many. Laptop keys tap gently. Faces are relatively relaxed, but focused, perhaps trying to pre-empt what products may be available, what deals can be done. The man next to me taps some figures into a calculator, nods gently to himself and looks stoic. We speed through Shanghai's sprawling outskirts and on through the rural grasslands of Zhejiang province, the route offering fleeting glances of small agricultural villages and emerging light-industry towns. The scenery becomes more mountainous as we enter the eastern part of the Jin Qu basin; peaks can be seen in the distance and industry feels less present. Then, just as cities and manufacturing seem to fall from mind, the route suddenly emerges from the undulating foothills, abruptly giving way to a grey urban expanse. This is Yiwu, the 'sea of commodities' (as its promotional website claims), a promised land for the international wholesale buyer and the place that boasts the highest concentration of all existing small products on the planet.

I disembark at the small grey station building along with the businessmen (they *are* all men) feeling conspicuous with my rucksack and casual clothes. We wind our way along the platform, through the slightly downtrodden underpass and out into the small station forecourt, to be greeted by the usual ticket touts and a small row of official taxis. It is all surprisingly low-key. I was expecting something rather more like emerging from behind the automatic doors of a plush international airport arrivals lounge. Instead, there is an air of pre-organized, quietly efficient, matter-of-fact business. Yiwu is obviously somewhere that most people come to frequently, get to know and understand how to negotiate. There are no signs to the markets, no business or translation services advertised, no wholesale agents waiting to meet foreign buyers; only immense, straight roads and austere grey high-rises. In its quiet efficiency, Yiwu (at least in terms of first impressions) is far from the glossy international hub promotional sources would have us believe. I am, well, frankly, underwhelmed.

A dour taxi driver takes me to my hotel. He seems bored with the whole affair. He eyes my rucksack slightly suspiciously, aware that I am not the average visitor to Yiwu, not being male and in business attire. Dropping me at the hotel door, he turns and points down another immense straight road, saying 'markets that way'. I nod my thanks and walk into the hotel foyer – it is marble, and exceedingly clean, with a water fountain and flowers, yet somehow dated. I had decided to avoid the international chain hotels, choosing instead one of the earliest hotels to be built in Yiwu, whose walls had witnessed the passing of many coteries of senior Communist Party officials. There is something delightfully austere and serious about the place, despite the showy foyer with its gleaming hard surfaces. It says success, but not decadence; wealth generation, not pleasure. My room is on the eleventh floor – 'seventh floor upwards is for Westerners', I had always been told in Shanghai, and as a Westerner, it seemed impossible to be placed lower than the seventh floor even if one asked. From its small, dusty window, I can see over the whole city and out to the beginnings of the mountains. I suddenly feel very aware of just how prime Yiwu's geographical position in the Yangtze River Delta (YRD) is.

In fact, Yiwu is perfectly placed for its function, just close enough to Shanghai, but with the space to expand and gather resources from the whole YRD. It is a key transport hub, with express trains to Shanghai, and at least eight inland flight routes to other major cities. Since the 'reform and opening' policies of the 1980s, it has developed its small commodity industry to go from being a traditional agricultural town to the key driver of a huge regional economy, not only in Zhejiang province, but also in the YRD economic area as a whole. The relative productive capacity of this area is incredible. The YRD constitutes less than one per cent of China's land area and only 5.8 per cent of its population, yet creates approximately 20 per cent of its GDP.[1] According to the latest statistics, it contains more than 800,000 private companies manufacturing predominantly small, inexpensive commodities such as socks, toothbrushes and plastic cups. In certain types of manufacturing it has usurped the established industrial success of the Pearl River Delta, which has now moved to producing larger, more durable consumer goods – fridges, TVs, etc.

Not surprisingly, this success has caused physical expansion. Since 1982, Yiwu's ground area has increased from 2.8 km square to 18 km square, not least due to the now-famous 'number four document' in 1984 which entitled private Town and Village Enterprises (TVEs) to the same tax incentives as collectively owned TVEs. More importantly, the document also granted TVEs the same policy treatment as State-Owned Enterprises (SOEs), therefore effectively equating private firms with SOEs. Its impact on potential private entrepreneurs was huge. According to Huang (Huang 2008: 97), within one month of its announcement, rural residents in the county of Yiwu raised 10 million Yuan and established 500 businesses. It is not surprising, therefore, that within the following two years, the city of Yiwu's ground area increased at its fastest ever rate and was such a success within China that before long there were attempts to transport it outside of national boundaries. The Yiwu model had become a transportable entity within its own right – something that could be transplanted wholesale within the boundaries of other countries.[2]

Yiwu now consists of Huangyuan Market (established in 1992), Binwang[3] Market (established in 1995) and China Yiwu International Trade City (first established in 2002) which includes Futian Market. Each market contains around five smaller markets, specializing in specific product areas, and together they cover an area of approximately 2 million square metres, containing around 58,000 company booths displaying around 400,000 products.[4] Local word has it that more than 1,000 containers leave Yiwu every day, largely bound for Europe and the United States. Almost everything is geared around the city's fame as the world's 'small commodity city', an official status bestowed by the Chinese government in 1982. It is almost impossible to contemplate the impact Yiwu has had globally, supplying a huge quantity of the world's small commodities and drastically increasing the availability of cheap everyday products in the West. I take a deep breath – it is time to descend from my vantage point into the fullness of these strange and remarkable 18 square kilometres.

The road from the hotel to Binwang market is straight – dead straight. It leads me almost directly from the hotel foyer to Binwang's impressive atrium – a direct route from centralized communism to market socialism. It is as I am heading down this vast straight intersection that the sense of being underwhelmed I had initially experienced begins to leave me, and a slow recognition of the vast production capacity of Yiwu starts to take its place. The city's raison d'être of manufacturing can most evidently be seen in its layout – all main roads head towards a commodity market. Yiwu is a built-for-purpose manufacturing leviathan, promoting as its overwhelming priority, the 'natural flow' of goods and people through urban space. Cars drive fast in Yiwu, speeding past me as I walk, and people speak loudly and in staccato tones. As a waiter later informs me, there is an accent specific to Yiwu which is very harsh – even the words of lovers sound angry', he says. I am not the best judge, but I cannot help but agree.

As I draw closer to the market building, the sides of the road begin to be lined on and off with groups of women sitting by the roadside, knitting. They perch on small stools, their fingers moving deftly and with the practised habit that can only come from years of repetition. I continue on towards the Binwang market building. Outside the market, brand new shiny Mercedes and BMWs are parked in neat rows, strangely juxtaposed with rows of trolleys and small forklift trucks placed in readiness for goods to be moved out to the containers that will transport them to the West. Yiwu, despite elements of glamour, is a strange combination, remaining curiously down-at-heel in places and stoically immersed in its own methods of operation. There is a showy-ness sometimes, but for the most part, it is concerned mainly with functionality – if things do not get done and done quickly, Yiwu is nothing, and it knows it.

The atrium of Binwang market is shiny, polished and bedecked with huge plants and laminated banners advertising goods and services. Looking upwards I can see that it is a vast, three-tiered warehouse, a Noah's Ark of China's small commodities. Should the rains come and the plains flood, Binwang will provide a prototype for each of the god of industry's creations. I feel miniscule, like a Gulliver exploring all that the new, open, efficient China has to offer. Once beyond the atrium though, the never-ending corridors of stalls are less glamourous and once again exude an air of functionality, zoned according to commodity and with their representatives sometimes crouching together in groups to eat cheap noodles out of plastic bowls. Ahead, behind and to either side of me, as far as the eye can see, are long, perfectly straight corridors, flanked by immaculately arranged stalls, each around 3 metres square, their contents unforgivingly lit by the industrial strip lights above. Each stall represents a factory and contains one example of every commodity that factory makes in all its variations – one blue six-inch vase, one yellow six-inch vase, one blue ten-inch vase, one yellow ten-inch vase, and so on and so on. I head to the crafts area, where I had agreed to meet Jay (not his real name), a UK wholesale buyer I had contacted via an online forum a few months previously.

Jay, it turns out, is an energetic Mancunian in his late thirties who has been coming to Yiwu regularly for the past five years. He says he doesn't work for any of the big chains, but seems to wish to avoid telling me who he does buy for, emphasizing the 'freelance' nature of his work. (In fact, I had begun to notice even before coming to China, how many buyers were rather unwilling to talk about who they worked for.) He emphasizes that many retailers in the United Kingdom do not want to use intermediary companies, but do not have the time or knowledge to come to Yiwu themselves and deal with factory representatives – they want someone they can trust … and trace!', he says. This afternoon his mission is to find some well-priced 'household ornamental' goods that can be sold for £1 and still provide a good profit for the retailer. 'I used to do household cleaning stuff and cosmetics', he says, 'but that kind of stuff is pretty straightforward really. The trick is making sure it's legitimate, because the profit margin won't move that much on that sort of product. Household crafts is more interesting, more challenging, and you do need to actually see the stuff. I like that – having to touch it and judge the quality and make a call on what wholesale price is worth paying. Today is really just a scout about for me. It's been a while since I was here and I need to walk about a lot and get a feel for what's out there. No deals today … well, unless there's something totally amazing', he chuckles. 'So, do you just want to follow me round, is that it.' 'Yes, that's it', I smile.

Ornamental flowers are the first port of call – they are unavoidable. A whole row of stalls stretching into the distance displays brightly coloured lilies, sunflowers and made-up creations – a plasticized Garden of Eden, half a kilometre long and 10 metres wide. Jay does not stop long. 'I don't need to look at them really,' he says. 'I know I'll order some of them – they're a stalwart product, they always sell and they can always be got at a good price.' He turns left into the next aisle, a more varied one, specializing in pots, bowls, vases and the like.

I am struck by a stall selling small vases decorated in a Chinese style. They are mimics of the kind of 'Chinoiserie' style that were so popular in the West towards the end of the nineteenth century – a mishmash of Chinese and Japanese motifs, many with dragons and traditionally clad figures. It seems strange to see them in this avowedly twenty-first-century context and produced in such mass quantities for such an 'un-precious' price. 'Good price, good price,' says the stallholder. As we turn away, Jay explains that negotiations often begin with the stallholder offering a 'good price', but that it is 'China price' that really counts. I look bemused. He explains that he has noticed there seems to be different set phrases used at different points in the bargaining process. It starts with 'good price'; then, with some shaking of heads and imploring on his part, 'good price' becomes 'best price'. This is communicated by the stallholder as if it is a final offer (and sometimes it is), but if he then starts to walk away, the stallholder will often call him back and try to improve the offer. A few sums tapped into a calculator, maybe a quick phone call (sometimes faked), lots more shaking of heads from both parties, and if he was lucky, the wholesaler would look stoic and say, 'Ok, I'll do you a very special price – China price.'[5] Not only was 'China price' the lowest possible price, but there was a more personal implicit hierarchy at play here. Unlike a 'good price', which was nearly always followed by the phrase 'good for you, good for me', 'China price' seemed to contain recognition on the part of the stallholder of the stronger bargaining power of the buyer. China price was 'good for you', but not so 'good for me' – it recognized China's cheap labour and begrudgingly gave in to its exploitation.

If this dealmaking was, in part, as a result of certain acceptances on the part of the Chinese stallholders, it was also to do with a set of assumptions on the part of the Western buyers (and indeed this applies to the Western shopper when abroad more generally) as to their 'right' to a discount price. As a result of the huge disparities between the cost of labour power in different parts of the world, there is an increasingly entrenched expectation on the part of those from the West that commodities should be able to be bought at little more than the price it cost to produce them. In fact, it is this expectation that drives the bargain store commodity chain, and that means the 'squeeze' in the chain is always at the Chinese end. Within this expectation on the part of Western buyers and their understanding of the global situation is also an assumption that this access to products at barely more than the cost of production is somehow 'common-sense' and that the structural injustices involved need not be addressed. Language itself points to these structural inequalities – 'to bargain' (from the French bargaignier) is fundamentally at odds with 'the bargain' unless relationships remain unequal. The seller can only earn a 'fair price' for the commodity, at the same time as the consumer pays a discount price for the commodity if the bargain buyer's money is worth more than the bargain seller's. To return to that familiar phrase of Chinese traders – 'good price – good for you, good for me'; this captures the structure of unequal value between buyers' and sellers' money, exposing the way in which bargaignier and bargain are caught in a set of structural inequities.

Our wandering continues, through realms of pots, boxes and baskets; clocks, candles and figurines, past a stall with a display of miniaturized scenes in glass domes and bottles. Jay pauses, seeing I have lagged behind – 'too naff', he says, 'stores won't take them on the whole. Plus only the really small ones will come in at the right profit margins, those kind of detailed products always cost more per unit – more labour time needed.' I do not doubt he is right, although I wonder about some of the more independent bargain stores. I have seen them stock such things – copies of Victorian-era flower and butterfly domes, or the ubiquitous ship-in-a-bottle. I stop beside one that shows a crudely formed lighthouse emerging from a stormy rubberized sea, as a small, yet still proportionately too large, sailing vessel clings on to the wave at an impossible angle. The vessel is a representation of a classic 'clipper' sail ship – so-called because they could 'clip' days off the usual time for a sea voyage. Clippers were the main trading vessels of the late nineteenth and early twentieth centuries, typically with three masts, square-rigging and a sharply pointed hull designed to slice through the water. Many of the most famous examples of trading vessels are clippers – the Cutty Sark,[6] for example, Thermopylae[7] and the Flying Cloud.[8] It was clippers which carried cargos of exciting new products back to the West from India and China – spices, silk and the much sought-after tea from China. Many of these clippers, the Thermopylae for one, were specifically used in the tea trade between Britain and China. Such ships were potent symbols of British trading power, new global adventure and the prowess of empire. (They were also, of course, symbols of the worst examples of colonial behaviour – such as the opium wars).[9] It seems strange to see such a scene of empire here, in the vast halls of the latest trading powerhouse – a reappropriated relic, sold without irony or care to the former colonialists.

Jay is getting into his stride. He speaks quickly and directly to a man inside a booth selling garden ornaments – fifty or so lurid gnomes smile bemusedly down at him from their shelves with expressions that suggest they know better than him and can see through his ruse. The man reacts fast, beckoning Jay over to his small desk inside the booth and tapping figures into a calculator. Jay nods slowly and brings out his own calculator to tap in some more sums. He pulls a face that expresses 'so-so' and makes to move off. The man taps in some more figures and holds up his calculator screen to Jay again. Jay nods his appreciation cautiously and asks for a business card, saying he needs to talk to people his end but that he will be back tomorrow, definitely. The man shakes his hand. Jay walks out looking quietly pleased. 'Good deal,' I ask. 'Unusual,' he says. 'Usually you get slightly bigger garden ornaments like that for a bigger price, and that's no good for the people I work for. This is very small garden ornaments but for a much lower price. I think it might work. I think my boss is going to say that people don't want garden gnomes that small,' he laughs, 'but perhaps people with small gardens or just balconies in inner-city blocks may be a market for them. We always have to consider where our stores are, and most of them are in areas of high-density housing, so I think there's a case for this … but I need to think about it.' I nod. 'I have seen slightly larger gnomes in similar stores,' I say. 'I spoke to a woman who had bought one … although I'm not sure that store ever re-stocked them.' Jay has a glint in his eye – 'You want to watch yourself,' he smiles, 'you'll be addicted to this game like me if you're not careful.' I turn back to see the gnomes smiling their knowing smiles. He might be right.

Onwards we go, and my eyes are beginning to blur with the bright lighting and the sheer amount of detail to take in on each side. One booth has an array of indoor water features – miniaturized Zen gardens with grey plastic rocks – many of them plugged in to show them off better. The tinkling of calm water seems strangely out of place in such a business-like environment. In fact, many stalls in this area display low-end versions of 'exotic' artefacts from the East. There is a whole stall of laughing Buddhas, model Tibetan monasteries, miniature Taj Mahals and various synthetic bonsais. Jay is unmoved. 'Too risky,' he says, 'ornamental is one thing, but it's got to suit the widest possible taste.' 'Like what,' I ask. 'Picture frames, candles, vases, fruit bowls.' 'Nothing with specific cultural meaning?' I say. 'I hadn't thought of it like that, but, well, just not stuff that will limit the potential market. That stuff, it's kind of kitsch isn't it. Most of our customers want functional stuff or the kind of ornamental stuff that everyone has.' He pauses, 'I mean, if you were looking for some kind of ornament with real character would you go to a pound store?' I smile. 'It depends how serious a statement I was trying to make with the ornament,' I reply.

ii) Yiwu – World-famous 'Commodity City': History and Non-place in the Paradise of Things

I am struggling through a bowl of congee in the breakfast area the following morning, when I overhear two men talking about taking a day off to go and see some local history. I am intrigued. I was not aware that Yiwu had any 'history' beyond its fame as a commodity city. It turns out that despite Yiwu's identity being largely based on its productive capacity, official promotional materials also draw upon celebrated characters from its dynastic past, pointing to famous residents from the Tang (618–907 BCE), Song (960–1279 BCE) and Yuan (1271–1368) dynasties, as well as more recent prodigies, including educationalist Chen Wangdao, literary theorist Feng Xuefeng and historian Wu Han. This concern with proving historical credentials is well illustrated by Xiuhu Park. It is to there that I head off through the fine, grey drizzle, just as the mountain mists begin to descend on Yiwu, obscuring the tops of the grey high-rises in the distance.

I enter Xiuhu Park through a faux historic gateway, painted in traditional black and red, beyond which lies a view of a large lake surrounded by pagodas and gazebos and interspersed with grey hump-backed bridges linking its decorative islands. In fact, it is not only the gateway that is faux. The entire park is a recent creation, constructed in 2003 around the pre-existing lake, complete with man-made hills and islands. It strikes me as somehow slightly strange that Chinese landscape architecture should now itself be creating false landscapes in the style of its traditional landscapes just as the likes of Capability Brown did in nineteenth-century industrializing England. Ahead of me stands the only part of this built environment which dates further back than the late 1970s – the leaning Da'ansi pagoda. Incongruously juxtaposed between the faux gateways, its ancient weathered bricks are set against a backdrop of smooth grey-pink 1980s' high-rises. It is the only remnant from Yiwu's dynastic days; days when, as a small village, Yiwu spawned poets and authors, educationalists and thinkers, rather than the legions of small-business entrepreneurs that it teems with today. Squinting, I can almost remove the tower block from view, framing the pagoda against the sky. Seen alone like this, it symbolizes an older China and the Yiwu of Tang days. Unsquinting brings back into frame once again the modern high-rise beyond, and the pagoda gains its more recent layer of symbolic value: a layer gifted to it by the Yiwu of current times, the Yiwu keen to embellish its trading reputation with a cultural–historical tradition.

What is strange about Xiuhu Park is that it seems to be desperately attempting to provide a history for Yiwu, giving it place-ship in a way that seems incongruous

Figure 2.1 The Da'ansi Pagoda framed against 80s-built tower blocks.

with what it has become, when actually Yiwu in many ways has created its own sense of place since the mid-1980s. In many ways Yiwu fits perfectly the picture painted by Mark Auge when he spoke of 'non-place' as temporal and transient, the classic spaces of postmodernity – airports, supermarkets, motorways – spaces lost in a kind of global blandness (Auge 1995). This is certainly the feel in the commodity market buildings, and Yiwu does indeed owe much to its temporal elements – it is defined by the number of commodities produced and sold every hour, the quantity of containers that leave every day, the sheer number of deals brokered within its markets. While the city authorities are keen to promote Yiwu as a nice *place* to live and an incredible physical site of activity, they also cannot help promote it as time – as an astounding *temporal* phenomenon in which one lives the *speed* of commodity exchange *as part of* one's place. Yi Fu Tuan acknowledges this tendency when talking of how certain places are promoted in more 'abstract' ways – the promotion of certain cities as places of great efficiency and exciting hubs of activity. As Tuan argues, these methods often tend to belong to cities which are either literally newly built or 'new' in their current form:

> A city does not become historic merely because it has occupied the same site for a long time. Past events make no impact on the present unless they are memorialized in history books, monuments, pageants.... An old city has a rich store of facts on which successive generations of citizens can draw to sustain and re-create their image of place .... New cities, such as the frontier settlements of North America, lacked a venerable past; to attract business and gain pride their civic leaders were obliged to speak with a loud voice. Strident boosterism was the technique to create an impressive image, and to a lesser extent it still is. The boosters could rarely vaunt their city's past or culture; hence the emphasis tended to be on abstract and geometrical excellences such as 'the most central', 'the biggest', 'the fastest', and 'the tallest'. (Tuan 2005: 175)

True to this description, in Yiwu, it is the impressiveness of speed and efficiency which are often promoted as its defining features, and this also fits neatly with Auge's description of time's presence in non-places: 'what reigns there is actuality, the urgency of the present moment. Since non-places are there to be passed through, they are measured in units of time' (Auge 1995: 104). Also true to Auge's description of non-place, Yiwu has a certain degree of anonymity, at least for some of those who live there and for many of those who visit. The nature of its business means it tends to revolve around the ability to attract large numbers of transient business people whose presence renders the city more fluid in its relations. Visitors often experience the anonymity there (especially if they are Western and less 'readable' to the Chinese inhabitants) as a kind of liberation from their usual identity (as indeed tourists and travellers do in unfamiliar environments). A business person can forget other elements of their identity and simply *be* the business interaction, the vehicle for the moment of exchange.

Yet, despite its emphasis on the temporal and its high degree of anonymity for some, in other ways Yiwu has more of a sense of place than can be understood at first glance. It is not, for example, 'non-specific culturally and historically' as Auge suggests non-places are; rather it is the kind of specific culture localized in time and space and the kind of 'community' in which people are familiar with one another's personal histories that he associates with the antithesis of non-place – anthropological place' (Auge 1995: 34). The reason for this is that many of the businesses set up in Yiwu at the beginning of the reform era were joint ventures between people who had been in the same *danwei* (work unit) in the Mao era. In fact, Kellee Tsai argues that workers from the same factory often become private entrepreneurs selling products that reflect the focus of their former employer and that this can explain why there are networks of people specializing in specific products (Tsai 2002: 176–7).

The *danwei* was the principal form of social organization (and of implementing party policy) under Mao's rule. It is most commonly translated as 'work unit', but was far more than a place of employment, providing housing, food, clinics, childcare, schools, as well as social respectability or 'face' (mianzi). Belonging to a *danwei* was obligatory, not only by Mao's rules, but also because it was incredibly difficult to survive without the shelter and food it provided. In fact, because the *danwei* provided all that was necessary for daily survival, it was often connected to the notion of the 'baoxialai' or social guarantee, colloquially referred to as the 'iron rice bowl' (tiefanwan). The *danwei* was created as part of the Maoist push towards collectivization and typically would house people in shared dormitories and feed them in shared canteens. It was like a very small, walled, close-knit town, at the front gate of which stood a guard who would check if a person's papers were in order before letting that person in. *Danweis* provided not only a means to produce goods, but also, due to their close-knit nature, a means to maintain a steady supply of political intensity and therefore activists who could be mobilized for party campaigns (Dutton 2005: 164). This combination of producing tangible commodities alongside political fervour suggests that *danweis* were creating what Boris Arvatov (1997) calls 'socialist' objects[10] – those that contained socialist ideologies within them. For all these reasons, a shared *danwei* experience was often a very powerful factor in people's lives, both during and after Mao's reign, and those who set up in business together after the *danweis* had been largely dissolved certainly knew one another's personal histories very well indeed. Indeed, Tsai argues that current-day workers' abilities to overcome common grievances are frequently enhanced due to collective action which comes about as a result of their shared *danwei* in the past (Tsai 2002: 176–7).

In addition to these shared histories, Yiwu also represents a specific historical trajectory in China's economy – a trajectory that very much gives it identity for many of its inhabitants. Yiwu's way of operating is based upon the 'Wenzhou model' – a mode of economic organization that is historically specific to Wenzhou city in south-east Zhejiang province. The model can be seen as characterized by four key features: (1) that it consists of numerous small-scale private enterprises; (2) that it specializes in wholesale petty commodity markets; (3) that it is built on tens of thousands of mobile traders who facilitate the flow of materials and (4) that it is made possible by various forms of non-governmental financial arrangements. The nature of these operations means that the Wenzhou model works to maintain low costs in return for low profit margins; this, in turn, means scale is required in order for the low profit margin per unit to still deliver economic viability overall.

These characteristics stem from the time of the Southern Song dynasty, when Yonjia county (in which Wenzhou is situated) in Zhejiang province started to drift from the main stream of neo-Confucian[11] thought and set up the Yonjia School. Unlike other proponents of neo-Confucianism – namely Zhu Xi and Lu Jiuyuan – who urged people to become officials, the Yonjia School under Ye Shi placed emphasis on business, arguing that traders too could be the backbone of society. Therefore, unlike in other provinces, in Wenzhou, commercialism was celebrated. Furthermore, Ye Shi's influence extended to later thinkers from Zhejiang province, such as Wang Shouren and Hunag Zongxi, who became the most important philosophers of the Ming and Qing dynasties, respectively, insuring the enduring appeal of Wenzhou's operations.

If the Wenzhou model was viewed with suspicion under Confucianism, it was positively controversial under Mao and indeed banned even before full collectivization began to take place. Under Maoist logic, it was deemed to be particularly capitalistic in nature as it was seen to rely upon individualism and small-scale entrepreneurship (i.e. at the level of the family unit). Mao's specific concern with this small-scale model was born out of his belief in collectivization – itself a product of his adherence to the Leninist policies China followed until the mid-1950s. However, following the coming to leadership of Deng Xiaoping in 1978, the reform and opening policies initiated saw Wenzhou become the first city to set up private enterprises and shareholder cooperatives. It carried out reforms in its financial system and structure and developed a commodity economy very early on in the reform era. This economy was based on household industries and specialized markets and sat nicely alongside the new national rhetoric of creating individual entrepreneurs of all Chinese citizens. Deng's reappropriation of neo-Confucianism at the time encouraged intra-family lending in order to set up family businesses under the guise of familial loyalty and taking responsibility for one's well-being.

Over the course of the 1990s, changes to what was seen as acceptable economically and the further development of 'market socialism' saw the Wenzhou model become the official economic paradigm model for China. Contemporaneously, however, Deng recognized that when this paradigm was allowed to unravel in its 'unofficial' forms, it did not suit the new ordered, 'civilized' look that China wanted to promote. The markets that Wenzhou migrants set up in certain quarters of large cities were cleared time and time again and eventually razed, and many migrants were forced to return to Wenzhou. The message was clear – we want the model, not you. If you want to be part of it, clean up your act. This 'cleansing' was most dramatically put into action with the razing of Zhejiangcun[12] in Beijing, a manufacturing area comprised of the largest collection of migrants in any Chinese city – 100,000 since the late 1990s. (See Li Zhang 2001; Xiang Biao 2005.) Zhejiangcun was located in Fengtai district in the south of Beijing and specialized in clothing manufacture. Its rapid population growth, from just six families in 1984 was in large part down to the relaxation of the rules on Hukou, allowing migrants temporary urban Hukou, but was also due to the way in which, post-opening up, Hukou played a lesser role in determining the ability of people to migrate within China (illegally) as it was no longer necessary in order to gain food, which was now available on the open market.

Neatening up the actual markets, however, was not the only thing necessary if the Wenzhou model was to genuinely be able to be sold as 'modern', innovative and quick to respond to the needs of a global marketplace keen to commission everything and anything at 'China price'. Therefore, once the model was in the hands of the State, the all-important new economic paradigm was made to undergo various changes which centred around two key themes – 'greening' and rationalizing. The environmental concern was a complicated mix of the necessity to portray the model as 'responsible' and 'green' to international corporations who were considering using China as a production base, subject to general 'ethical' standards, and as a popular reappropriation of Confucian principles of 'harmony' and 'balance'. In Yiwu, what resulted from these twin desires was the very Xiuhu Park through which I am wandering – the creation that provides the '11 square metres of public garden per inhabitant' that the official website triumphantly announces.

Yiwu is then the embodiment of the new, state-endorsed Wenzhou model, and its absolute reliance upon the model is important for understanding another key part of the logic of the bargain – the necessity to operate on the basis of high quantities of inexpensive units. The Wenzhou model is always a numbers game. The logic of the bargain is held in place by the idea of the combination of quantity and cheapness – a direct reflection of the model used to maintain the bargain commodity chain. This combination is absolutely about anonymity and is defined by speed rather than place – not only the anonymity of the markets in Yiwu or the invisibility of the pedlars in Shanghai, but also the anonymity of the bargain stores themselves – the ways in which their functionality denies them the 'character' one might consider other stores to have.

If, however, anonymity is definitive of bargain logic across the commodity chain, this is not to say that those places that make-up the bargain chain are purely and simply about anonymity. Place squeezes through in spite of anonymity – people have sentiments towards their local bargain stores; dock workers have fierce allegiances to their places of work; and even in Yiwu, the overwhelming features of non-place do not completely rule. The practising of the Wenzhou model in Yiwu reflects the ancestral links of many of its inhabitants and therefore very much embeds a sense of history within the city, albeit one that has had to battle for recognition and is now shaped to the requirements of market socialism and indeed Western business concerns. What's more, this history is tied to a specific group of people, from a specific district, so is very much 'anthropological' in the sense that Auge speaks of. Yet, today's Yiwu was not the geographic site of this anthropological history – the roots of the Wenzhou model were effectively *transported* to the Yiwu that was set up in the late twentieth century. Therefore, its inhabitants have a lived environment in which history on the whole consists of *replicas* of past China, which can only serve to show people what Yiwu *never was*, but what other parts of China certainly were. History is something of an abstraction in Yiwu and not simply in Auge's sense of being absent. Yiwu is celebrated for poets who were geographically situated within it and whose achievements are unrelated to trade, and contemporaneously for its trade capacity, the history of which is unrelated to its geographical location. Its history then is a series of 'blips' in time that the Yiwu authorities attempt to join via the architectural references seen in Xiuhu Park.

It is in Yiwu's more functional (less decorative) built environment that we can see a genuine continuity from Confucian, through Maoist, to reformist times. In fact, in wandering Yiwu's streets, the city starts to display an increasing number of examples of new construction that echoes both a dynastic and a communist past. As David Bray argues, the current-day *xiaoqu* (small districts) are very much influenced (it would certainly appear) by the previous *danwei* (work unit) form (Bray 2005: 35). Just like the *danwei*, the xiaoqu in Yiwu and elsewhere are planned neighbourhoods in which housing is integrated with communal facilities such as nurseries, clinics, restaurants, shops and sports facilities. A spatial repertoire used for the production of communist objects and fervour is now put to the service of the production of market-socialist objects and fervour.

However, as Bray points out, the history of this historical form goes much further back than Mao. Despite being a quintessential mechanism of the Communist Party under his leadership, the *danwei* can trace its roots to the traditional courtyard house designed to complement the ethical codes of Confucianism. For Bray, then, the form was first reappropriated by socialism and only then by market socialism (Bray 2005: 35). This third-time re-employment of the courtyard form cannot, of course, operate without its historical legacy. It brings with it both Confucianism and Maoism, continuing them into the new *xiaoqu* spaces and providing a built continuity between the dynastic past, the Maoist past and the market-socialist present. In fact, the commercial developers of these areas even focus on creating spaces for *linli guanxi* (neighbourhood *guanxi*),[13] such as the *danwei* used to provide, proving just how deeply the ideological remnants of the *danwei* are ingrained in current practice – the 'mimetic effect' Bray mentions (Bray 2005: 156). So, the *danwei*, born of Confucianism and appropriated for political ends, finds itself now, in the post-reform period, reappropriated for economic ends as part of the general dominance of economic logic, as Michael Dutton asserts:

> The once all-encompassing work unit that took care of all aspects of a worker's life is being transformed into an economic enterprise, while peasants, once tethered to the land by a caste-like system of household registration, are being transformed into 'free' workers and drawn into the city in ever-increasing numbers. (Bray 2005: 268)

The history that asserts Yiwu as a 'place' then is to be found not in monuments, plaques and statues, but in the fabric of its everyday spaces, in the *unintended* aspects of both Confucianism and Maoism that entered into its creation and being. As Auge says, place has history as a day-to-day creation and is 'historical' for its inhabitants since their own pasts are captured there and they have built up memories there (Auge 1995: 55). The creation of this day-to-day history can even be witnessed in the behaviour of many of the wholesale buyers who visit Yiwu. Despite never staying long enough to find a sense of place in the same way an inhabitant would, some buyers want a sense of familiarity and community. They, therefore, choose to stay in the large Western chain hotels rather than the ex-state-run hotels, despite the fact these hotels do not necessarily have better facilities and are often further from the markets. Many told me they enjoyed the kind of ad-hoc community that briefly built up in and around these hotels, especially around busy trading times of the year.

It is also worth considering that Yiwu will increasingly gain a more solid sense of place, as it starts to become seen as typical of a specific era in China's history – one in which it was attempting to marry market economics and socialism. As Auge points out, markets too can gain history: 'whether they are shrinking or expanding, the space in which they grow or regress is a historical space' (Auge 1995: 59). It may be that in the future, Yiwu's markets are hailed as the instigators of new forms of capitalist relations, in a manner not dissimilar to the way Venice's markets are regarded as the birthplace of older capitalisms. Visiting Yiwu may then become part of what Auge describes as 'a turning back on the self' (Auge 1995: 92); an awareness of oneself as part of a geographically located spectacle, created as a result of mythmaking surrounding a specific place that causes its image to be stronger than the place itself.

This awareness of the place Yiwu is likely to occupy in future histories is certainly true for a young Western couple I meet who have made Yiwu their home. They tell me how they struggled to garner any feelings towards the place at first, but that they realized, even then, that they were part of a very interesting piece of global development and history. When struggling to make Yiwu feel like home or find anything 'homely' about it, this was a great comfort to them. Jen tells me – 'When we came here, I was quite depressed for a while, and I guess a little shocked, because I knew it would feel very different to us, but I thought I would be able to make it my home even then … and I wasn't able …. I couldn't feel like that about it. And the business was hard you know – it took a long time to have any success. But, I mean, we came here before Yiwu was really known about and when I started to see it becoming well-known I felt different. I realized it was becoming famous, you know, globally, and all of a sudden, I felt proud. I was amazed! This place I could not make my home … and suddenly I was proud of it. It was completely illogical, my reaction, but it really helped me feel a sense of home towards Yiwu.'

Yiwu's relatively new-found fame can also be seen amongst the manufacturers. I thought back to wandering around the markets with Jay and remembered how he had explained that sometimes when stallholders were really determined to sell, they would draw upon the place-ship and kudos of Yiwu as a tool to convince him. 'If they thought they were losing me, you know, if they thought I was about to walk away, they would start to tell me how this was Yiwu and I wouldn't do any better anywhere than this. They would say how efficient and fast it was, and how cheap, and how this was the *world*-famous Yiwu … you know … *YIWU*! … and it didn't get better than this.' This world fame, though, is based on an essentially economic phenomenon – Yiwu's markets. Surely, this means that if it is gaining place-ship, it is because 'the market' is becoming accepted as 'place'. This is, in fact, Auge's concern with non-place – that their 'contracts' may become the most common way of interacting with location and their (fake) features of place may gain total legitimacy. The point is a wholly political one for Auge; non-place is primarily economic and therefore cannot be separated from the proliferation of corporate control and profit-logic, and the systematic destruction of the means to escape, refuse and reappropriate the latter two elements (Auge 1995: 103). By this logic, non-place uses its 'blandness' to hide its politics, when in reality it is a *political* location, whose apparently non-political brandings and nondescript spaces serve to hide its potency as a corporate player. But what is happening in Yiwu is not a hiding of economics (and therefore politics) – it shouts them loudly! – but rather the economic realm (the market) having politics above and beyond 'contracts' in the first place. The corporate nature of the market in Yiwu, is underplayed and interspliced with personal histories and ways of operating from the *danwei* days, as well as a long history of struggle for the Wenzhou model. While the logic of the bargain may revolve around anonymity then, locations along its chain have important recourse to place-ship.

I head away from Xiuhu Park and back towards the foyer of my austere hotel, where I am due to meet Ben (not his real name), a wholesale buyer from the West who has been coming to Yiwu for the best part of a decade. He probably wants to check out I'm not a journalist before he lets me follow him round the markets tomorrow, watching him do his deals. He seemed very cautious when I messaged him online. I'm not quite sure how I'm going to prove to him that I'm not. The sun is beginning to fall behind the outline of the mountains and the air is distinctly chill. Despite its various historical strands, it's hard not to feel that Yiwu is an uncaring non-place once the evening comes.

iii) Reciprocity, Risk and the Denial of Copyright Culture in Yiwu

Ben is a surprise. He's young – in his late twenties and well spoken. He works for what he describes as a 'large thrift store chain' and is rather ashamed of being a wholesale buyer. He thinks it is a 'dirty game'. I try to get to the bottom of why he feels this way, and he explains that manufacturers are always looking for the next 'wave', the next hot product, and that they just continue to jump on the back of trends in order to make a few pence more profit. 'I know they have to do it,' he says, 'I just can't help but think that it's so cut-throat.' He tells me it quite often happens that a manufacturer wants to switch production, so sells his old moulds in order to purchase different ones, and since he can no longer be part of the commodity chain for that specific product anyway, he does not mind if the buyer of those moulds makes more or less the same item he was making. 'Once a manufacturer believes demand for a certain commodity to be on the wane, he doesn't mind someone else taking their chances with the same commodity,' he says. 'Nobody wants to be tied to one product for ever anyway, the risk of someone making what you used to make is out-weighed by the ability to switch to the latest hot product.' To me this sounds rather vibrant; Ben says he has seen it too much and admits he is perhaps cynical due to 'overexposure.'

Ben's experience sounds familiar. A few weeks earlier in Shanghai I had met an American logistics manager named Jeff, who had told me how his company had wanted to buy a bulk load of plastic light pulls in a certain blue-green colour. He had gone to established companies in the Pearl River area, and they had done sample runs for him, changing the size and shape to his specifications and using a slightly different tone of one of their set colours. They were no good; the colour was not close enough. Then, he had a call from a young factory owner from Yiwu, who had heard from a friend of a friend that a Western businessman was looking for light pulls in an unusual colour. 'I can make them,' he said, 'give me a week to show you.' Jeff had replied that it was not possible to make the colour on the basis of already established formulae and that he did not want to deal with more people who would try to convince him it was a close enough match, when it clearly was not. He put the phone down and thought no more about the conversation. A week later the phone rang again. It was the young factory owner saying he had a sample for Jeff to see. Jeff said he was leaving in two days and did not have time. 'I am downstairs,' said the voice. Jeff moved to the office window and sure enough in the street was a young Chinese man holding some boxes and waving up at him. The boxes contained a sample run of fifty light pulls, in exactly the shape, size and colour Jeff had wanted. He was amazed. He gave the factory owner a contract on the spot.

I am beginning to enjoy these anecdotes and the sense of vitality they bring and admit as much to Ben. 'Ah,' he says, 'but this is a real issue for China, and I don't just mean individuals…. IPR [intellectual property rights] is a big deal for Westerners and China is trying to prove it understands its importance by bringing in new laws. But the factory owners often ignore them, even though the laws are often there to protect them too. They don't want protecting. They want to go on being able to switch production to make something that has already proved itself a success whenever they choose. They don't understand the issue with copying … well … sometimes they do … but it doesn't suit the way they work you see. They want flexibility, and IPR doesn't give that.'

The dilemma at play is an interesting one. For the great majority of small-business owners in Yiwu, making very basic products at low prices, the 'risk' of a product being copied is a small price to pay for the ability to be able to create spontaneously what is demanded, and, while it sometimes causes problems for specific individuals, it keeps Yiwu as a whole thriving. Here, risk allows for a spontaneity which creates a safety of sorts, a safety that at first glance seems to defeat itself, as its logic runs almost entirely contrary to the logic of large global corporations. 'Risk,' in current discourse, and applied to financial or business transactions, is risk as defined by the rationale of big business – Jack Ma's 'whales',[14] as opposed to the rationale of huge agglomerations of 'shrimps' present in Yiwu. In fact, despite its 'big market' status, Yiwu is operationally far more aligned to the 'small networks' part of its own model; so, risk is effectively reformulated in Yiwu and forces a reconsideration of the assumptions of classic Western risk discourses.

Such discourses are based on a rationality of the West in which 'risk' is a category which remains constant, rather than one more dependent upon situation. For example, whilst preventing the stealing of designs in Yiwu (the right to intellectual property) is often deemed necessary, for the manufacturers of small, ubiquitous products, it could heighten the risk of large Western companies only using a handful of producers and the rest not surviving as a result (the right to put oneself forward for work). For Yiwu, it is crucial that wealth (even small parcels of it) is spread, if the whole is to survive. In a commodity chain based on the existence of many small players making many small units for small profits, those profits must fall to the many. If designs are protected, profit starts to fall to the few, the few grow large and the majority must fall off. Sooner or later this defeats even the Western agendas in which copyright was deemed necessary, as the newly grown companies are large enough to start competing head-on with the Western companies. This kind of example exposes the way that classic risk discourses tend to be culturally myopic (i.e. Western), and in fact, in being so, enable the purporting of risk discourses as something removed from the culture 'out there' as if it is therefore neutral and distanced. Risk is made apolitical and stripped of any agenda, when, of course, it has a deeply ingrained agenda, and the desire on the part of Western businesses to see Yiwu prove it can maintain IPR laws is testament to this. To be sure, there are also many manufacturers in Yiwu who welcome the concept and practice of IPR – especially those making slightly higher-end products where design differentiates a product greatly. But there are also many who do not, and this cannot be simply explained by seeing them as 'unethical' or 'fly-by-night' (as I often heard them called). Rather, many (not all it is true) are simply working on a different business logic.

Also, it is worth considering that the notion of individual rational choice utilized by risk discourses – economic man with his internal 'hedonic calculus' weighing up losses and gains as a neutral tool – may not be quite so straightforward in the context of a culture in which remnants of collectivism and a different view of oneself in relation to others remain. This ignores the way in which Yiwu, to a large extent, operates as a mutuality of many small players, in which to share the risk (by ignoring IPR regulations), is often part of 'sharing the wealth'. This was a phrase I heard frequently from buyers in Yiwu. It was used to refer to the tendency of businesses to stay small and remain in areas of business within the same commodity chain, so as to be able to share knowledge and resources. If successful, a small-business owner tends to start up another small business in a linked industry, rather than attempting to buy out companies making similar products to his own in a bid to be the biggest. For example, if he makes plastic bowls, he may buy a small plastic recycling plant, so as to be more in control of the raw materials needed, and a small trading company in Shanghai, so as to be able to attract sales through different channels. These additional small companies, which are often staffed by members of the same family or close family friends, will then give work to one another by sending clients through one another's companies, thus 'sharing the wealth'. If the bowlmaker wants to switch production to another product, he can do so relatively easily as long as IPR is not in the way. He risks another company copying his designs, but he is also enabled to be spontaneous and utilize whichever raw materials are more available and therefore cheaper.

Sometimes 'sharing the wealth' was used more scathingly. Two young Russian wholesalers in Yiwu were adamant that you had to 'do your sums, make a decision, and do the deal, there and then, on the spot. If you wait, you will find other people get involved and you do not know what is going on. They [Chinese manufacturers] try to share the wealth, so you have to say yes before they can bring someone else in on the deal. There are many layers, you know, many layers that you do not want.' Back in Shanghai, another wholesale buyer, John, had told me how he had recently travelled down the coast to Ningbo to meet a factory owner he felt he may well potentially want to do business with. When he arrived, the factory looked as though it could easily cope with his requirements, and the price quoted was a good one. 'But the guy I am dealing with has involved another guy in the deal and I can't work out why,' he said. 'I don't really want to deal with both of them even though they still seem to be able to offer a good price, because I like to know what's going on and who's getting what bits of money. I don't like it. Why is he there? Why do they always have to share the wealth?'

Similarly, Jeff in Shanghai had explained to me how about eight years ago he had an agent from Singapore who was introducing him to several companies in Asia. 'We were paying a retainer to him, for his services, plus all his expenses,' said Jeff. 'He introduced me to the owner, Mr W. in Suzhou, and someone I thought worked for Mr W. We did the deal and began purchasing small aluminium tubes. We paid about one dollar for each. About two years into the relationship I received a call from Mr W in which he stated that he could sell me the product for only fifty-five US cents if I could get those other two guys out of the middle. I told Mr W I had no idea that the other guys were involved and to immediately stop paying them and send me revised pricing. Fortunately, he did and I fired the guy in Singapore, but that could have turned out very bad if we had had to find another manufacturer at short notice.'

Ben had a rather more nuanced understanding of the situation, saying 'it's normally that there are more layers involved than you think, not that the manufacturers are literally sharing out the profit between them. When people say "wholesale" in China, it's often second or even third-hand wholesale. That's why you have to come to Yiwu and make sure you deal with a factory that's actually based in Yiwu – that way you're most likely to get the real wholesale price. If you go to someone in Shanghai, they've probably already got their stuff from here and marked it up a bit – they're just selling it on. Sometimes there are different layers of the process who do know each other and are part of the same agreement to supply a certain buyer, sometimes without that buyer knowing – I have heard of that happening, but often it's just that there are a lot of layers! But, you know, it's a way of operating here, someone owes someone a favour, so finds a way they can be useful to a deal they're doing, brings them in on it you know, so that they can maintain their relationship with that person and count on them to return the favour in the future – that's good *guanxi*. It doesn't necessarily mean they are charging any less good a price, and I've learnt that you can't just go in there and clear out the dead wood, get rid of those extra guys. You have to say, is the deal right for me? If so, you have to do it, and not worry about what's going on with them – that's their problem, as long as the price is right for you.' He laughs – 'Yiwu's only a one-stop wonder if you make it work for you!'

Guanxi is unignorable in Yiwu, as it is across China, and has seen many large Western business players struggle. For example, when Lee Kai Fu controversially left his position as corporate vice president at Microsoft to work for Yahoo, he wrote a report stating that Bill Gates had made various '*guanxi* mistakes'. These included boastful public relations campaigns, failure to make long-term commitments, failure to properly nurture local talent, and most importantly, failure to lower the price of Microsoft software so as to make it affordable to Chinese consumers. Gates was seen as benefiting before contributing, and according to Lee, he should have expected the vast amount of pirated software, considering its contextually high price. The fakes were a direct result of his bad *guanxi*.

For Gates and many Western business people, the struggle to accept *guanxi* is to do with the way it enables strong ties and favour-giving to determine how and with whom business is done. Within the Western model this is seen as allowing practices reserved for the family or community realm to enter the market – a realm seen as entirely separate. It is this separation that Gudeman attempts to blur when he argues for an understanding of the economy that consists of both 'market' factors and 'anthropological' factors. His analysis sees economy as consisting of two realms: community and market, community being associations, and market being anonymous short-term exchanges (Gudeman 2001: 1). In the community realm, which is localized, material goods are exchanged through relationships kept for their own sake, whereas in the market realm, which is global, short-term relationships exist purely to achieve a project or secure a good (Gudeman 2001: 10).

This attempt to join market and community in a new conception of economy is inspired by the view, which Gudeman shares with Mark Granovetter (1973), that while anthropologists employ an oversocialized view of human action (embedded communities), economists employ an undersocialized one (disembedded communities).[15] So, following this logic, in non-market economies, there is more instrumental action than anthropologists recognize, and in market economies, there is more embedded action than economists concede (Gudeman 2001: 19). This is a useful acknowledgement of economic and anthropological typecasting of situations and works towards a sort of market–community merger alongside an acknowledgement that these realms take on many of each other's features – as in Yiwu. Michel Callon's attempt to argue for seeing market relations as merged with community relations is worth mentioning here. His mission is to continue Polanyi's work by arguing that economics, rather than being a descriptive tool, actually *performs* the economy (see Callon 1998, 2007); economic ideas entangling themselves with materialities in order to achieve their efficacy and durability. However, as Bhaskar Mukhopadhyay points out, despite Callon's positioning of subjects as agents entangled in a web of relations and connections, he is far from being a proponent of the idea of the network as a mechanism of collective effort. For Callon, networks inherently contain structural asymmetry, agonistic struggle, coercion and violence, and here he is engaging with Polanyi's concern in regard to the violence entailed in the process of disembedding, or 'making market', as Mukhopadhyay puts it (Mukhopadhyay 2010). This latter frequently involves dispossession, exploitation and the destruction of markets structured on other principles. This is largely the case – indeed the razing of Zhejiangcun and the closure of many other 'unofficial' markets provides a perfect example. However, in Yiwu, built-for-purpose as it was, the making of market did not involve a disembedding in Polanyi or Callon's sense. Rather, it involved the making of a new phenomenon – one we could perhaps call the *market life-world* – in which market and community were instantly already combined, both through cultural history and the built environment. In fact, the ways in which older systems of reciprocity play out in Yiwu and newer systems of contractualized protection are tacitly ignored stand testament to the entangling of market and community.

In comparing classic cases of making-market (such as the colonial relations Mukhopadhyay uses as his example) and more recent (and unusual) cases such as Yiwu, it is difficult not to cast the market lifeworld as the latest highly successful invention of a capitalism determined to enter into every vestige of everyday life. If we accept this as the case, where does this leave us with defining how reciprocity works within a merged economy and market? In opposition to both the traditional anthropological view that reciprocal ties are the basis of society and the neoclassical economist view that sees these ties as evolving from individual interests, Gudeman believes reciprocal ties to be *tactical* acts. As such, they extend the community base to persons outside of its borders as a way of 'groping with uncertainty at the limits of a community' (Gudeman 2001: 80), in order to gain power or maintain independence. So, for Gudeman, refusal to reciprocate can be interpreted as a lack of desire to create mutual relations, or an inability to do so, which means it cannot be viewed as a norm of social life (as the anthropological tradition would have it) nor a function of self-interest (as neoclassical economics would argue). For Gudeman, anthropologists are still caught in a dialectic with Western economists, as both offer essentialist views, the anthropological view being relational and the economistic view being atomistic; one reinforcing relationships and altruism, the other the individual and egoism. In contrast to both these positions, Gudeman sees reciprocity as 'part of a system of practices in which participants express, conserve, lose, and gain position in the sphere of social value' (Gudeman 2001: 89–90). So, reciprocity as a tactical act is about negotiating the value of one's position, a position with a value which is social, not economic. As he says, 'reciprocity is not the core of society but its expression ... neither a primitive isolate nor the atom of society but its badge' (Gudeman 2001: 92). But what determines the social value of a position gained through tactical reciprocity? Surely, the value is defined by the amount of choice the position confers upon its owner. If reciprocity is based on tactics, used to gain greater influence in some way, then the way it is played out is to do with individual people carving out ways to gain more life choices, or at least be less constricted in life choices. It is about the creation of a feeling of greater freedom in the ways in which to survive and can be mutual as well as individual. It is not 'maximizing' in the classic sense; that is, it is not manifested in attempts to make profit; rather it is concerned with maximizing choice through increasing personal potency within the surrounding framework. (Of course, this may also inevitably revolve around questions of wealth and profit.) In short, it is, once again, about being a tactician; attempting, just as the pedlars in Shanghai did, to gain as much autonomy over one's survival practices as possible.

The manufacturers and wholesale buyers of Yiwu, then, through this specific form of reciprocity, are proving that they too cannot be strategists, forced as they are to operate according to the short-term, spontaneous logic of the bargain.

What emerges from all this is a portrait of a place that is intrinsically set up to operate as a shared space, on both a micro and a macro level. Its very infrastructure is designed in such a way as to cause numerous small enterprises to gain through practising mutuality. Unlike the Guangdong (Canton) market, Yiwu allows buyers to order small quantities and to mix small amounts of various commodities as part of an order. It operates more like a domestic supermarket than a cash and carry. Containers to be shipped can be shared between any number of people. The success of one company, far from being seen as the downfall of another, is simply seen as potentially attracting more money to the area. One simply has to stay ahead of the game, make the next hot product for a hot price. This modus operandi creates forms of solidarity which are at one and the same time 'new' and built upon older forms. This is not, however, to suggest some essentialist vision of Yiwu as a place somehow displaying 'communist' characteristics within a capitalism of its own – individualistic behaviour does, of course, exist in Yiwu, is even perhaps dominant. However, it *is* the case that risks are often calculated with the whole in mind, simply because the whole is more likely to turn up insurmountable risks to the individual. Yiwu exposes the mistaken impression of risk analysts that it is *direct* individual choice which determines action. As Mauss emphasized, our sharp division between freedom and obligation, just like that between self-interest and altruism, is an illusion thrown up by the market, whose anonymity allows us to ignore the fact that we constantly rely upon others (Mauss 1990).

The modus operandi in Yiwu not only brings into question the way risk is thought about, but also forces us to pull apart well-established binaries which have become taken for granted in the history of Western philosophy – market/community, commodity/gift, exchange/use, monetary/non-monetary, modern/traditional, capitalist/non-capitalist, anonymous/associated, reciprocal/non-reciprocal. Such binaries tend to continue the idea of the 'gift' economy being somehow intrinsically 'moral', as opposed to the immorality of the 'commodity' market. More recently, it can be found in Polanyi's (Polanyi 2001) assertion that when kinship is present, reciprocity is apparent and dominant, but when the market economy prevails, things are better understood by formal economics – presumably a formal economics which assumes a non-reciprocity relationship. For Polanyi, as for Aristotle, this transition from what he called 'embedded' to 'disembedded' economies (i.e. land and labour becoming separated from the social fabric through money and exchange) was a devastating moral transformation. Again the moral is equated to kinship relations and the immoral to the market relations. Again there seems to be an unproblematic line separating the two. From the standpoint of this tradition, money corrupts reciprocity.

Therefore, what we have arrived at, in terms of our interpretation of reciprocity, is a rather contradictory position which asks us to embrace individualistic accumulation, but for the good of a mutuality; in effect creating of us Bauman's 'walking contradiction' of the 'good consumer' (Bauman 2000) who must spend, but must not overspend or spend wrongly. (This same contradiction can be seen in recent statistics of China's development, which show how as poverty in China decreases, so inequality increases, and provide 'evidence' for those who assume as inevitable a Smithian process in which, in order for us all to rise, some must rise further than others.) Reciprocity has become embedded in consumption by this reasoning and rendered invisible; to return a 'favour' given to us by 'the market', we must spend for the good of everyone. But this is only the case if we allow that 'market' is distinct from 'community'; by disallowing the opposition we can, perhaps, reclaim reciprocity. The city of Yiwu, from the very outset of its modern conception, defied all opposition of 'market' and 'community', being ideologically defined by its 'small commodity city' status, and reliant upon its past live–work (*danwei*) relations. In Yiwu, market relations *are* community relations. Reciprocity is claimed by the collapsing of the two into each other.

iv) Yiwu versus alibaba.com: The Power of the Anti-inventory

It is mid-morning, around 140 kilometres north-east from Yiwu. The mist that earlier had hung above the sparkling surface of the West Lake has lifted, revealing the iconic forms of its long, low walkways, with their crenellated sides and half-moon gates. The air is clear and moist. Sound does not travel quite like it does elsewhere, rather, it hangs, just briefly, in the dampness, before disintegrating into the urban quagmire. Opposite the lake, a group of older Chinese men and women sit on benches playing traditional instruments and singing. Others, mainly men, are crouched on the pavement playing cards for nearly worthless Fen. A man in his mid-twenties shows off his Kung Fu moves to friends, saying 'Jackie Chan, Jackie Chan!' His friends stop a Western tourist and politely ask if they can take a picture of themselves with her on their mobile phones. Above them all, the ever-smiling face of Jack Ma beams down from an immense billboard, surveying the scene with that familiar owl-like glint and irresistible optimism.

This is Hangzhou, birthplace of Jack Ma (or Ma Yun to give him his Chinese name), China's popular and highly successful entrepreneur and role model. It was here that, at the age of twelve, Ma cycled miles every morning to wait outside hotels and offer to give guided tours to tourists in an attempt to learn English. It worked. His English is near perfect. Perhaps rather prophetically, this was 1976, the year Mao died, bringing an end to the Cultural Revolution and soon after, a beginning to the reign of Deng Xiaoping, along with its reform and opening policies. Twenty-three years later, as much of the world was in a state of pre-millennium fever, concerning itself with era-marking extravagances or panicking about the 'millennium bug', Ma quietly and confidently launched alibaba.com. The site is a business-to-business (b2b) marketplace which links wholesale buyers to manufacturers, serving 12 million members from 200 countries, figures that are increasing constantly. It now has offices across China as well as in Europe and Silicon Valley, with over 5,000 employees, and is China's largest e-commerce company and the world's largest and most successful online b2b marketplace for small to medium-sized companies.

'Lee' (his chosen 'English name' – a derivative of his own) is a business graduate from Shanghai, here to attend the Hangzhou Trade Fair, where he hopes to make contacts and gain employment in trade logistics. I point to the Jack Ma billboard: 'He's a popular man.' 'Yes, he is very popular.' Lee informs me, 'a huge national role model. A recent survey found that one in ten school children wanted to be like him.' 'What is it about him they like?' I ask. Lee pauses for a second or two, before explaining that Ma came from humble beginnings, the son of hardworking parents in rural Sichuan province, so his rise is inspirational for the huge numbers of young workers from rural provinces trying to carve out a better life. 'He is a symbol of what can happen in the new China,' says Lee, 'and people want to believe that.' I nod, 'He's been very clever to base his business online – especially before many people were doing that in China.' Lee agrees. He thinks it was because Ma came from nothing that he dared to take more risks than others – he would go back to nothing if he had to because he knew how to cope with it. So he invested in the internet even before it had taken off in China, which meant he got there first and cornered that market with hardly any competition. 'Do you think he would have got where is today without the Internet?' I ask. 'No,' says Lee, 'definitely not. He would be successful, but not to the extent he is now,'

According to the China Internet Network Information Centre, in 2006 alone, China's internet population increased by 24 per cent, to 137 million people – one tenth of the population – compared to a minute coverage five years earlier. Without doubt, the sudden and large increase in internet coverage and usage in China has hugely contributed to Ma's success. Within the bargain store commodity chain, the internet has been, and is, a fast flow, both in terms of the speed with which it was put to use by Chinese manufacturers and in terms of the extent to which it caused the chain as a whole to operate more quickly. Thousands of small manufacturers signed up to alibaba.com and began receiving orders from Western companies. Because alibaba.com did not require buyers to purchase in bulk, these orders tended to be relatively spur-of-the-moment decisions requiring quick turnaround schedules. Just-in-time economics had reached new levels in the bargain store commodity chain and it was in no small part due to the likes of alibaba.com. It is, in many ways, the ultimate just-in-time business.

Unlike so many of the key places along the bargain store commodity chain – the recycling workshops, the container ships, the dockside warehouses, the display stalls in Yiwu, even the 'stocky' displays of the bargain stores – places of stock-piled commodities, alibaba.com resists the inventory. It is a virtual inventory, an anti-inventory, a menu of things which will only be brought into existence if and when they are purchased. Yet, conceptually alibaba.com fills up space and time, making promises of future labour and motivating new desires, new needs, at the click of a mouse. As Jack Ma once pointed out in a company speech, 'we're better than Yiwu, when we want to expand we just add another server.'

However, the anti-inventory comes with its own issues. Trust becomes even more crucial. Comments and forum threads on wholesale websites are revealing when it comes to alibaba.com in the light of its territory-based equivalent – Yiwu. A wholesale buyer, relatively new to the business, who had just started using alibaba.com, asked advice from others on the forum, saying, 'How do I go about narrowing down my choices? Have you guys eliminated suppliers based on location, rating, or other criteria? Slightly lost as to where to start!' One reply stated, 'I know where you're at. I experienced the same thing two years ago when we switched to alibaba from our traditional suppliers. It feels like the whole of China's on there right? The ratings tell you something, but not enough. I would attempt to make contact with about six companies, tell them you have contacted others and that good and honest communication is important to you, and see which one gets back to you quickest and with the best response.' Similarly, another user was considering using alibaba.com to buy products made in Yiwu. 'I want to shift my purchasing more to online, but I'm thinking I'd still like it to be Yiwu-based, as I have bought from there for the past five years and believe it to have more integrity than other areas. But I can't tell whether the Yiwu-based firms on alibaba are displaying in the markets, or just happen to have a workshop there. I want one that has a regular stall. Any advice?' Amongst the replies was one that said, 'You can ask the supplier for their stall number and check it out on one of the Yiwu websites, but I've found that if someone is in Yiwu they are nearly always connected to the markets because it's not worth them being based there otherwise. Even if their factory doesn't have a stall, they are making products for another factory that does.'

As Ben explains to me, 'trust is incredibly important in Yiwu because its USP (Unique Selling Point) is that, unlike with alibaba.com, you can come and see the goods, meet the people, shake hands, etc., but this is only a useful USP if it counts for something – if there is trust. If there isn't, and you think it's risky either way, you may as well buy the goods online and save yourself the time and the costs of the flights out here.' Both Yiwu's local authorities, though, and Jack Ma are keen to garner the trust of wholesaler buyers and agents. Ma has set up various mechanisms to inspire trust in buyers, including his 'alipay' system (described on alibaba.com as 'a secure, trusted and convenient way for individuals and businesses to make and receive payments online and on mobile phones') and the 'gold suppliers' approval scheme. For their part, the Yiwu authorities have attempted to implement an equally rigorous programme of what could perhaps be termed ethico-legal cleansing. Informal market practices (such as unofficial loans) have been cracked down on and manufacturers were given clear legal constraints and codes of conduct – the Wenzhou model has been 'rationalized'. Being China's most famous and most prolific city for small commodities, Yiwu is a testing ground and leading example in the building of new legal frameworks for Intellectual Property Rights (IPR) and has strategic importance at the national level and in the establishment of cooperative international relations. Therefore, the authorities there are keen to appear as adherents of international legal and ethical standards on trade practices. As party secretary of Yiwu, Lou Guohua says, 'We know that the prosperity of the market heavily relies on credibility. Quality control and credibility establishment is key for Yiwu to be integrated with the world' (2014: China Economic Net website).

In 2008, Yiwu released a White Paper entitled 'IPR Protection in Yiwu', which elaborated upon Yiwu's IPR protection in terms of patenting, trade-marking, copyrighting and judicial protection. It stressed how Yiwu has developed a multilayered network of protection and adopted monitoring and interconnecting mechanisms from various departments, enabling booth-owners' complaints of infringement to be handled immediately through information sharing and mutual supervision. Yiwu is the only county-level city in China to have an IPR protection service centre and was the first to create an international coordination in IPR involving over 200 members from 8 countries, including the United States, France, Germany, Japan and the United Kingdom. Yiwu's Trade and Industry Department describe this operational style as 'small network' supervision of 'big market' functions; a practice which has come to be known as the 'Yiwu mode' of IPR protection.

However, this newly evolved legal framework is largely concerned with protecting higher-end 'brand' products, as part of a concern with upgrading and protecting the types of commodities China as a whole makes, and with guarding against the loss of credibility counterfeit trading brings upon Chinese manufacturing. For the smaller manufacturers who remain ensconced in the low-end sector, new IPR legalities have little relevance, as 'brand' and 'fakes' are non-issues in the realm of mundane and ubiquitous objects. Furthermore, as previously mentioned, because of the short-termism and volatility of commodity chains for inexpensive commodities and the simplicity of the products manufactured, companies often switch production very quickly, ignoring IPR protocols if and where they exist.

If the introduction of IPR and the contractualization of manufacturing in Yiwu (and indeed in China in general) are part of the new China, then it is easy to interpret the less formal practices as part of the revolutionary era. As Michael Dutton describes with rich detail in *Policing Chinese Politics* (Dutton 2005), one of the main ways in which the period of economic growth that China has entered into since 1978 and the reform and opening policies of Deng have manifested themselves is through the introduction of the Western-style 'contract'. This contract has effectively created a new form of 'policing' which constitutes a replacement of the political form of policing that China had in the past – the 'mass line[16]' – thus delinking politics and policing. For Dutton, the replacement of mass line with contract equates to the replacement of the Schmittian friend–enemy binary by a legal–illegal binary. This friend–enemy binary evaporated quickly with the beginning of the reform era and in the wake of Deng's extreme pragmatism.[17] This transition transformed the single political question of friend–enemy into 'a multitude of discrete and largely non- or even de-politicizing questions'. Furthermore, 'what slowly came to undergird all these disparate questions of the reform era was the single issue of profit and loss' (Dutton 2005: 18). Thus, Dutton argues, the logic of profit promoted in the reform era saw political capital replaced with money, and the end of a long period of political intensity (Dutton 2005: 18).

> The desire to replace the Maoist-induced collective dependence upon the politicized state with a notion of rationally calculable individual obligation was central to Deng's reform campaign. It was the contractually based notion of individual obligation that fuelled China's economic reform program and, as a result, the development of a substantive legal code would, by necessity, become an essential component of this process. (Dutton 2005: 263)

The issue, for Dutton, is one of commitment politics. Whilst prior to reform the either-or choice of class struggle was reiterated in its simplest form, in the post-reform period, social questions have been condensed into monetary forms ordered around the contract. Therefore, 'in each and every domain ... the practices once undertaken out of passionate commitment to a political program were now to be underwritten and disciplined by the dominant economic distinction of profit and loss' (Dutton 2005: 314–5). Dutton paints this transition as one which has created a 'new, passionless world of the commodity society', in which 'the excitement of revolution gave way to the faux excitement of manufactured commodity desire' (Dutton 2005: 315).

Similarly, Xiaobing Tang (2002) suggests there are two distinct responses to everyday life in China. At the height of the Cultural Revolution, it was something to be overcome by a heroic commitment to communal living, whereas, as China moved into the post-revolutionary period, emphasis was placed on transcending the everyday and ameliorating anxiety through the consumption of lifestyles and commodities. Tang sees these two strands as 'related social discourses: an anxious affirmation of ordinary life and a continuous negotiation with the utopian impulse to reject everyday life' (Tang 2002: 129–130). Tang describes a revolutionary mass culture as emphasizing 'content over form, use value over exchange value, participatory communal action over heterogeneous everyday life ... production oriented rather than consumption oriented' (Tang 2002: 128). Hence, he argues, revolutionary mass culture is profoundly romantic in form and utopian in vision but may become compelling in hindsight:

> Only in absentia does this revolutionary mass culture reveal itself to have been a heroic effort to overcome a deep anxiety over everyday life, often at the cost of impoverishing it. When everyday life is affirmed and accepted as the new hegemony, when commodification arrives to put a price tag on human relations and even on private sentiments, participatory communal action may offer itself as an oppositional discourse and expose a vacuity underlying the myriad of commodity forms. (Tang 2002: 128)

For Tang, Mao nostalgia[18] in the current era in China is a sure sign of the yearning for this past heroic culture and the collective anxiety that the market economy has given rise to. However, consumerism also works to contain and dissolve the anxiety of everyday life by translating collective concerns into consumer desires (Tang 2002: 129). Whilst comfort is sought in past ideas by some, it is sought in things by certain others, and for Tang, this typifies the difference between revolutionary mass culture and the new urban culture. Whilst the former needed to project a life that was wholesome but abstract, the latter needs to present a secular existence full of concrete expectations and fulfilments (Tang 2002: 130). The two responses are indicative of the existence of both revolutionary and post-revolutionary subjectivities in current-day China. The contractualization of manufacturing relates to the post-revolutionary subjectivity, whilst deeply embedded, informal practices relate to revolutionary subjectivity.

In fact, Yiwu provides a good example of the more complicated subjectivities existing in current-day China; its spatial relations force a nuanced analysis of the often unquestioned assumption that the shift from *danwei ren* (*danwei* person) to *shehui ren* (social person) corresponds unproblematically to the rise of the market and the privileging of individual interest. (See Cao Jinqing and Chen Zhongya who put forward a relatively straightforward connection between market economics and non-collective identities, 1997.) In reality though, subjectivities are created by a constant reappropriation of deeply ingrained features from the 'old China' and the subsequent rearrangement of them as part of the 'new China'.

Perhaps it is Dutton's use of the word 'faux' that is important here, because the problem with setting up pre-reform politics in opposition to post-reform economism is that the binary does not acknowledge the current sense of 'revolution' and 'excitement'. As Dutton says, 'commitment produces the ethic of the heroic' (Dutton 2005: 313), but the current 'commitment' on the part of China to play developmental catch-up is also played out heroically by many of its people. These two forms of heroism, the former with its strong political and conceptual base, the latter with its determination to improve lifestyle (note, not 'lives'), are precisely what is shaping current-day China and creating a new politics in which market logic is pitted alongside a fading socialist allegiance. Whilst radical theorists such as Raymond Lotta[19] are staunchly against the possibility that politics can exist vis-à-vis marketization, Giovanni Arrighi tends towards the opposite view. In *Adam Smith in Beijing*, he makes clear his conviction that 'even if socialism has already lost out in China, capitalism ... has not yet won' (Arrighi 2007: 24), saying 'add as many capitalists as you like to a market economy, but unless the state has been subordinated to their class interest, the market economy remains non-capitalist' (Arrighi 2007: 332). It could be argued, of course, that the desire to create a *xiaokang* does, in practice, precisely translate to the class interests of capitalism subordinating all others.

Charting a nuanced path between these two arguments is Wang Hui in the celebrated work *The End of the Revolution* (Wang 2009). For him, whilst the forces of marketization are a very real and powerful presence – probably the dominant one in today's China – their potency does not mean that China can be described as following a neo-liberal path in a simplistic or well-trodden sense. The reason for this lies in the historical trajectory of China's relationship with other communist powers. As Wang points out, China began supporting non-aligned movements in the mid-1950s and gradually shed its suzerain[20] relationship with the Soviet Union, establishing its own socialist system and achieving independent status on the international scene. Therefore, China is highly self-reliant and its reform and opening policies were self-directed and had an internal logic (Wang 2009: xix–xx). In particular, he cites Mao's works *On the Ten Major Relationships* and *On the Correct Handling of Contradictions Among the People* as providing the foundations for the new state theory (Wang 2009: xxv). That said, Wang is far from romantic about the extent to which marketization has come to dominate present-day China saying, 'notions such as modernisation, globalisation and growth can be seen as key concepts of a depoliticised or anti-political political ideology, whose widespread usage militates against a popular political understanding of the social and economic shifts at stake in marketization' (Wang 2009: 13). For him this marketization is linked to a two-fold process of depoliticization involving the 'de-theorisation' of the ideological sphere and the sole focus of party work becoming economic reform (Wang 2009: 7).

> In the socialist era, we saw how the strength of the two or many social forces fluctuated in concert with one another, and how the 'far left' and 'far right' were overcome; but as marketization reforms become the predominant trend, the absence of checks and balances from socialist forces between the inner workings of the state, the inner workings of the party and the entire social sphere will quickly shorten the distance between the state and special interest groups. (Wang 2009: xxv)

In Yiwu, the question of subjectivity is perhaps simply overruled by its presence as the mechanism behind a huge brand – 'Made in China'. Its own self-image as a phantasmagorical utopia of commodities is as yet mirrored by the West's fascination with the sheer scale, speed and efficiency of China's rise. This association manifests itself in popular cultural imagination in images of China as the world's factory; a full-to-overflowing production fiend, of epic proportions, as witnessed in Baichwal's previously mentioned *Manufactured Landscapes* (2006). Here, in one scene, a tracking shot over two minutes long captures the longest production line in the world. It is clean, bright, and most of all, it is fast. Nimble fingers are a blur on screen due to the speed with which they go about their work. It is impossible to tell what they are making and how, the motions are so fast; what is clear is that their actions are second-nature. This is China as the world's factory – a full-to-overflowing production fiend of epic proportions; a utopia of commodities, whose subjects strive robot-like in the name of a glorious great leap to the present. As Arrighi argues (with a nod to de Vries's landmark work), China's revolution is indust*rious*, not simply industrial (Arrighi 2007).

It is through such depictions and imaginings that inexpensive, ubiquitous commodities have carved a place for themselves as 'Made In China' objects. Indeed it may even be the case that, contrary to the beliefs of many economic commentators (e.g. Huang 2008), China does not lack a global brand as such – 'Made in China' *is* a brand. Whilst it, of course, cannot be assessed economically alongside 'company brands', its cultural and psycho-social status bears an uncanny resemblance to other 'brand identities', providing clear opportunities for consumers to gain awareness of its connotations and even feel a fondness or 'brand affinity'. This occurs despite its low-end produce, in much the same way as people have fondly dubbed Primark 'Primarni' in a sarcastic nod to it certainly not being Armani. In fact, 'Made in China' has done what 'Made in Spain' in the 1980s never managed to do; it is not an embarrassed apology for low-end products, but rather a triumphant announcement of use value at a bargain price. And Yiwu is its chief protagonist.

On a chilly December morning, I check out of the ex-state-run hotel with its ghosts of past communist officials and its formal arrangements of flowers reflected in the overpolished marble floor and head for the train that will take me back to Shanghai. Yiwu has been a fascinating yet melancholy place; soulless in many ways, yet full of so many era-defining personal histories. Now I, like the commodities made here, will head out to Shanghai before parting company with them momentarily as I get on a plane back to the West, and they take their chances on the high seas.

3

The Container Port: The Overflowing Spaces of Felixstowe and Los Angeles

i) Defetishizing 'whizzy capitalism'– The Slow Foundations of Hyper-speed

It is a late autumn afternoon and a small crowd has gathered along the blustery dockside viewing area at the port of Felixstowe in Suffolk, England. Those gathered are keen to witness the arrival of the largest container ship the world has ever seen. The vessel is almost a kilometre long and moves eerily into harbour to be greeted by the inevitable flurry of press interest and local curiosity. Its cargo is of toys, household products, gadgets, clothes, decorations and trinkets – as the headlines attest, it is 'bringing Christmas from China'. Many, if not the majority, of these products are from Yiwu. Down on the dock itself, huge cranes are poised ready to begin lifting the containers from the ship according to a sophisticated, highly computerized, logistics plan which charts to the inch where each will be placed in readiness for distribution across the United Kingdom. The tiny figures of men on the dockside, dwarfed by the enormity of this floating island of merchandise, seem sublimely ridiculous – men out of time and place, running to keep up with things larger and less stoppable than they have ever experienced. The watching crowd appear awestruck. Some ask in low voices how it will stop and how it stays afloat. The scene is a twenty-first-century version of such early industrial spectacles as the first great train rides or the churning cogs of giant factories. And, despite its computerization, it is cumbersome and heavy like those earlier miracles. The small coloured blocks on the computer screens of the logistics team translate into heavy, creaking lumps of metal, stained with sea-spray and demanding upkeep. The fluidity of the operation remains curtailed by the dictates of the iron cages. The click-happy world eases slowly and creakingly into focus. Just-in-time economics will not be hurried at this particular juncture.

Perceptions of capitalistic growth in recent decades have focused increasingly heavily on speed – especially when it comes to China's development and the impact of this on the ability of consumers in the West to have access to commodities quickly and cheaply. The great manufacturing dragon is cited time and again as undergoing the fastest industrial revolution ever known, and as providing commodity chains that are the epitome of fast capitalism. Message a manufacturer in China one week, and your product will be with you the next, simple as that, goes the myth. But underneath this layer of hyper-speed are older, clunkier facets which provide the foundations for such velocity, and nowhere are these more evident than in the slow-heaving container ports of the West, such as LA and Felixstowe.

Felixstowe port has always been privately owned, despite being requisitioned, along with all other British ports, during both World Wars, before being sold to foreign interests for the first time in the 1970s. Thus, it escaped much of the problematic transition from a nationalized to a privatized entity following the Thatcher government's decision in the 1990s to create the Associated British Ports Company: a corporatized entity which would subsequently be sold by stock offer. In fact, Thatcher's decision to sell-off twenty-one ports to a private company in 1981 was the trigger for governments in various other countries to do the same, and many ports became owned by private interests, including stevedoring and transport companies, and leading ocean carriers. Governments effectively became landlords, renting out the waterfront space to private companies, and by the end of the twentieth century, 'nearly half the world's trade in containers would be passing through privately controlled ports' (Levinson 2006: 239). Prior to this sell-off, government investment had been crucial to the development of ports and Felixstowe and Hong Kong were the only exceptions – all other major container ports were developed at public risk and expense. This created a natural affinity between the two ports and in many ways it was no surprise when in 1991 75 per cent of the port was acquired by the Hutchison Whampoa Group, Hong Kong – the world's leading port investor, which has interests in forty-seven ports across the globe.

Hutchinson Whampoa began life as two separate nineteenth-century companies – Hong Kong and Whampoa Dock established in 1863 and Hutchison International established in 1877. In the 1960s, Hutchinson International gained a controlling share in Hong Kong and Whampoa Dock, which led to a complete takeover in 1977 when Hutchison Whampoa Limited was created. The company ran into trouble in the late 1970s and was rescued by Hong Kong and Shanghai Banking Corporation (HSBC) which took a 22 per cent stake in the company. However, by 1979, HSBC had sold its stake to Cheung Kong [1] for HK$639 million. This move cemented links between the then burgeoning Chinese manufacturing industry and British importers, and facilitated shipping and trade links, making Felixstowe the United Kingdom's largest container port and the arrival point for most goods from China.

Of course, this facilitation of trade links coincided with the development of mass container shipping, a factor which has single-handedly had the largest impact on the volume of global trade. The shift from break-bulk to containerized cargo shipping is universally acknowledged to have begun with Malcolm McClean, a trucker from North Carolina who decided to try his hand in the world of freight shipping. McClean was constantly emphasizing the necessity of speed in ports, insisting on the logic that a ship only earns money when at sea and that costs quickly rise when in port, therefore the quicker loading and unloading can be undertaken and the ship can be back at sea the more money is saved. It was him who reasoned that it was a waste of space to include a vehicle's undercarriage and that all that was really needed was the trailer itself. The *Ideal X* was based on this premise and was the first container ship as such (Cudahy 2007: 27). A wartime tanker with a specially fitted inside deck, the *Ideal X* left New York harbour on course for Houston on 26 April 1956 with 58 brand new trailer trucks fastened inside it – containers as they would come to be called (Cudahy 2007: xi). The ship heading into Felixstowe that late autumn afternoon as I stood and watched with the crowds contained closer to 9,000 containers.

This increase in the amount of 'stuff' travelling around the globe is indicative of the way in which the container industry, and indeed the ports themselves, developed. As Levinson points out, in 1960, twenty-eight carriers sailed the North Atlantic, 'from the mighty Cunard Line to such one-ship minnows as American Independence Line and Irish Shipping Limited', but worldwide container shipping capacity increased by more than 20 per cent in a single year four times during the 1970s. By 1977, all major shipping routes had been 'containerized', causing longshoremen almost everywhere to lose their jobs in large numbers as a result of the redevelopment of ports (Levinson 2006: 245). Scale became all-important:

> Companies such as Sea-Land, US Lines, and Hapag-Lloyd, wanted to be in every major trade, either with their own ships or with an arrangement that allowed them to book space on somebody else's. The more ships they had, the more ports they served, the more widely they could spread the fixed costs of their operations. The more far-flung their services, the easier it would be to find loads to fill their containers and containers to fill their ships. The broader their networks, the more effectively they could cultivate relationships with multinational manufacturers whose needs for freight transportation were worldwide. (Levinson 2006: 233)

In addition, this quest for scale not only meant there were more ships on the world's oceans, but that they were bigger. For example, the *Fairland*, the first

Sea-Land ship to cross the Atlantic in 1966, was only 469 feet long, whereas the purpose-built container ships of the late 1960s were about 600 feet long, and the vessels launched in the early 1970s were about 900 feet long. In terms of the amount of 'stuff' this enabled to be transported, whereas the ships entering service in 1978 could hold up to 3,500 20-foot containers, by the 1980s, they were carrying 4,200 20-foot containers, and by 1988, they could not fit down the Panama Canal (Levinson 2006: 234). This increased size meant the new container ships were not able to be used very flexibly. However, what they could provide was massive savings in costs *if* they travelled between two deep-water ports. So it was, that the major trade routes became fewer, but saw the passing of increasing numbers of ships between them – Hong Kong, LA, Rotterdam, Antwerp, Yokohama and Felixstowe were crucial and, as these super-ports mainly traded only with one another, the world's 'stuff' was beginning to increasingly pass only between this handful of places.

One of the key features of these super-docks was that they made minimizing the time spent in port even more crucial. As Levinson puts it, big ports meant bigger vessels able to dock and faster handling times – as well as distribution networks up to the task (Levinson 2006: 235–6). The more containers a port could handle, the cheaper the price per container would be. In this race to the bottom, size and speed were the key factors, and it no longer mattered where the markets for the goods delivered were within any given country – freight train routes changed due to the unusual location of deep-sea ports. London and New York were no longer the obvious choice for docking as it made more sense to pay less for the dock and then send the goods via train to the more populous areas. 'Non-traditionally' located docks such as Felixstowe and LA suddenly came into their own.

In many ways, the onset of container shipping was the end of a story of the sea that began with a deeply rooted biblical (and indeed pre-biblical) repulsion of it as a sinister, dark unfathomable force, filled with monsters and unknown dangers – a fearsome primordial substance. By the mid-eighteenth century, the beginnings of colonial adventures meant the world's oceans were becoming better mapped and more easily traversable and during the nineteenth they began to be associated with restorative health and hedonistic pleasure. But it was the sheer sense of management of the sea that container shipping brought, that is perhaps the final end point in a conception of the sea as all-powerful. And this too has something to say about whizzy[2] capitalism and the determination to see it as smooth and untroubled. Whilst the oceans of the world are in many cases highly navigated tracts, this 'management' does not prove a smooth tale of trade efficiency by any means. Perhaps some of the sense of the dark and unfathomable ought to return to current-day rhetoric.

I have an appointment with Len – a seasoned dock worker. The café is small, with plastic chairs which cannot be moved from the iron they are moulded to and Formica-topped tables, some of whose edges are beginning to peel off. The walls are painted in a thick gloss paint which appears somehow greasy in the early summer heat. A constant waft of cigarette smoke is blown in through the open door. Nobody seems to mind. A huge blackboard with a vast array of combinations of all things fried adorns the wall, high above the counter. Behind it, a ruddy-faced woman looks at me expectantly. Groups of men sit at each table. I notice how very few of them are sitting up straight. The atmosphere is dour; pleasant enough, but dour. I order a tea. Len is a large man in his early fifties, with huge hands and a rugged smile. He agrees with me when I suggest that things must have changed a lot at the docks during his time working there. He says in some ways there have been improvements; for example, the work is not as physically demanding as it used to be. Some of those sat around him disagree, but he waves them off saying they're young and don't know what it used to be like. However, he bemoans the way the scale of computerization has made the job less sociable, saying, 'there's no spark now, you know, people don't have a laugh, there's not the old spirit there used to be, it's a job now, not a community.' The man beside him chimes in saying, 'it's only a community when things go wrong, like when Dennis Burman died.'[3] This causes much agreement and rousing of those surrounding us – the man has touched a nerve. 'Things like that ... it's sad', says Len, 'they're the things that keep us together ... shouldn't be ... but they are.' I ask how, in this day and age, such a thing could have happened. 'That's just it, isn't it,' he says, 'they think 'cos it's all clean "n" that now, and people sit behind computer screens controlling where all the containers go, that there aren't some of us still out there, all weathers, operating the cranes – doing dangerous stuff, not like the old dockers would've had to do of course, but still. It looks neat on the screen don't it, but it's still pretty tough down there on the ground, getting it all done under pressure ... and now it's busier than ever. There's stuff coming in all the time ... we've broken world records at Felixstowe y'know.' I nod. I do know, only too well.

I'm curious about this idea that behind the on-screen efficiency is a layer of operations that are still slow, awkward, heavy, physical and dangerous. It seems very much part of the false idea that capitalism is simply fast in the twenty-first century, without slower mechanisms supporting it. 'Would you say the work you do at the docks has sped up?' I ask. 'I mean, do you think the whole dock is having to work faster and things are coming in and being unloaded faster?' Len shakes his head. 'There's more coming in. That's a fact. But there are computers to help with that. Sometimes I think we're expected to work faster, but then, you think about the days when they hulked things around without cranes, you know, before big container ships and that – those guys were under much more pressure to work faster than us. It's still big, heavy work, there's a limit to how fast it can get ... there's just more of it, that's all, and the port's grown so big.'

He pauses…. 'Dennis didn't die 'cos he was being rushed – he died 'cos the cranes were in the wrong place.'

In Len's relating of the way the dock works, how it has changed and what it is like to work there, there is a clear distinction between the idea of the amount coming in to the port – its ability to process vast amounts due to its sheer scale – and the fact that the actual work on the ground is still slow, heavy and lumbering. In other words, there is a distinction between volume and speed: the filling up of time and space in Felixstowe does not simply translate into rhetoric on speed as has become so common in discussions of globalization (e.g. Robertson 1992; Castells 2000; and Friedman 2006). Speed is often emphasized at the risk of neglecting rupture, stultification, apathy and the cumbersome nature of the labour of unseen others. This rhetoric has been particularly difficult to analyse and critique as it cuts across traditional political divides: speed as both a negative and positive impulse has been used by both the left and the right. In fact, as Tomlinson points out, Gramsci was an early admirer of the Futurists[4] and Lenin enthusiastically embraced the speed-regulation of Taylorism (Tomlinson 2007: 9).

Paul Virilio's account is perhaps the best example of the speed-as-bad rhetoric. He argues that the speed at which something happens has the ability to change its essential nature and things which move with speed always quickly come to dominate that which is slower. Therefore, territory is first and foremost a matter of movement and circulation; possession of territory is about speed of contact (Virilio 1977: 47). For Virilio, speed is an engine of destruction and it is speed, not class or wealth, which is the primary force shaping society. For example, he argues that Western man has only appeared superior and dominant because he is more rapid; he has survived due to being part of the most powerful dromology, as opposed to being part of either a 'hopeful' population who aspire to finally reach the speed they are accumulating or a 'despairing population' who are forced to live in a finite world due to the inferiority of their technology (Virilio 1977: 47).[5] There is, of course, much to agree with here and an obvious application to the world of super-ports across the globe – it is undeniable that the fastest ports and trading routes are those that have come to dominate. However, Virilio's speed is a mono speed. It does not contain layers, or collateral damage or pockets of slowness – it is an all-encompassing dromology. Somehow, this does not quite seem fully representative of what is at play in the distribution networks of the low-end commodity chain. Speed alone does not win. The logic of the bargain relies upon speed certainly, but also on the ability of the collateral damage caused as a result of that speed to adapt and repair itself quickly – an ability often built upon the less speedy elements within the chain.

Despite his insistence on speed as all-powerful, interestingly Virilio does not see it as a potentially revolutionary factor, perhaps because he sees it as the norm; thus to break from the norm, to create revolution, we must slow down or stop: 'The time has come it seems, to face the facts: revolution is movement, but movement is not a revolution. Politics is only a gear-shift, and revolution only its over-drive: war as continuation of politics by other means would be instead a police pursuit at greater speed, with other vehicles' (Virilio 1977: 18). Virilio's concern with speed is that it enforces intensive (quantitative) growth; for him speed is problematic as it negates space through the reduction of distances: the '*strategic value of the non-place of speed has definitively supplanted that of place* [original italics] and the question of possession of Time has revived that of territorial appropriation' (Virilio 1977: 133). Whilst this insistence on 'slowing' as revolutionary has its merits as an argument, it does not take into consideration the ways in which we are immovable and apathetic already; it is caught up in its own rhetoric of dromology and assumes all in life is at a pace which guarantees 'slower' as a force to be reckoned with. In the bargain commodity chain, slower has already been requisitioned to be the backup when speed goes wrong. It is perhaps only startlingly new combinations (or rather, clashes) of fast and slow that may bring about revolution – we will return to this idea shortly.

It is worth briefly mentioning other writers too who generally berate speed. In his *Tyranny of the Moment* (2001), Thomas Hylland Eriksen's concern is that slow time – time when we are able to think without interruption – is becoming extinct, as information technology permeates every area of our lives. Thus, culture lacks a sense of its past and future and so is essentially static. Similarly, James Gleick's *Faster: The Acceleration of Just About Everything* (1999) is concerned with our biological, psychological and neurological limits and the extent to which technology pushes these to the extreme. Ben Agger's writing on 'fast capitalism' is in much the same vein as the above two examples, but provides a more nuanced argument. In its first conception in the book *Fast Capitalism* (1989), Agger concentrated largely on an argument which posited the changed position of writing in society as indicative of an erosion of the mind and the ability to form a serious critique. He attributed this erosion as stemming from the fact we can no longer see how a book is independent from the world and therefore how its contents could oppose the dominant world. For Agger, people were insufficiently distant from the world, lacked perspective to form critique and were inculcated with conformist values due to the way in which the world appeared to have no outside and thus no exit. Most crucially, for Agger, fast capitalism was capable of speeding up the rate at which people lived out the historical possibilities presented to them (Agger 1989: 17–20).

In his subsequent works (such as *Speeding up Fast Capitalism*, 2004), Agger has broadened his analysis to include the impact of information technologies, namely the internet, on work, families, childhood, schooling, food, the body and fitness. He sees the internet as having quickened the pace of everyday life and impacted upon consciousness, communication, culture and community, by making everything turn faster. Whilst in some senses this is a return to 'whizzy capitalism' and the idea of information flows necessarily speeding up life somehow in a more general sense, Agger is not attempting to argue for a new era of capitalism or indeed a capitalism with as yet unseen features. He fully acknowledges that 'there is nothing new about fast capitalism other than the rate at which it happens' (Agger 1989: 6–7). Rather, his concern is that this faster rate is that of a society characterized by administration and that revolt against this is now subsumed within the everyday and so is extremely difficult to access. In some ways, therefore, Agger arrives at a very Lefebvrian point – that the issue is one of bureaucratization of everyday life and that the battle must be won *from within* this quotidian existence. Fast capitalism, in this version, is perhaps far more understanding of the existence of its clunkier aspects – Agger's is a critique of capitalism's *mode* rather than its speed per se, and in this sense is, therefore, far more aligned to an understanding of the logic of the bargain. Bargain logic is not about speed pure and simple; it is about the way in which the *idea* of speed has embedded itself within other rationales. The commodity chain must turn faster, but this relies upon fast repair and adaptivity as much as speed.

Fast repair does not feature in Thomas Friedman's (2006) speed-as-good rhetoric. In contrast, he is of the ilk of writers who tend to see globalization as an unproblematically positive force – an incredible, exciting, and most importantly (and erroneously), democratizing phenomenon. *The World is Flat* cites countless examples of outsourcing and flexibility in the tone of one entirely dazzled by the sheer scale and potential of the globalizing tendency. It is perhaps typical of what Hutnyk sees as clichéd writing on speed; that which accentuates electronic flows and global linkages as if in a rapture of celebrating some enthralling novelty. For Hutnyk, the acceptance that everything is a blur in capitalism belies the non-happening of reality: 'it is not uncommon to find gee-whizz declarations of hyper-intensity of capital flows that seem only to lead to stasis and quietism' (Hutnyk 2004: 59). Hutnyk's comments here have much to say when considering the functioning of ports, with their hyper-efficient and clean computerized dock systems, yet their intrinsic requirement for men of flesh and blood to control heavy mechanical devices that haul bulky, dirty things about slowly and with effort. Speed rhetoric often suggests a certain culture of 'clean'; fast things do not get dirty. Implicit in this is also the suggestion that clean equals safe; slow things are not only dirty, but also dangerous. Yet, in reality, 'fast things' are supported still by grit and grime, sweat, and now and then, unfortunately, accidents and death.

In fact, it may be useful to turn the depiction of the hyper-speedy commodities chain on its head by looking at the occasions when the smooth functioning of the chain is ruptured. Seen in this light, the chain becomes a long line of micro (and not so micro) catastrophes, with gaps between catastrophes constantly teetering on the edge of collapse. The whizzy commodity chain suddenly becomes a flow of constant ruptures. This can be seen in numerous examples of the danger of cargo shipping and the potential for it to go wrong. On 8 April 2009, for example, the container ship the *Maersk Alabama* was hijacked by Somali pirates off the coast of Africa, who held the captain, Richard Phillips, hostage. He was eventually released and returned to work fourteen months later. The episode was made into a film by director Paul Greengrass and released in 2013. Also, thousands of containers are lost at sea every year. Most famously, on 10 January 1992, during a storm in the North Pacific Ocean, 12 40-ft containers were washed overboard from the *Ever Laurel* as it travelled from Hong Kong to Tacoma, Washington, United States. One of the containers held 28,800 'floatees' – a child's bath toy made in China that comes in the form of red beavers, green frogs, blue turtles and yellow ducks. When this container somehow came undone, the floatees escaped, as they did not take on water (so therefore did not sink) and were only fixed to backing card that quickly disintegrated. The work of Seattle oceanographers Curtis Ebbesmeyer and James Ingraham who tracked the floatees, as well as other spilt cargos (such as the 61,000 Nike running shoes that had washed overboard in 1990), is now the subject of Donovan Hohn's 2011 book *Moby-Duck: The True Story of 28,800 Bath Toys Lost at Sea*.

Container ship captain 'Bob' (not his real name) works for a major cargo shipping company and tells me that there have been a couple of occasions when containers have fallen overboard during high seas. 'We have even sometimes seen them go,' he says. 'Usually you only lose one or two, but others around them slide and move and crush others, so you lose more goods than simply the ones that go overboard, 'cos most of that stuff becomes unsellable as a result. Fortunately, staff are usually OK … apart from being sick sometimes! … but it's a dangerous game sure enough.' In fact, the danger of container shipping does tend to be recognized (if not talked about) by ship captains, who to this day have insisted upon maintaining the tradition of giving container ships names, as opposed to simply the company and a number as 'they would not be willing to go down with a ship that was identified only with an impersonal number' (Cudahy 2007: 27).

It must also be acknowledged that ports still, to this day, attract various aspects of life that could in no way be considered 'smooth' or 'efficient' in the manner in which the computerized logistics operations of twenty-first-century ports are often described – sex workers, and people and goods smuggled in, for example. While situations today are not quite like those in Elia Kazan's 1954 film *On the Waterfront*,[6] the 'smoothness' and 'speed' of operations does still belie a rather murkier undercurrent. As Bob admits, 'you're always wondering what's in the containers. You know, I've kinda got used to it now, but I do still often hope that everything's as it should be in those things and that I'm not carrying anything illegal. I know other Captains who've found out much later that a container from one of their ships had immigrants hiding in it…. I don't know if they were all alive when it got opened. I didn't like to ask him. That kind of thing actually scares me more than the idea of being hijacked. It's usually the Captain hijackers go for,

Figure 3.1 Freight trains transporting containers through Vancouver.

and I can take responsibility for my own risk, maybe my own death you know, but I don't want to be anything to do with the death of other folks. I don't want to have to live with that.'

There is also the environmental rupture caused by the necessity to dispose of containers and ships that have come to the end of their working lives. In fact, shipbreaking as it is called, is one of the most dangerous occupations on the planet, not to mention one that creates much environmental damage. It involves the complete dismantling of a vessel's structure in order that it may be used as scrap materials or disposed of, and due to cheaper labour and fewer safety regulations, the vast majority of shipbreaking is carried out in the developing world. Chittagong in Bangladesh has become the location of one of the largest shipbreaking yards in the world. Vessels no longer able to be used have been taken to Chittagong since the 1970s and the yards there break down around 250 ships in a year. Workers, with no safety equipment, many of whom are children, pull apart the hulls by hand. Not surprisingly, many are harmed or killed by inhaling noxious fumes, electrocution, falling debris and explosions and fire due to residual oil.

The problem with both the positive and negative rhetoric on speed, then, is that they take speed (rather than rupture) as a constant – an unchanging element upon which to base a moral judgement; whereas in reality, as Tomlinson (2006) points out, there is ruly speed (regulated) and unruly speed. This acknowledgement is a pleasing development on the good and bad speed rhetorics that tend to posit speed as a mono speed. However, it still does not capture the complicated nature of the myth of speed – something which comes in many forms, and which behaves differently and is perceived differently, depending upon the effect it has in any given situation. Indeed, ruly or unruly speed can be perceived differently *by the same people.* For example, some proponents of unruly speed – speed which 'clears out dead wood' in the economy and forces out those 'not up to the job' – are frequently also in favour of interfering in the running of the economies of other countries, in order to 'regulate' them. This returns us to the idea of new combinations, or clashes, of speed that may bring about change.

Joe is a dock worker at Felixstowe and relates how he struggled with the changes when the port began to become heavily computerized:

> Lots of operators were laid off, skilled people and all. They just didn't need 'em. The computers could do it, you know, even control some of the cranes. Lots of people re-trained, or were forced to re-train really. I s'pose in the end some of 'em liked it once they got used to it, you know, being indoors more, and it don't take such a toll on your body like. It's a real change though, some people like being out and about you know, they don't wanna be in front of a screen, they like to see things happening and know that they did it themselves – directly. I just couldn't get used to it meself, couldn't get me head round the idea that I didn't need to go anywhere or talk to anyone to work out a problem you know, I just had to sit there and work with the screen. It was a real shock to the system I can tell you.

The sense I get from Joe is that the nature of work at the dock in one way or another alters his own rhythms – forces them into patterns and ways of working that do not feel natural to him. To use Lefebvre's way of describing this, the 'rhythms of the other' are forced upon the 'rhythms of the self', making the latter impossible to maintain and leading, potentially, to crisis (Lefebvre 1992: 99). Lefebvre calls this 'dressage', which he defines as the way a person bends and is bent to a group or society and its ways, and likens to the process of animals being 'broken in' in which they modify themselves, or are altered (Lefebvre 1992: 40). For him it is this 'dressage' that determines the majority of rhythms.

It feels somehow intuitive to speak of rhythms in an automated environment such as a port. I think of Kracauer's argument in *The Mass Ornament* where he asserts that only an industrialized, post-Fordist country could develop an entertainment aesthetic such as the 'tiller girls' with their uniform high-kicks; bodies in unison as a machinic form. Automation inevitably leads to rhythm, and the enforcing of rhythms, to power, whether on an individual human or a far grander scale. This crushing of different types of time – namely that of cyclical rhythms by linear (automated, not-of-nature rhythms) – represents for Lefebvre a colonization of the everyday. Speed, however, is a culprit, as it detracts from the 'natural' rhythms at play and therefore disenables the recognition of specific 'moments' that could be used as a basis to trigger social change.

For Lefebvre, everything has a rhythm – trees, people, cities, universes; some of these rhythms are linear – the time of watches and clocks; and some of them are cyclical – the time of day, night, seasons and biological rhythms. In short, 'everywhere where there is interaction between a place, a time and an expenditure of energy, there is rhythm' (Lefebvre 1992: 15), but that rhythm is not always, in fact rarely, under the control of those most involved in its daily operations. (We could apply this to the bargain commodity chain by acknowledging that neither the dock workers nor the manufacturers nor the pedlars, and perhaps not even the consumers, are operating under their own chosen rhythms.) In fact, Lefebvre argues, rhythm is *imprinted* on people, and with this comes power – 'for there to be change, a social group, a class or caste must intervene by imprinting a rhythm on an era, be it through force or in an insinuating manner' (Lefebvre 1992: 14). Rhythms, in other words, and the question as to which ones are dominant, are political. The changing of them is not about speed, but about power. For him, all crises have their origins in rhythms[7] as different rhythms interact to create new rhythms by different repetitions falling at different points, rather like different time signatures playing at the same time (Lefebvre 1992: 44). So, rhythm is specifically about changes in repetition – for there to be rhythm, there must be repetition, but not monotonous repetition. In other words, mechanical repetition is not rhythmical – rather 'strong times and weak times', as well as 'stops, silences, resumptions' are (Lefebvre 1992: 26).

Everyday life is the site at which these linear and cyclical rhythms have to interact the most and therefore create new rhythms. Linear 'work' time and cyclical time that cannot be governed by socio-economic systems represent polyrhythmia (multiple rhythms), but they are not eurhythmic (united in rhythm). Rather, they create arrhythmia due to the way in which their beats clash. (Arrhythmia is the lived equivalent of musical 'flamming').[8] Therefore, the everyday is the theatre for 'what is at stake in a conflict between great indestructible rhythms and the processes imposed by the socio-economic organisation of production, consumption, circulation and habitat' (Lefebvre 1992: 73). The interaction between the cyclical and the linear – domination of one over the other, rebellion of one against the other – is complicated and intricate and causes an 'antagonistic unity' between the two (Lefebvre 1992: 76). It is precisely this antagonism that enables us to understand the bargain commodity chain not as a smooth, 'whizzy' trajectory, but rather as a series of conflicting rhythms which have the potential to create blips, or what Lefebvre calls, 'moments'.

Lefebvre began developing this theory of moments as early as the 1920s as a response to the popularity of Bergsonism. In his autobiographical work *La Somme et la Reste* (1989), Lefebvre pits his own notion of 'moments' against Bergson's[9] 'durée', emphasizing the spatial as part of these moments, whilst simultaneously underscoring his thinking on time as just as foundational for him as that on space. Unlike Bergson, he privileges the instant rather than the durée – his greatest influence here being Nietzsche's 'augenblick' in *Thus Spoke Zarathustra* (1969) – a moment where past and future collide, presenting new opportunities. Importantly, this meant that Lefebvre's time/space was quintessentially nonlinear – time and space were seen as interrelated, as time *with* space. This meant that the moment was not defined by clock time. It could be a split second of insight or a short period in history in which opportunities seemed to come to the fore. For David Harvey, Lefebvre's moments are to be understood as 'revelatory of the totality of possibilities contained in daily existence … during their passage all manner of possibilities – often decisive and sometimes revolutionary – stood to be uncovered and achieved' (Lefebvre 1991: 429). Similarly, Rob Shields describes a moment as 'times when one recognises or has a sudden insight into a situation or an experience … a flash of the wider significance of some "thing" or event' (Shields 1998: 58).

This rejection of clock time was part of Lefebvre's desire to understand time as experiential rather than linear. (It also has poetic resonance with the French Revolution and the attempt to create a new calendar, and with the 'revolution' of Paris 1968, and the cry to 'shoot the clocks' in order that workers would not leave the protests at 5 p.m.) It was this dislike of linear time that had always perturbed Lefebvre when it came to Bergson and the notion of durée. Lefebvre detested the idea of time as progress along a teleological path; preferring instead the recognition of time as made up of instants, some clear, some blurred, some that pass quickly, others that linger, some lacking in potency, others with a potentially revolutionary clarity. Additionally, Lefebvre wanted to make time personal, to give it insight and feeling, to allow the experience of it passing to be variable – all of this was part and parcel of his wider 'humanist Marxism'. Time was lived ('vecu').[10] Moments had the power to take one out of the everyday, even if one must be returned to it. However, when time is 'full', such as it is in the linear regularity of ports' logistics, its rhythm is regular, even automated, in order to fit the most in as efficiently as possible. This lack of variation in the way time is experienced (i.e. no 'flamming' of different rhythms) makes 'moments' less likely to occur. This is rather aligned to Agger's thoughts on bureaucratization being the real issue when it comes to fast capitalism.

Lefebvre attributes the phrase rhythm analysis to Gaston Bachelard, which may well explain the use of the word 'elements' in the title of his book on rhythmanalysis. (Bachelard had written on the psychoanalysis of the 'elements' fire, water, dreams and earth in his *The Psychoanalysis of Fire, Water and Dreams, Air and Dreams and Earth and Reveries of Will*.) It was probably Bachelard's *The Poetics of Space* (1969) and *The Dialectic of Duration* (2000) which most informed Lefebvre's thinking. In the latter, which is essentially a critique of Bergson, Bachelard had contradicted Bergson's view of time in two key ways, both of which were to inform Lefebvre's work on moments and rhythms. First, in contrast to Bergson's notion of the 'durée', Bachelard had posited time as fragmented and discontinuous. In doing so, he had intentionally laid out his view of time in direct contrast to that of Bergson. Whereas for Bergson time continued as a flow between events, for Bachelard, it was to be understood as being made up of an infinite succession of momentary and discrete instants, which have no extension and are isolated from each other. As Ann Game asserts, in Bergson's duration,

> There is a complete permeation of moments: past, present, future melt into each other.... There is, if you like, a process of referral. The present bears traces of the past, such that no element is ever simply present; with each new moment the whole changes, so that everything remains and yet changes – hence the principle of qualitative differentiation and an undoing of sameness. (Game 1995: 194)

In other words, there are memory traces (much as there are for Freud). For Bachelard, however, duration is experienced through instants and is, therefore, discontinuous, having neither extension nor flow. Crucially, this means the instant is constantly breaking with the past, the new does not have a history and therefore, the present is not inscribed in the past as Bergson suggested. In fact, past and future are empty and time is only the present instant, which never passes, as we are constantly moving into a new instantaneous present (Bachelard 2000).

This presentism, however, provided Bachelard with a problem. If, as he suggested, instants are static and there is no flow between them, what mediates between them in order to cause one instant to give way to another? Bachelard's answer was to posit a dialectical relationship between the instant and nothingness, in which being is defined in contrast to its opposite, nothingness, and is, therefore, seen as a movement to overcome nothingness. Thus, and here we see the alignment with Lefebvre, what remains from the past is what begins again, and only that which starts over again has duration. This starting over again, a series of instants, creates a *rhythm* – and so 'duration' for Bachelard is constructed by rhythms.

Secondly, Bachelard had insisted upon framing moments and memories within space. For Bergson, time is the time of becoming. He argued we mistakenly think of it in spatial terms, projecting it into space, as a line of time marked by discrete moments. For Bergson, this was abstract, static time, and as Game points out, in critiquing abstract space, he almost exclusively emphasizes time – 'If he does not precisely reduce space to time, Bergson nevertheless privileges time over space' (Game 1995: 195). However, what lay behind Bergson's critique of this spatially oriented, abstract time, was a concern with understanding time as *lived*, sensuous and characterized by qualitative differentiation (Bergson 1950). So, despite their strong differences, Bachelard and Bergson were perhaps aiming at the same point, albeit from very different places – a conception of time as lived.

In fact, Bachelard's work *can* sound remarkably close to that of Bergson or Freud. In *The Poetics of Space*, he says, 'various dwelling places in our lives co-penetrate and retain the treasures of the former days' (Bachelard 1969: 5). This sounds remarkably similar to Freud's 'memory traces' and Bergson's account of the past entering the present, and certainly does not posit time as a sequence of discrete states. However, as Game points out, whereas Freud and Bergson talk of traces in *time*, Bachelard talks of 'dwelling places' and so spatializes the temporal assumptions of Freud and Bergson. For him, lived time is dependent upon spatial specificity – space is necessary to give quality to time and duration is dependent upon qualitative, lived space. Bachelard is exploring space that has been lived in with all the partiality of the imagination, rather than attempting to look at space in its positivity[11] (Game 1995: 200–1). So, Bergson's lived time of duration becomes abstract time unless there is space; it is space which quickens memory and gives time life.

Bergson's version of lived experience, then, because it was bounded in time, not space, is existentialist in an individualistic sense – his lived time is that of the individual and his own memory. In contrast, Bachelard's lived time relies upon memories in space – space occupied by others and which may not always be our own. Therefore, Bachelard's memory traces came from past space-bound moments which could be *public*. (It was for this reason that Lefebvre was able to conceive of and posit the moment as potentially *mutually experienced* – a notion which was far more suited to his desire for the moment to be capable of inciting *public* revolution, rather than simply private, existential, 'romantic' revolution.)

I wonder about this treatment of 'moments' as I remember the China-price ship-in-a-bottle in Yiwu – a 'moment' of maritime history calcified in the form of a commodity bound for transportation on a very different kind of ship to the classic sail ship represented in rudimentary form and suspended from the inside of the glass bottle by a somewhat less than subtle dab of glue. Was this object a 'moment' in history, mutually experienced, by various peoples across the world, not least in China as a result of the horrific effects of the opium wars? If so, did this make it a moment that had, in the present day, gathered new connotations; a symbol of British trading power, global adventure and the prowess of empire, that served as a national reminder of the age of discovery, but which had, in the nineteenth century, become a holiday souvenir as the great Victorian day-at-the-seaside become an established British phenomenon. Perhaps the 'moment' captured was one that enabled new meanings – a refilling of the bottle with different fragments of colonial memories.

Alternatively, to relate the idea of moments to the bargain store commodity chain is to recognize that it is made up of the fragmented continuity Bachelard conceived of. In other words, the commodity chain is best seen as a set of micro catastrophes – a multiplicity of fractures which themselves, by interacting (in time and space) with other fractures, create the 'rhythm' of the places along the commodity chain. This interaction of micro catastrophes (with their opposing rhythms) is what Lefebvre would call arrhythmia – the bargain store commodity chain is flamming. Global urges come up against local concerns (global ethics vs. local developmental ambitions); human endeavour strikes against the realities of nature (the urge to work vs. decomposition of raw material and tiredness); environmental aspirations are taken over by consumerist ones. Potentially, 'moments' can arise from these clashes, or flams, but they do not do so easily, often simply being absorbed by them and becoming part of their coping mechanisms. Sometimes, however, operations are forced to change to some extent due to the enforcement of one rhythm over another, as the following incident perhaps shows.

ii) Strike! The Dockside Politics of Abundance

On 27 November 2012, clerical workers at the Ports of LA and Long Beach went on strike to protest against the threat of their jobs being outsourced to China or elsewhere. They had worked without a contract for thirty months. Their role involved filing invoices, arranging visits for customs inspectors and, most crucially, ensuring that cargo moved off the dock quickly and onwards towards its final destination. The strikers themselves, members of the International Longshore and Warehouse Union, were relatively few in number – around 450 – but their actions meant that thousands of dock workers who were members of a sister trade union refused to cross the picket lines. Their eight-day strike, which shut down ten of the fourteen terminals at the ports, therefore, paralysed the United States's busiest container complex which handles 44 per cent of all container cargo arriving in the United States by sea. In just one week, it cost the region billions of dollars and caused concerns over the potential for shortages of pretty much everything as ships sat out at sea waiting to be able to unload.

Eight days later, the strikers won modest increases in wage and pension benefits over the life of a new four-year contract, as well as guarantees from the management that no more than fourteen jobs would be outsourced over those four years. The port gates reopened, and the huge consignments of goods that had been stuck waiting out at sea began to be unloaded and sent on their way. The strike had created standing itineraries of goods. Had Malcolm McClean still been alive, he of all people would have recognized just how expensive the unmoving stillness of those huge container ships off the coast would be. This break in the commodity chain was absolute proof of the way that speed brings abundance (in the form of millions of commodities), but that abundance is entirely at the behest of speed. It is an abundance that must keep moving if it is not to bring ruinous debt upon those transporting it. But it is also an abundance that becomes a norm and something that (we are told) must be gained at all costs. As Hannah Arendt argues,

> We have almost succeeded in levelling all human activities to securing the necessities of life and making sure they are abundant. Everything we do is supposed to be part of 'making a living' and those who oppose this are becoming fewer and fewer [therefore] all serious activities are called labour and every activity which is not necessary either for the life of the individual or for the life process of society is subsumed under playfulness. (Arendt 1958: 126–7)

Labour is key here. Arendt's concern is that securing abundance has become an activity under which people labour, yet which does not improve their lives – a fact they are unable to see. She says, 'the danger is that such a society, dazzled by the abundance of its growing fertility and caught in the smooth functioning of a never-ending process, would no longer be able to recognize its own futility' (Arendt 1958: 13). Arendt explains this inability to see the lack of improvement by explaining that homo faber, the fabricator, works with his hands, conducting himself as lord and master of the earth in a process of self-reification. His production is seen as that of a god; just as the watchmaker creates the inner workings of his watch, homo faber creates a micro universe (Arendt 1958: 139). Homo faber, therefore, has complete confidence in his tools and a conviction that every issue can be solved and every human motivation reduced to the principle of utility. He, therefore, equates intelligence with ingenuity and holds in contempt all thought which cannot be considered as part of the first step towards the fabrication of an artificial object. This matter-of-fact identification with fabrication and action leads him to reify the labour that went into creating the object. What Arendt questions is not so much homo faber himself, but the elevation of labouring to the highest position – the shift from the thing itself to the fabrication process (Arendt 1958: 305–6). This, in turn, means abundance is held in high esteem.

Perhaps it is the fact that labouring is inherently a process that poses the problem here, as it emphasizes production (a process) rather than the thing itself, meaning that worldly things become no longer primarily considered in their usefulness but as more or less incidental results of the production process which brought them into being. Therefore, the end product of the production process is no longer a true end, and the produced thing is valued not for the sake of its predetermined usage but, as Arendt says, 'for its production of something else' (Arendt 1958: 307–8). She continues, 'use has lost out to utility, in the form of utilitarianism under Bentham's formula "the greatest happiness of the greatest number"' (Arendt 1958: 307–8). What man is now trying to produce is 'happiness', so object things became bound up in the desire for, and pursuit of, happiness. As we will see, this can also be related to the way in which the bargain store shopper sometimes desires simply the *feeling* of being able to consume, rather than the object itself, and enjoying the 'freedom' the bargain store provides. This is precisely the consumption of utility as opposed to use; an addiction which is not related to the object, but to the quest for the mini thrill of consuming. It is perhaps a withering away of the thing. At the same moment as the thing symbolically (in the economy of libidinal desire) reaches its highest peak yet, the thing itself melts away to nothing; becoming almost entirely disposable.

Abundance, then, can be seen as a feature of economies that revolve around high levels of quantitative growth. For many, the issue with this is that quantitative growth (via capitalism) is linked to uneven development. For example, as Neil Smith argues, uneven development is a function of capitalism, rather than vice versa. Therefore, uneven development must not be viewed as in any way inevitable, natural or unavoidable. He says,

> Uneven development is the hallmark of the geography of capitalism. It is not just that capitalism fails to develop evenly, that due to accidental and random factors the geographical development of capitalism represents some stochastic deviation from a generally even process. The uneven development of capitalism is structural rather than statistical. The resulting geographical patterns are thoroughly determinate (as opposed to 'determinist') and are thus unique to capitalism. … Uneven development is the systematic geographical expression of the contradictions inherent in the very constitution and structure of capital. (Smith 2008: 4)

This assertion of capitalism as the cause of uneven development is in direct contrast to the traditions of regional geography which were once dominant and which accounted for regional development (locally and globally) by the availability of resources and raw materials. However, as Smith points out, the underdevelopment of certain areas cannot simply be explained by nature – with the development of the productive forces under capitalism, the logic behind geographic location retreats more and more from such natural considerations' (Smith 2008: 141). What makes nature alone insufficient as an explanation is two-fold: previously, economic development was tied to natural conditions by (a) the difficulty of overcoming distance and (b) the necessity of close proximity to raw materials. As Smith argues, the development of the means of transportation meant the first natural obstacle (distance) diminished in importance, and the general increase in productive forces made the second obstacle also less important, since raw materials today are the product of an ever-increasing number of previous labour processes (Smith 2008: 141). (In fact, Smith gives plastic as an example of a material that the rules of regional geography cannot apply to, making his argument particularly relevant to the low-end products of the bargain store commodity chain.)

So, while the explanations of commercial geography may have been suitable for the age in which they were developed, it is now necessary to consider economic and sociopolitical factors, and in doing so, it is impossible not to recognize the way in which underdeveloped spaces are put to the purposes of more developed ones. As Smith argues, uneven development is the exploitation of geographical unevenness, *but also* creates systemic inequality, as it works not only to find less developed areas, but also to guarantee that those areas always exist. Therefore, it is not simply a 'gap' between more and less developed regions, but the 'systematic product of previous capitalist development and the fundamental premise of the future of capitalism' (Smith 2008: 207).

If uneven development is unavoidable in the context of quantitative growth, what then is the alternative? More concern with an accompanying qualitative growth perhaps? For Lefebvre, this is part of a Marxism which understands Marx to have referred to *economic* growth only as part of the means necessary for man to achieve totalness. This is to refuse to see Marx as economically determinist, even in *Das Kapital*, insisting instead as Lefebvre does that there are two types of growth in Marx: industrial expansion, which is quantitative, and development, which is qualitative. Whilst the former is continuous and therefore easy to predict, the latter is discontinuous, proceeding by leaps and involving unforeseeable accidents and the sudden emergence of new qualities (Lefebvre 1972: 29):

> The two aspects, though never completely separate, do not necessarily go hand in hand. Quantitative growth (the forces of production) may unfold gradually over a certain period and only later be followed by a qualitative leap forward. Economic growth is possible without the intervention of the working class, social development is not. (Lefebvre 1972: 162–3)

If this greater emphasis on qualitative growth is to be considered, one important aspect to recognize is that speed does not necessarily translate into economic (quantitative) growth. As Stephen Kern points out, speed presents itself in its functional, developmental aspect, as the prime condition for economic growth and the material development of everyday life. Therefore, on the whole, the world has chosen speed time and time again (Kern 2003: 129). Yet, it has not realized that 'speed' in and of itself is often simply an appearance and does not necessarily translate into growth of any sort. Development does not always occur in socially perceivable ways. As Tomlinson points out, speed is, after all, only linked to capitalism because it is the outcome of the pursuit of the maximization of profit (Tomlinson 2007). When speed is normalized as part of a discourse on capitalism, it includes the assumption that being 'speedy' constitutes an even process of quickening, which bears fruit for all. As Tomlinson says, 'there is a fundamental tacit consensus in modern societies that progress should be as swift as possible. If progress is defined as change for the better, then delay is always a matter for either apology or rationalization' (Tomlinson 2007: 22). Of course, in reality, speed is uneven and cumbersome at times, creating disadvantage as well as advantage and increasing inequality. For Tomlinson, the reason the notion of progress is so easily and wrongly melded with that of speed, is due to a lack of long-term purpose – 'the continued, gestural use of "progress" in political or economic discourse in a sense restricted to short-term demands, agendas and goals. A public discourse which seems in fact … to have largely abandoned the attempt to define long-term collective purpose' (Tomlinson 2007: 73).

Perhaps this less long-term outlook mirrors the normalization of the idea (and reality) that 'stuff' being on the move has become the most profitable way to operate. Inventories make losses. Stagnancy and long-term planning (especially if entrenched in deeply held political philosophy) is seen as bad. Quick, spontaneous decisions, fast distribution and reacting to on-the-ground situations are seen as good. As Levinson says, 'inventories are a cost: whoever owns them has had to pay for them but has yet to receive money from selling them' (Levinson 2006: 266). Moving stuff, on the other hand, represents profit. The discovery of just-in-time manufacturing in the early 1980s is a key moment here. Originated by Toyota Motor Company, just-in-time manufacturing was specifically motivated by the elimination of large inventories. By 1985, 'logistics', previously used only as a military term, had become a business function. Retailers realized they could manage their own supply chains and did not need wholesalers. (Wholesalers are often only used in China due to lack of confidence in dealing directly with Chinese manufacturers.)

In many ways, the bargain store commodity chain is a story of relatively small areas full of small objects – a chain of inventories. The dump, full of half-decayed, remnants in huge piles as high as small hills; the city of Yiwu with its commodity markets full from floor to ceiling with the world's products; and now the container facilities at ports such as Felixstowe and LA where the purchases of the West finally begin to be dispersed and scattered. If space is full in these places, though, it is not necessarily indicative of global trends. It is tempting to see them as typical, as everything filling up, speeding up, becoming full of things, but it is more true to reality to see them as abnormalities, spaces flying in the face of the norm – continual movement (albeit not always fast movement or rupture-free movement).

This brings us back to the LA dock strike and the idea that the only real break to what has become the norm is perhaps to stop, completely. This was Walter Benjamin's suggested tactic in his *Thesis on the Philosophy of History* (one that Virilio's earlier argument echoes in many ways). Here, he posits the state of emergency, not as an exception to the norm, but as normality (an idea Agamben was later to draw upon). Catastrophe is not, therefore, what will happen if the system collapses, but rather the continuation of things as they are because the present is a series of catastrophes. Benjamin's answer, then, is to rupture this continuation by pulling the 'stop-chord' on the 'runaway train' of 'progress'.[12] It is not much of a leap to apply this to the conception of the bargain store chain as a series of catastrophes, and the only real rupture being a complete halting of it.

Lefebvre's understanding of fullness is interesting: 'Le temps est bondé (jam-packed) et la vie parait pleine à craquer. Or elle est vide. Pleine comme un oeuf, vide comme l'abîme' (Lefebvre 1961: 94 in French version of *Critique of Everyday Life*). Here, he is describing modern life as at once crammed full and ready to crack (pleine comme un oeuf/ pleine à craquer) and yet completely empty (vide comme l'abîme). The phrase 'pleine come un oeuf, vide comme l'abîme' literally translates as 'full like an egg, and empty like the abyss', but 'pleine comme un oeuf' is a colloquial French expression in its own right usually used to describe something that is full to the point of bursting. Indeed, what is lost in the English translation is the sense of pregnancy; the idea that to be 'full like an egg' is to be, precisely, *full to the point one might crack* – there is an inherent sense of a bursting point, or at the very least of an uncomfortable fullness held together by a fragile membrane. This metaphor suggests, then, that time (and space) are not simply 'full', but that this fullness is unsustainable, and that when the fullness 'cracks', the consequences could be messy.[13]

All this considered, it is still the case that, as Levinson argues, the true importance of the revolution in freight transportation is to be found not in its effect on ship lines and dock workers, but in the impact containerization had on the 'hundreds of thousands of factories and wholesalers and commodity traders and government agencies with goods to ship' (Levinson 2006: 246). And this, in turn, influenced those who owned or ran stores. Goods could be ordered far closer to the time when they would be needed in store, so trends could be jumped upon and business that relied upon fast turnaround of inexpensive product units could come to the fore – not least bargain stores. Sanjay (not his real name) runs a small independent store in south-east London and tells me how he decides week to week what to order. 'I really keep an eye out for what sells in other stores, not just mine,' he says, 'but I only order them at the last minute if they are still selling well when I need to put in the order. I am always pushing things to the last possible minute in order to make the best decisions. This is good because it means I am very responsive to my customers on a week to week basis.' He explains that he has not always run a bargain store and that he does not think he could do it without this level of responsiveness. 'For me this is the fun in running a store,' he says, 'being able to predict what will sell well and jump on the case if I'm right. I like it being that spontaneous. I s'pose it's a bit like me having a bet with myself all the time.' He laughs. 'I usually win my bets,' he says, 'but that would be pointless if I couldn't get the stuff so quickly and easily.'

For Sanjay too then, the bargain store commodity chain appears as smooth and 'whizzy', despite the underlying slow foundations of the world's ports.

It is to the stores that the following chapter takes us, to meet another type of tactician – the shopper-tactician – and to learn how those characteristics of the logic of the bargain play out in the hands of the consumer.

4

The Bargain Store: Buying and Selling in the West's Spaces of 'Cheap'

i) Shopping for Kicks: The Immediacy of Bargain Store Shopping

A pedestrian crossing bleeps out its signal and six or so people on either side of New Cross Road move to step off the curb, hesitating only to check that a nearby siren will not imminently be followed by the emergency vehicle emitting it. I round the corner onto Deptford High Street. Despite the ongoing regeneration of this area of south-east London, which has seen the creation of semi-glamorous apartment blocks around the docks, the high street continues to reflect the multifarious minorities who have settled here and the low level of income. Its shops are Halal butchers, African beauty outlets, small vegetable stalls, charity shops, pawnbrokers and bargain stores. The chain-owned bargain stores are gaudy and neat, with wide aisles and bright lighting. They are expanding at an astounding rate – especially since the financial crisis hit. The independent stores are small narrow spaces which require careful negotiation. Crammed and sprawling, their contents spill out onto the street; a vast and often bizarre array of artefacts: always the pile of brightly coloured buckets and the fronds of plastic flowers; tuppaware towers up to the lime-green bird cages; mobile phone casings form the backdrop for an array of rubber gloves. From feather dusters to garden gnomes, washing baskets to model Tibetan monasteries – Chinoiserie, islamery, household drudgery; the exotic and ubiquitous are held together in these places, levelled by their low-price status.

The chaotic, sprawling nature of the independent stores seems not so far from Benjamin's descriptions of the jumbled visions of the Parisian arcades:

> In the crowded arcades of the boulevards, as in the semi-deserted arcades of the Rue Saint-Denis, umbrellas and canes are displayed in serried ranks: A phalanx of colourful crooks. Many are the institutes of hygiene, where

gladiators are wearing orthopaedic belts and bandages wind around the bellies of mannequins. In the windows of the hairdressers, one sees the last women with long hair, they sport richly undulating masses, petrified coiffures. How brittle appears the stonework of the walls beside them and above: crumbling papiermache 'souvenirs' and bibelots take on a hideous aspect: the odalisque lies in wait next to the inkwell; priestesses in knitted jackets raise aloft ashtrays like vessels of holy water…. Over stamps and letterboxes roll balls of string and of silk. Naked puppet bodies with bald head wait for hairpieces and attire. Combs swim about, frog-green and coral-red, as in an aquarium; trumpets turn to conches, ocarinas to umbrella handles. (Benjamin 1999: 93)

In much the same way as the arcades described above were destroyed by the Haussmannization[1] of Paris, so too Deptford High Street is undergoing its own micro process of Haussmannization. Its narrow, crammed spaces of ephemera are being forcibly replaced with the bright, open spaces of chain bargain stores, their wide aisles and strip lighting echoing the long gas-lit boulevards of Haussmann's newly designed Paris. But the bargain stores are a long way from the display-conscious department stores that also came into fruition in the era of Haussmannization; rather, they are more akin to the early thrift stores with their functional aesthetics, or indeed the proletarian store with its emphasis on supply according to need. It is no coincidence that Woolworths (generally thought of as the first thrift store) is also often seen as the forerunner of bargain stores. Its layout was functional in the extreme, announcing wares strictly according to category and with nothing but table-top cabinets to view products laid out in.

Figure 4.1 The sprawling contents of a pound store in London's Deptford.

The philosophy behind Woolworths was in a similar vein to that of the French entrepreneur Eduard Leclerc (1926–2012). Leclerc had opened his first store in his home town of Brest, buying his goods directly from manufacturers and placing them on shelves in unpacked boxes with little regard for 'display' of any kind. His model proved successful and Leclerc became a household name in France.

Leclerc, however, was to face an ongoing battle with those who chose to emphasize display, namely a certain Bernard Trujillo. Trujillo, originally from Columbia, heavily influenced French commerce by stressing the importance of piling high and lowering prices. In his view, this piling high must be carried out alongside the creation of 'islands of losses' (loss leaders) amid 'oceans of profit' and stores which were 'a permanent circus' rather than having long-term window displays which he saw as 'coffins' of merchandise (quoted in Bowlby 2000: 166). Trujillo is credited with creating Modern Marketing Methods (MMM). For him, the key issue was 'display'. A shop should be a piece of showmanship in which loss leaders encouraged the consumer to buy more profitable commodities. Leclerc, on the other hand, believed in delivering the lowest price for the consumer *throughout* and was prepared to make less profit on each unit than anyone else. (In fact, his strategy is much aligned to Jack Ma's 'shrimps not whales' strategy previously mentioned.) Leclerc spurned the use of marketing as being against the interests of consumers, a conviction which earned him the mocking title 'L'epicier' (The Grocer) from Trujillo.

With hindsight, it is, of course, clear that Trujillo's emphasis on display and creation of MMM has dominated the development of retail practices across vast tracts of the globe, but it is Leclerc's philosophy that continues to triumph when it comes to low-end stores. Indeed, with the rise of agglomerative manufacturing and the current huge exponential increase in low-end stores, it could be argued that the battle between these two great entrepreneurs has yet to be settled. The 'stocky'[2] display of the bargain store window, frequently obscured by piles of products, is about as far removed from Friedberg's idea of the shop window as a glamorous cinema screen as it is possible to be (see Friedberg 1993). But the stocky display works in the bargain store as it does not simply prove a disregard for display (although is certainly indicative of that), but is also a powerful signifier of the presence of inexpensive products. The stocky window can immediately be read by the consumer as a guarantor of 'bargains' within. The lure of the bargain store is in direct contradiction to the pursuit of luxury in other stores – its lure is not that of the rare, or hard-to-own, but purely and simply that of the bargain. It follows, therefore, that this lure has an aesthetic of its own which is specifically concerned with fullness and sprawl, because the bargain relies upon the abundance of its units and the accompanying suggestion that they are to be 'snapped up' as they will sell quickly (or there would not be so many available). The stocky display also, then, suggests a certain urgency.

It may also be that the argument about price versus display (or access vs. aesthetics to put it another way) has almost eradicated itself in many contexts – the store that disregards methods of display and is, therefore, *perceived* as disregarding commercial considerations 'acquires a kind of counter-prestige from the very fact of being seen not to participate in them' (Bowlby 2000: 72). This was certainly true for many bargain store consumers I came into contact with who expressed the pleasure they gained in 'a shop that does what it says on the tin', 'the honesty of the £/$/€ store', or 'the way it's so functional'. For example, one shopper – Helen – explained how she enjoyed the temporary ability not to have to think – to 'put her head on hold' – that she felt the pound store gave her:

> Once you're in, you're in, and you can't get out until you've gone up and down all the aisles, so you can't wander and take your own direction. It's kind of a relief because you have no decision-making to do, you have to do as the shop's layout tells you … and also, everyone's in the same boat as you … none of you can choose where to go, you just go up and down the aisles and stop when you see something that interests you. Funny really, because normally I would hate things that told me what to do- you know, like I hate to see people behaving like sheep – but for some reason I enjoy it in the pound stores, it's like a kind of relinquishing of responsibility. I enjoy the dumbness of the pound store…. I guess it's like allowing yourself to be a sheep sometimes, but without the guilt trip [laughs] … yeah, knowing that you're not really a sheep because when you leave the shop you're thinking and making decisions again.

The stocky display, then, works because it suggests a certain ease and availability. Yet, crucially, it firmly posits the idea that this availability may not last – these displays are not the 'coffins' Trujillo accused Leclerc of creating. There is an immediacy that underlies the whole process when it comes to bargain store shopping.

I walk with Linda, dodging the market stalls, the prams and now and again the fruit that topples from its precarious pile only to be scooped up and thrust to the ground by a market trader whose movements speak of the many years his body has known this work. Linda fluctuates between a nervous concern that what she says is of use to me and an animated pleasure that she can share her thoughts with someone. 'I've been doing this for years,' she says, 'years and years. Sometimes I hate it and sometimes I love it, but it's so familiar to me. I feel like I know every crack on the pavement. I do all my shopping on this street. I only go to a supermarket once a month. Everything else I need is here, on the stalls or in the bargain stores on this street.' Linda is a ball of breathless energy. Grey-blonde, around fifty, and, I get the impression, not easily defeated by life. Turning sharply she heads into a shop through a narrow opening between piles of plastic buckets and children's stools. The strings of plastic flowers above waft gently in the breeze created by her passing. Inside, she's looking for plastic cups, plates and cutlery for her young niece's birthday party which she has agreed to host. She spots a pack of ten plastic jumping frogs and takes those too saying, 'that'll keep them occupied for another ten minutes, won't it! There's no point spending lots of money; people think you have to, but kids are happy with the simplest of things, and it'll all get ruined anyway, so it's best to buy stuff you don't mind throwing away. After all, it's only stuff isn't it.' I ask whether she only feels like that because of the low price of the 'stuff' in question. 'Well, I guess if it was worth a fortune I wouldn't say that, but I *choose* not to care about stuff. I mean, it's not that the stuff makes me feel I don't have to care about it, it's that my feeling towards stuff means I only buy things I don't have to worry about. That's just my attitude. I'd rather have it when I need it, use it, and get on with life.'

Linda's attitude is one in which the ability to immediately buy and consume something is seen to fit a pre-existing personal choice not to care about objects or 'stuff'. This not caring (or apparent non-caring) both requires, and is fed by, the ability to purchase what is needed at short notice, spontaneously and without too much worry over the price – it is characterized by immediacy, that great pleasure, some might even say right, of late modernity. As John Tomlinson argues, immediacy is not only present in consumption, although this is a key area of expectation. He points to the internet, delivery speed, news coverage and just-in-time manufacturing as all indicative of the way in which immediacy has become a *cultural* principle (Tomlinson 2007: 74). As such, immediacy is not simply concerned with 'mechanical velocity' (although technology enters into the discussion, of course), but rather it is connected to a culture of instantaneity, rapid delivery, ubiquitous availability and the instant gratification of desires (Tomlinson 2007: 74.) Crucial, for Tomlinson, to this culture of the instantaneous, is proximity, the sheer 'connectedness' of people and the ability to be in constant communication with others through various technologies – telepresence (Tomlinson 2007: 74). It is this which closes the gap between now and later; between desire and satisfaction, or, to put it in Freudian terms, which decreases the space in which the 'pleasure principle' resides. In fact, as Tomlinson argues, 'the culture of immediacy ... involves as its core feature the imagination that *the gap is already closed* [original emphasis] ... the sense of being without the intervening middle term. Immediacy – closure of the gap – is therefore most generally *the redundancy or the abolition of the middle term'* [original emphasis] (Tomlinson 2007: 91). The important factor for the consumer now is not how many possessions they can amass, but the speed required in order to do so – in other words, how *immediately* available commodities are (Tomlinson 2007: 125).

Contemporaneously, (and consequently) the requisite immediacy has rendered the quality of manufacture of these items, whilst not necessarily inferior, less important, as they are not required to last as long. In fact, the desire on the part of the consumer is for them *not* to last a lifetime, in order that they may be replaced with the latest fashion relatively frequently and the 'pleasure' of purchasing may be relived *ad infinitum*. Gilles Lipovetsky describes this as a 'second generation presentism' which is not pure hedonism (like its sixties' forefathers whose desire was to break away from the traditional attitudes of their parents), but rather 'hyperconsumption' – a modernity in which 'the politics of a radiant future have been replaced by consumption as the promise of a euphoric present' (Lipovetsky 2005: 35–7). Seen in this light, the immediacy the bargain store offers can be read as a rebellion against waiting.

I witness this change in attitude towards consumption between generations when out with Tracey. She is eyeing some cushion covers and pondering how they would provide a small change to her lounge – 'I get bored with how the house looks sometimes … you know…. I want to change it in a little way … cushions are good for that … cos I can't afford a new sofa. My mum and dad wanted to give me theirs, 'cos they want a new one, but I feel weird about it 'cos they've had that all my life, you know, since I was a baby'. She smiles fondly, 'We were constantly being told not to put our feet on it and not to muck it up … 'cos it had been expensive for them to buy, you know … but it's too much part of my childhood for me to have it in my house now and I don't want something that I'll feel I can't get rid of.' Tracey's sentiments show how both steady accumulation (such as that of her parents) and continued accumulation and disposal (such as her own) were and are practices which emphasize possession, albeit in the latter case that possession is more momentary. The key difference is that immediacy has closed the gap, while patience, in contrast, means 'deliberately leaving the gap open' (Tomlinson 2007: 151), and so is the antithesis of the driving spirit of immediacy.

In theory, immediacy can also be seen as a move against labour (as opposed to credit) or at least a shift in emphasis from productivist to consumerist. However, as Tomlinson points out, this shift must not be viewed simplistically, because for most people, the necessity to work still exists – credit culture only *attempts* to create the feeling that spending is removed from labour. (Baudrillard makes a similar point, arguing that buying before one has the money is actually living in reverse due to being forced to work after the act of buying as it were and therefore not owning our own future time (Baudrillard 2005)). What has changed, Tomlinson maintains, is the belief in progress and betterment through industry, the dignity of labour and the virtues of providence and accumulation. In contrast, values are now consistent with the need for consumers to spend freely in the interests of avoiding systemic crises (Bauman 2007a: 126). Zygmunt Bauman makes a related point:

> The consumerist syndrome consists above all in an emphatic denial of the virtue of procrastination and of the propriety and desirability of delay of satisfaction … [the] consumerist syndrome has degraded duration and

elevated transience. It has put the value of novelty above that of lastingness. It has sharply shortened the timespan separating not just the wanting from the getting ... but also the birth of wanting from its demise .... Amongst the objects of human desire, it has put appropriation, quickly followed by waste disposal, in the place of possessions and enjoyment that last ... *the consumerist syndrome is all about speed, excess and waste'* [original emphasis]. (Bauman 2005: 83–4)

In many ways, this is a truism, although it is hard to read both Tomlinson and Bauman without feeling there is a certain suggestion that careful saving followed by thought-out spending is somehow intrinsically 'better' than spontaneous spending. There is a danger in such arguments too easily leading to a moralizing discourse on the perils of consumer society, which berates consumption for its own sake, rather than seeing it as indicative of other features – such as the enforced reliance upon credit or the status attached to the ownership of certain types of material things. This said, it is difficult to remove the concept of immediacy totally. To some extent, a change in the culture of consumption inevitably requires an ability to compromise immediacy every so often. Perhaps the point is not to allow immediacy to become inextricably linked to a moralizing discourse which berates immediacy *for its own sake.* In fact, Tomlinson himself spots the danger in making waiting in itself, a moral crusade, acknowledging that waiting only became moral out of necessity and that the issue at stake is that 'contemporary consumption is characterized by the expectation of *delivery* rather than of satisfaction' (Tomlinson 2007: 128).

Bernard Stiegler offers what are perhaps more 'practical' reasons why closing the gap between consumption and disposal (reconsumption) might be considered a bad idea. This reduction is related to what he calls 'the proletarianization of the consumer' (Stiegler, quoted in Crogan 2010: 161). In an interview with Patrick Crogan, Stiegler interprets Marx's definition of the proletariat as not being about pauperization, but rather as resting upon the deskilling of the worker – Marx describes the proletariat as a worker who had skills and *savoir faire*, but who has been dispossessed of them by the introduction of machines. Stiegler points out that this is also precisely what Adam Smith had said almost a century earlier in *The Wealth of Nations* (1991 [1776]), but he had not made a political theory out of it. Similarly, Gilbert Simondon has called this deskilling 'disindividuation' on the basis of the logic that when individuation comes through the singular knowledge a person possesses, if this is taken away from that person, the individual is disindividualized (1954). For Stiegler, the same process of proletarianization that the worker experienced has also now rendered the consumer less capable of knowing how to live (*savoir vivre*)[3]: 'from the moment when marketing invents the service society ...we see how the consumer is himself deprived of his savoir vivre. The producer was deprived of his skills or abilities (savoir faire), the consumer is deprived of his savoir vivre' (Stiegler, quoted in Crogan 2010: 161).

This is how, according to Stiegler, the proletariat consumer is left with nothing but his purchasing power, just as the proletariat producer was left with nothing but his labour power – 'so he will work to earn the little bit of money he uses to be able to buy what he produces, having lost everything; he has no knowledge in work anymore and no knowledge in life. So he is unhappy' (Stiegler 2010: 162). In the context of the bargain store commodity chain, Stiegler's argument here is useful in acknowledging how cheap products can rarely be fixed – they do not allow for repair even if one knew how – so the knowledge of repairing (and indeed the thought to do so) declines and dies. Either because the object cannot be fixed (e.g. plastic products don't have joints one can fix back together) or because the consumer does not know how to fix it, he or she has no choice, therefore, but to re-buy and can do so due to the low price. This, of course, is crucial to the operations of the bargain store chain as it secures the continued increase in the number of exchange interactions and so maintains economic growth. A bargain store commodity, therefore, has both physical and psychological built-in obsolescence – the physical kind first described by Vance Packard in his classic *The Waste Makers* (1960) and the psychological kind conferred upon the bargain store commodity by its price tag. This too fits Stiegler's vision of the dispossessed consumer, who can do nothing but attempt to gain pleasure in spending on the most ephemeral and inexpensive of commodities.[4]

Immediacy, therefore, within the bargain store commodity chain and twenty-first-century consumption in general, rests not upon the immediate gratification of the desire for an object which satiates a need or want, but upon the immediate gratification of the desire simply to possess it (regardless of whether or for how long it satiates a need). The pleasure in the logic of the bargain store commodity is, therefore, one step removed from traditional consumer desire in that the object itself is not expected to satisfy (at least not for long); satisfaction comes instead from the ability to possess in a carefree manner, or in a way that causes the consumer to feel that he or she has somehow 'beaten' or 'tricked' the market. This is to step away from fears over 'false needs'[5] emphasized by the Frankfurt School theorists and which Lefebvre defined as 'neatly outlined hollows to be stopped up and filled in by consumption … until satiety is achieved, when the need is promptly solicited by devices identical to those that led to satiety … thus incessantly re-stimulated' (Lefebvre 1971: 79). 65). Such rhetoric is outmoded and irrelevant in the context of the bargain store commodity chain. The failed promise of the commodity has long been exposed, and to little general concern. The consumer realized long ago that commodities lie. What rules now is a different (false?) promise – that of the spending thrill.

I try to get to what lies behind the spending thrill as Linda and I move on to another pound store. 'Have you been planning your niece's party for long?' I ask. 'Well, I s'pose I had a rough plan,' she says, 'Why?' 'You don't have a shopping list,' I reply, 'is it all in your head or are you making it up as you go along?' Linda laughs and says that it's all in her head and that she knew she'd be able to buy things cheaply to entertain her niece's friends. 'Do you think the fact you knew you'd be able to buy them cheaply meant you could be more last-minute about the party?' 'Well yes, I s'pose it did … yes … cos I didn't have to think about putting money to one side, I knew I'd find stuff. That's the same with most of what I buy though, I mean, it's only really big things that I think of in advance … and I don't particularly have much money you know … but, well, everyone can afford pound shop stuff can't they … even when you're really skint you can buy a little something in the pound shop.' We pause. 'Is it nice to be able to buy something for yourself in the pound shop?' I ask. 'Well … it's always nice to be able to buy yourself something, isn't it…? Guess I'd rather buy myself something in Selfridges yes, but you're still treating yourself aren't you … even in a pound shop … even if it's rubbish … it's still nice to buy a little something.' Linda is aware of the lie of the commodity, but still takes pleasure in the ability to buy it – pleasure is transferred to the moment of exchange, rather than the thing *in itself.*

This emphasis on exchange and the (apparent) practical and psychological necessity of purchase is a key feature of what Lefebvre calls the 'society of bureaucratically controlled consumption' (Lefebvre 1971). This is specifically *not* 'consumer society', which, according to Lefebvre, is simply born out of statistics whose raison d'être is to show that the purchase of consumer (so-called) durables has increased. For Lefebvre, this is correct, but trivial, as it can easily be agreed that there has been a transition from penury to affluence and from the man of few needs to the man of many. Rather, what concerns him,

> is the transition from a culture based on the curbing of desires, thriftiness and the necessity of eking out goods in short supply, to a new culture resulting from production and consumption at their highest ebb, but against a background of general crisis. Such is the predicament in which the ideology of production and the significance of creative activity have become an *ideology of consumption* [original emphasis], an ideology that bereft the working classes of their former ideals and values while maintaining the status and the initiative of the bourgeoisie. It has substituted for the image of active man that of the consumer as the possessor of happiness. (Lefebvre 1971: 54–5)

So, in the society of bureaucratically controlled consumption, it is not 'the consumer nor even that which is consumed that is important in this image, but the vision of consumer and consuming as part of consumption'. Therefore, as part of this process, man's awareness of his own alienation is repressed by the addition of a new alienation to the old (Lefebvre 1971: 54–5). This is useful in understanding why the bargain store is such a fixture in society and is popular for reasons above and beyond the fact that it is perceived to provide cheap products and enable people to spend less. In fact, it is the ability to buy and to gain the sensation of spending which is key, as much as what is actually bought. In enabling this for the consumer, bargain stores redefine poverty as freedom, telling even the consumer 'underclass' that they are 'free' and making other classes of consumers feel that they are enjoying 'novelty' forms of consumption as they marvel at their guilt-free spend.

All this is not to suggest, of course, that just because the nature of 'false needs' has changed (or indeed that the concept was flawed from its conception), there is not still an erroneous view of the nature of happiness! For Lefebvre, the problem stems from there being an abundance of commodities, which creates uneven development and the emptiness of boredom for the consumer (Lefebvre 1981: 41). This understanding of abundance as emptiness is clearly linked to a reading of Marx's understanding of the state of non-having as a 'state of very positive having – the having of hunger, cold, sickness, crime, degradation, stupor, every conceivable inhuman and anti-natural thing' (Lefebvre 1972: 84). Lefebvre takes Marx's idea of not having as having and includes the reverse within his thinking – having as not having. In volume three of *Critique of Everyday Life*, he states explicitly that both having and not having are devoid in different ways as life is full yet so empty and that emptiness comes from boredom and privation: 'On the horizon of the modern world dawns the black sun of boredom, and a critique of everyday life has a sociology of boredom as part of its agenda' (Lefebvre 2002 [1961]: 75). Privation for Lefebvre, is linked with 'private life' etymologically and philosophically, with the 'world' being there to 'plug up the holes, fill in the cracks, camouflage frustrations, etc.' (Lefebvre 2002 [1961]: 90).

In many ways, Zygmunt Bauman says a similar thing when he states that 'were the "excessive" taken away, the norm would be restored. The truth is that were the excess out of the way, the void would yawn where the norms were supposed to reside' (Bauman 2001: 86). For both Bauman and Lefebvre, then, excess is more than simply being too much; rather it is a fundamental lack of the ability not to need in capitalistic ways. This is useful in that it aids and clarifies Lefebvre's understanding of needs as abundance – an abundance which has disenabled people to utilize what is out there readily available. For Lefebvre during the 1970s, and certainly by the time he was writing volume three of his *Critique of Everyday Life*, there was, therefore, relevance, even a culprit, in the form of consumer society. For Bauman, this was certainly the case. He steadfastly attributes the reliance upon excess to the emergence of consumer society, seeing happiness and survival as fundamentally misaligned due to the former resenting limits and the latter being all about abstention (Bauman 2001: 86–7).

Happiness for Bauman is (wrongly) kept alive by the dream of excess; it is the 'trademark of modernity', but has no longer a finishing line, 'no more a dream of arrival, but the urge to be forever on the move'. And here he again connects with Lefebvre's interpretation of the void of abundance being caught up with a sociology of boredom, saying: 'The image of happiness is shaped in the likeness of a road movie: a picaresque string of adventures, each new and exciting for its novelty … but each one wearing off quickly, shedding its charm the moment it has been tried and tasted' (Bauman 2001: 88–9) Whilst happiness used to be 'burdened with delay', reward is now instantaneous. Of course, Baudrillard also talks of this instantaneous culture of consumption in the section on credit in *The System of Objects*, as previously mentioned. But if the disposability of bargain logic is also key to understanding how boredom can be satiated, abundance is key to understanding how needs have transformed themselves into the need for excess – the excess that creates the boredom.

Heather Hopfl's comments help frame this cyclical relationship. She argues that the supply of the excess is the major concern of late-modern social life and coping with excess passes as individual freedom – 'an oppressive drudgery masquerading as ever-extending choice. Matter fills up all space. Choice is bewildering illusion' (Hopfl 1997: 236–7). These tactics – those of filling space and portraying drudgery as freedom – are precisely those of the bargain store. Which returns us, of course, to Lefebvre's reasons for continuing to pursue alienation as his Marxist theme of choice, but also his insistence that it is a social rather than economic phenomenon – his 'humanist Marxism' (Shields 1998).

This said, there are fundamental differences between Bauman's interpretation of excess and Lefebvre's. Whilst both agree that it is what is thrown out that signifies most about a society and that is now the quintessential sign of an attempt to defy boredom – that it is transience of things that is an asset – for Bauman, this transience suggests that there is no attachment to things, whereas for Lefebvre, it is indicative of inappropriate attachments to things as opposed to 'entanglements'. Surely, to follow Bauman's argument, a disattachment from things ought to lead to excess becoming an empty notion, but it does not. So, Lefebvre's notion is in many ways more useful as it does not suggest that the ability to throw away is indicative of a dispassionate relationship with having and excess. For Lefebvre, the ability to throw away is more convincingly rooted in an argument which states that disposal is tied up with reconsumption (via the primacy of the exchange moment). The jettisoning of a thing already has the promise of new novelty, of boredom momentarily banished once again.

ii) The Freedom to Buy: A New Kind of Democratic Right?

The immediacy and spontaneity of consumption is very often and easily linked to a notion of 'freedom'. (Indeed, immediacy is classically linked to 'fluidity':

see Castells 2000; Bauman 2005, 2007a; Urry 2000, 2003.) In fact, the idea of
'consumer freedom' is now so embedded in Western culture that many aspects
of consuming are seen as 'freedoms', when previously they would have been
chores. Consumer freedom has become an equal to other types of freedom for
many. As Ben Agger says, 'freedom' is obtainable at 7-Eleven grocery stores,
not in egalitarian social relationships' (Agger 1989: 17).

9 a.m. Catford. South-east London. A fifty-person strong queue has developed
outside the brand new pound store that is about to open. Five minutes and
counting. It is cold and some people have been here for over an hour in their
determination to be the first customers and grab as many bargains as possible.
Jean had set her alarm early especially. 'My husband was appalled,' she told
me. 'He just could not understand why I would get up so early to go and stand
in a queue outside a shop. He said he could almost understand if it was the
New Year sales and there were designer labels and stuff, but that this was
ridiculous … and embarrassing … he said it was embarrassing!' I ask her why
he thinks it would be embarrassing. 'Well, I s'pose he was brought up to feel
that looking too needy for things is shameful you know … almost like being seen
to accept charity. He doesn't want our neighbours to see me queuing here. He
thinks it looks desperate and greedy.' 'And you don't see yourself as needy or
desperate,' I say. 'No I don't. I just like a bargain … and I don't really care how it
looks to other people … anyway, it's normal, look how many people there are in
this queue, and all sorts too.'

If Jean's sentiments showed how the behaviour her husband still found
'shameful' had become perfectly acceptable and part of an accepted culture for
her, Sue's attitude seemed to go even further. 'I think it's great that people can
queue like this outside a pound shop. I remember back in the eighties it wasn't as
acceptable to buy cheap stuff, you know, it was all about having money wasn't
it. But now, everyone wants cheap stuff, I mean everyone, not just people who
can't afford expensive stuff. I would've put my pound shop carrier bag inside
another carrier bag to hide it back then. Not now.' For Sue, finding a bargain
has become something everyone does, rather than remaining an activity limited
to those with less money. She epitomizes the main-streaming of the culture of
bargain shopping and does not question the logic it asserts that the consumer
is getting a 'fairer deal'.

To some extent, this culture can be interpreted as an example of Adam
Podgorecki's 'dirty togetherness' (Podgorecki 1986) as, initially at least, it
required the presence of cliques and close-knit networks within the context of
scarcity. However, unlike Podgorecki's notion, which is hinged on distrust of the
state, bargain culture was and is effectively a state-backed project designed
to maintain the economic health of consumer-nations. Nevertheless, the
success of this culture is in some ways surprising, as it hinges upon a pride
in the super-cheap, something which even thirty years ago may well have

struggled to take hold. Whilst searching for bargains would previously have been the sole prerogative of the less well-off or those priding themselves on being thrifty, it is now celebrated as a national 'pass-time' for all. The ability to spend is all-important and the truth of this spending is covered over with the myth of the bargain as providing 'freedom'. In fact, bargain culture could be better understood as providing a kind of grimy glue (to draw upon Podgorecki's notion), which allows for the entanglement of social relations in things previously found disgusting. For example, the sheer unabashed rush for bargains would, in the era of post-war consensus, have been seen as shameful and grasping. Now, public behaviour around the openings of new bargain stores proves how pervasive bargain culture has become and how deeply embedded the notion of the bargain is for the consumer. In 2009, local press reported police having to be drafted in to control crowds of shoppers at the opening of a new pound store in Halesowen.[6] Similar scenes were reported following the opening of the ninety-ninth 99p Store in Ashford, Kent.

This logic of bargain culture often requires additional pieces of information to surround the commodity, usually in the form of information or tag lines. In the case of the bargain store commodity, these are to be found in the form of signs outside stores which point not to the actual commodities themselves, but to how easily one's general concerns could be solved for 'only one pound/dollar'. For example, 'warm and dry for £1', or 'personal alarms – be safe for £1'. Others target even wider ideas such as 'choice' – 'something for everyone' and '£1 – your choice'. In these cases where buying a £1 commodity is attached to cultural ideas surrounding that commodity (such as freedom and choice), the culture surrounding the commodity becomes its mouthpiece. Or, to put it another way, we have to become addicted to the *idea* of the bargain in order for the bargain commodity to be addictive. And we are addicted.

The reason the bargain must be understood as ideological is because as a more tangible entity it is indefinable. What we tend to mean when we talk about 'getting a bargain' is that we bought something at a cost lower than we feel we would 'normally' have paid for it. However, as we are unaware of how much that commodity cost to manufacture, ship, etc., we cannot say whether what we paid was under the odds or not – 'getting a bargain' is based on social context rather than the commodity's inherent truths. Bargain store commodities are priced cheaply because they are made from cheap materials, by cheap labour and do not last, or they are, in fact, no less expensive than elsewhere, but their context within the bargain store convinces us that they must be cheaper than elsewhere. In reality, if the bargain commodity was as omnipresent as its idea, all bargain stores would be out of business! It is the *idea* of the bargain that is all-powerful. Of course, this is not to deny that some consumers do manage to make savings on the whole. For example, Helen is a 'market mavern'[7] and will only buy those items in bargain stores that she feels are genuinely cheaper than elsewhere, as opposed to being what she calls 'false bargains'. She admits to taking great pleasure in seeking out the best price:

> When I was regularly shopping in pound stores it was for certain things. I mean, I loved looking round them anyway, but I didn't necessarily buy just any old thing in there. I would say that I either bought certain things that really were cheaper than in other shops, or I bought funny little novelty things now and again.... Like, I'd buy cleaning products and bathroom stuff, and then I'd buy little ornaments and things like that, but I never bought kitchen stuff, because they normally break and then you have to buy another and then you've spent as much if not more than you would have done if you'd bought the corkscrew or whatever it was somewhere else. And I never bought socks or tea-towels because although they look cheap, you can actually get them much cheaper from supermarkets or other large stores.

In this way, Helen probably managed to buy the commodities that made the pound stores the least profit. Her behaviour and that of other maverns may mean the making of profit becomes harder, but in the bigger picture, it very much aids the survival of the concept of the bargain, because by accentuating the importance of price comparison, it promotes the thrill and pride of being a wise bargain hunter. It makes bargain hunting something one can 'be successful' at and therefore encourages consumers to involve themselves with bargain hunting almost as a pastime. The culture of price comparison may enable people to avoid bad deals, but it also encourages the gaining of pleasure from so-called 'playing the market' – feeling one has not fallen for its trickery.

Sometimes bargain culture relates itself in casual ways to other ideas, partnering with deeply embedded social histories. For example, in recent years, in the run-up to Christmas, 99p stores have begun to use a seasonal carrier bag with the slogan '99p stores – the spirit of Christmas'. Here, semantics play the role of causal factors in the psycho-cultural construction of the bargain by fixing together a notion with strong emotive connotations such as 'the spirit of Christmas' and that of '99p'. In this context, ironically, the bargain emerges as a way to return to a romantic vision of the past in which Christmas was less commercialized, and gifts were about considered thought rather than grand gestures or price. In actuality, the slogan, and quite possibly the feelings of consumers, has little to do with not needing to spend, and everything to do with spending in a way that makes people feel the gift they give is worth financially more than what they paid for it. This is the bargain masquerading as 'spirit', and in doing so, increasing its potency as a concept.

Of course, the culture of the bargain is a global phenomenon; it can be applied on a macro scale from one part of the world to another, as well as on the level of the individual consumer; it can seep into the global rhetoric of East versus

West in new and pernicious ways. This is particularly relevant when looking at the Western consumer who is caught between the necessity to economize, pressure from media sources to spend in order to keep the economy healthy, and the expectation that products made elsewhere will reach us at very low prices. For this strange combination of reasons, the Western consumer is used to the bargain, in fact, even expects it – as Slavoj Žižek says, 'in Capitalism, the *definition* of the "proper price" is a *discount* price' (Žižek 2002: 43–4).

This syndrome has been further analysed by Victor Alneng in his work on backpackers and Vietnamese traders (Alneng 2007). He argues that backpackers seeking and expecting the 'right price' (a low price) are part of a north-to-south tourism 'which cannot be truly sustainable if the monstrous global geopolitical and economic inequalities that pave its travel routes are not sustained too' (Alneng 2007: 4). According to Alneng, the quest for this bargain price is not driven solely by pure economic concerns, but also by a desire for authenticity, and 'a commodity can only have high value (authentically) if it has a low value (monetarily); it is only emancipated as a global souvenir if it is confined to the local in terms of price rate' (Alneng 2007: 9). This means, Alneng says, that 'the souvenir cannot be authentic if the local who sells it is inauthentic, and an authentic local is a poor local' (Alneng 2007: 9).

This 'balance' expected of producer-nations by consumer-nations is mirrored by the policies of consumer-nations towards their own consumption, creating what Bauman calls the 'walking contradiction' consumer who must spend, but not overspend, in order to be a good citizen (Bauman 2007b). This balancing act on the individual's level reflects a macro phenomenon which is what Lefebvre was attempting to define in his 'bureaucratic society of *managed* consumption' [my emphasis] (Lefebvre 1971). The same set of rationales that creates the 'walking contradiction' consumer also creates a convenient set of pretend enemies which allow consumerism to extol itself as the purveyor of all things good and reasonable – hence strange conflations of consumerism with democracy. For example, news reports during the Cold War often showed USSR citizens queuing for bread and portrayed them as deprived of *buying power*, due (apparently) to their communist regime. According to these reports, they were not deprived of basic sustenance and resources; they were deprived of *consumer choice* and their *right to buy*. Consumerism became democracy and vice versa. Thus, anything other than consumerism became totalitarian. Such is now the (ironically) totalizing nature of consumerism.

As Susan Nacey explains, this link between consumerism and democracy really came of age in 1950s' America and was solidified by a now-famous exchange between USSR Premier Nikita Khrushchev and then US Vice President Richard Nixon, in which the latter vociferously defended the merits of consumerism as being one of the greatest advantages of democracy (Nacey 2015: n.p.). The confrontation happened at Sokolniki Park in Moscow in July 1959, where, as part of an exchange of science, technology and culture between the two countries, an American exposition was showing products such as labour-saving devices, make-up, frozen dinners, cars, and, of course, Pepsi. As Khrushchev and Nixon strolled around the American pavilion together, Nixon equated consumer choice to freedom, arguing that the habit of making consumer choices lay at the heart of democracy. In response, Khrushchev argued that the abundance of choice experienced in the United States exemplified bourgeois extravagance and that function should be valued over outward appearance (Nacey 2015: n.p.). Nixon's diatribe would become the basis of many liberal thinkers who followed, perhaps most notably Milton Friedman's argument that a true freedom (and democracy) could only exist under free market capitalism.[8] In contrast, for Lefebvre (and, of course, many others), this linking of consumerism and democracy is complete mythmaking, best understood as part of a process of 'mystification'[9] in which people are given a false sense of freedom whilst becoming further disenfranchised (Lefebvre 2008 [1947]).

To relate this directly to the bargain store is to understand that for many consumers (even to some extent those who feel they have no choice but to shop there), there is a sense of 'freedom' in the bargain store – the store satiates the need to feel agency and therefore relates to desire in that it plays upon the need to need (in order to feel part of consumer society), rather than the need for objects to provoke desire. This is how the mundane 1 £/$/€ object has become an object of desire and it is also perhaps how the process has become deformed ('déformé' – to use Lefebvre's word) with desires no longer conforming to needs and needs no longer metamorphosing into desire in the same ways. (Admittedly, this assumes, of course, that we can neatly separate out desires and needs in the current age, as seems to have been possible for Lefebvre and others.) This current process remains connected to 'the suggestions and the orders given to [the consumer] by advertising, sales agencies, or the demands of social prestige' (Lefebvre 1961: 10–11), but in the twenty-first century, this prestige has become subtly but inextricably removed from the possession of the object itself. Rather, it is now embedded in the concept of the possession of 'freedom' through spending and in the familiar rhetoric of buying power (and what one does with it) as the last great vote.

This sense of freedom is evident amongst many shoppers I speak to. On one occasion, for example, I spend time with Sarah and Mark. It is a Saturday morning, and Sarah informs me that coming to the high street, wandering round the pound stores and then going for lunch in the café have become a casual tradition of theirs. 'I dunno,' says Sarah, 'it just chills me out. I like the simplicity of it, you know, it's no big deal, it's not like I'm off down Oxford Street to spend big money or something. We have fun looking at the nick-nacks and stuff. It's part of local life isn't it. It's something I like to do in my free time. I s'pose I like it 'cos it's easy … kind of mindless. I feel carefree when I know I can buy stuff.'

Similarly, Tracey had expressed similar feelings, saying: 'wandering round here, you know, it's relaxing isn't it. No big decisions to make. No rush. I s'pose I feel like when I'm pottering round the pound shop, it's a bit of "me time" you know. This is how I relax [she laughs] … that's kind of sad in a way isn't it!' She had also described how she sometimes goes to a particular pound store with her children on a 'mini spree'.

> I tell them we have fifteen pounds between us all, so we can each pick five whole things and put them in the basket. It's such fun because you feel you can throw caution to the wind a little and that you are choosing little treats for yourself in a quite extravagant way, only it's not extravagant 'cos we're only spending fifteen quid. And the kids love it, I think they feel it's so exciting to be able to choose five different things – five!

For both Sarah and Tracey, shopping has become a leisure activity. At a societal level, this acceptance of shopping as leisure fails to recognize the ways in which spending is precisely tied up with the necessity for work and monotony – we must 'buy' our leisure time with our work time, it is not free. Furthermore, and crucially, with the advent of shopping as leisure, the binary of work and leisure has gained the ability to retain itself, as not only must we 'buy' our leisure time, but we spend in our leisure time the money we then need to pay back via working. The way in which the bargain store is often described by those who shop in it as providing 'guilt-free' shopping (as well as products that are, or are perceived to be, cheaper) has enabled this syndrome to extend to even those on the lowest incomes, and there is little challenge to the idea of spending as a type of freedom. In fact, terms describing purchasing choices, such as 'working class freedoms' and 'ethical consumption', perpetuate this linking of the two concepts.

Daniel Miller's take on consumption is perhaps typical here (See Miller 1998a, 1998b, 2008). For him, consumption brings us closer to realizing our own link with materiality; it is the point at which goods are returned to the domain of personal relationships and taken out of situations of alienation (Miller 2006: 347). For him, shopping is a creative process, during which individuals are expressing their self-identity through their consumptive choices. Miller's shopper is one of agency (and therefore 'freedom'), in direct contrast to what he sees as the 'outdated' depiction of the consumer perceived as being at the behest of powerful market sirens. With Miller's brush, then, Tracey is painted as creative and as having choice; a person whose creating of a 'treat' out of spending money in a bargain store is to be celebrated in an unproblematic way. This does seem to rather negate the presence of Tracey's economic *necessity* to shop in a bargain store, and indeed her wider struggle to make ends meet. Perhaps, in the attempt to escape what he calls the trends of 'anti-consumption studies' through Veblen

(1994), Lasch (1979) and Marcuse (1964), all of whom he says are influenced by an 'ascetic version of Western Marxism' (Miller 2006: 342–3), Miller has too easily created a binary in which the answer to outdated 'anti-consumption' rhetoric is a kind of 'agency–consumer' rhetoric. (In fact, the consumer with agency is the most common trope of the postmodern in Consumer Studies – a simple reversal of the beleaguered consumer beset by 'evil' advertisers promoting 'false needs'.) This refuses to acknowledge that there is any sense in which the choice offered to the consumer is limited by what the market offers in order to remain profitable – on trends and norms and ideas not necessarily applicable to the individual consumer. As Bourdieu says:

> We no longer even have the option of not choosing, of buying an object on the sole grounds of its utility, for no object these days is offered for sale on such a 'zero-level' basis.... It follows that the choice in question is a specious one: to experience it as freedom is simply to be less sensible of the fact that it is imposed upon us as such, and that through it society as a whole is likewise imposed upon us. (Bourdieu 1984: 151)

Rather than attempting to choose between the consumer-as-dupe vision and the consumer-as-creative-agent vision, or indeed to decide to what extent the consumer is each of these, it is preferable to shift the question entirely and recognize the way in which the freedom (or non-freedom) of the consumer is much more about state interests for the economy than personal desires and the range of products available. What I mean by this is that the role of consumerism within developed societies shapes the expectations of a country's citizens and changes the way in which they feel about consuming and the cultural position it occupies in their society. 'Needs' have changed, and the creation of 'false needs' has moved to a different arena. Rather than causing consumers to believe that they need a specific commodity, it now causes them to believe that it is their duty to be a consumer even when they cannot afford it. This inevitably sees a constantly increasing emphasis on the amount of money available to the individual. And, the frequency of the occasion/interactions where money is needed is becoming greater (especially in regard to replacing inexpensive, non-durable items), as well as the amount of money needed more generally. As Lefebvre argues, money is the only way in which the individual can gain contact with the world of objects and 'the vaster this world of objects becomes, the greater the need for money' (Lefebvre 2008 [1947]: 161). (This does not mean, however, that within the fulfilling of this duty, the consumer does not exercise originality and choice; that he does not resist and reappropriate with impunity.)

This embedding of needs with money, according to Lefebvre, is part of the process by which 'every other need is adjusted and revised according to the need for money'. This leads to a situation in which 'the need for money is an expression of the needs of money'; the producer endeavours to create a need for his object (Lefebvre 2008 [1947]: 161–2) so that this need can be transformed into profit. The bargain stores' products are not advertised; needs are not created in quite the way in which Lefebvre talks of. In many ways, the bargain store is where the expression of the need for money has come to: it operates as a space of hyper-available goods, available to all, all the time (hence its comfort for many shoppers – the 'good old reliable pound store'), but this need for money is not even to satisfy 'needs' created directly by advertising, but to satisfy the more general need of 'spending' – a need which the last three to four decades have instilled in society. Money is needed in the bargain store simply in order to be able to buy frequently and give the feeling of freedom *to spend* – precisely 'the need for money is an expression of the needs for money'. The bargain store masquerades as running contrary to the idea of money reigning, when in reality it is the epitome of the necessity to spend.

This acknowledgement of the prevalence of the idea of the duty to consume and the way in which consuming is linked to freedom as part of this consumer society rhetoric and encouragement to spend has implications for the way in which we understand the beginning of 'consumer culture'. Most histories of consumerism understand its prevalence as something that emerged simply because consumption became 'mass' – things became available, affordable and therefore part of culture. They do not consider that in many developed societies, at the point consumption became 'mass', economies became heavily reliant upon it and strategic top-down messages increasingly began to make people feel that it was their duty to consume in order to keep the economy afloat. This is to differentiate between consumer society per se and consumer society that puts pressure on its populace to spend – perhaps this might usefully be called *obligatory* consumer society. In consumer society, while a trade economy may well require spending, this has not been deemed a crucial activity on the part of individuals by state powers; in obligatory consumer society, state powers consciously and openly make it the duty of individuals to spend on the basis of a rationale which constantly posits the risk of the nation-state failing if they do not (i.e. most notably in the Keynesian rationale of Western post-war economies).

Like consumerism, obligatory consumerism has its own historic gestation period. In Britain, this began to emerge as early as the seventeenth century through writers such as Nicholas Barbon and John Cary. As Frank Trentmann points out, they presented a new, optimistic view of popular consumption, encouraging ordinary people to pursue commodities in the belief that their desire for more goods would make them work harder, enabling enterprise and initiative in the place of idleness (Trentmann 2009: 197). In the eighteenth century, as previously mentioned, Bernard Mandeville asserted that the consumption of 'luxury' (or 'unnecessary') commodities was, in fact, what drove the economy and improved the wealth of all people (Mandeville 1997: 14). Similarly, Adam Smith asserted that 'consumption is the sole end and purpose of all production and the interest of the producer ought to be attended to, only so far as it may be necessary for promoting that of the consumer' (Smith 1991: 56). In the nineteenth century, Methodists attempted to prohibit the consumption of leisure pursuits deemed to be 'unproductive' in terms of them not generating any income as a result of being consumed. In the twentieth century, hundreds of thousands of conservative British women in the inter-war years became involved in 'empire shopping weeks', in which they felt it was their duty to pay more for their commodities in order to 'help their white brother-and-sister producers in the colonies' (Trentmann 2009: 201). In Britain, these messages were reversed during the Second World War, as the 'make do and mend' poster campaigns took hold, but although this left a lasting legacy for many, it was one that post-war advertising quickly attempted to undo.

Such a historic blip in the duty to spend does not exist in the United States. As Sheldon Garon argues in *Beyond Our Means: Why America Spends While the World Saves* (2013), spending is shaped by deliberate government policies, and while in most other parts of the world governments have created huge public-information campaigns to promote saving at certain difficult points, in the United States they have tended to use such events to galvanize spending, elevating it to a virtue, and even sometimes suggesting that it is patriotic. Garon gives the example of the policies put in place during the Great Depression when stimulus packages were specifically created to encourage and enable consumer spending and each Christmas during its ten-year period newspapers described a strong, even frenzied, Christmas shopping season in order to build confidence, even if this was more or less an outright lie. In more recent times, in a speech two weeks after the terrorist attacks of 11 September, President George W. Bush urged Americans to 'get down to Disney World in Florida.... Take your families and enjoy life, the way we want it to be enjoyed.' This was obligatory consumption of the most patriotic kind.

In China, the duty to consume is almost exclusively linked to the notion of the 'trickle-down effect' (albeit reconfigured to include strands of reappropriated Confucianism). The idea that the enrichment of the upper income levels (often due to tax breaks or economic benefits provided by the government) will benefit poorer members of society by improving the economy as a whole is proving pervasive (despite its inevitable side effect of increasing wealth inequality in China). This logic is embodied in the desire to continue the creation and expansion of the middle class (xiaokang) – itself a Confucian term. (It is important to note that this middle class ought not perhaps to be read in the same way as one might read the British middle class or indeed the American middle class, both of which have their own specific connotations, not to mention wealth levels.) Creating a xiaokang was part of Hu Jintao's 'scientific development' theory,[10] which emphasized sustainable development and social welfare in pursuit of a 'socialist harmonious society'. In perusing this harmonious society Hu chose to return to the Confucian language of balance and modesty by using the term 'xiaokang', meaning 'basically' or 'functionally' well-off or middle class but without huge wealth, living comfortably but ordinarily. The suggestion was that the enabling of all to reach this state would involve wealth distribution and create the desired 'balance' and 'harmony' within Chinese society. Deng Xiaoping had also used the term in 1979, positing it as the ultimate goal of Chinese modernization.

It is the economic necessity to spend and the notion of the 'duty' to spend that is the driving force behind the specific phenomena of mass consumer society in late modernity (in China and elsewhere). It is this economic drive which, in turn, causes products and services to gather the kinds of social signification which Bourdieu emphasizes and which theorists of the 'post-modern' have centred upon. To put it differently, 'signs' provided by commodities are not disenablers/enablers of consumer agency to escape socio-economic categorization; rather economic conditions are triggers for State policy to encourage the consumption of 'signs'/commodities. Furthermore, these are posited as an actualization of self-hood under the rubric of individuals being consumer-citizens, with 'consumer sovereignty' and 'consumer rights'. The argument, then, is not a simplistic choice between whether the consumer is duped or has agency, but a recognition that the agency given (which may indeed involve a certain amount of self-actualization) is part of a wider schema in which the subject's relationship with the State is being framed in terms of being a citizen with rights, when in reality, it is one of being a subject with responsibilities. Obligatory consumer societies, by their very nature, require subjects who take their responsibility to consume seriously. The era of obligatory consumerism changed the structure of the subject's position to the State and strategic relation to his or her own consumption as far as the State is concerned.

It is worth noting, however, that this individual-to-State positioning via the encouragement of consumerism has not been, and continues not to be, straightforward in China. The Chinese subject has not been easily convinced of the delights of consumerism, or indeed of his or her duty to engage with it. Successive changes in welfare policy in China have attempted to tackle this head-on by providing more of a safety net for Chinese citizens so that they do not rely so heavily upon savings. 'Golden week' holidays have been created specifically to provide time for travel to cities in which one might wish to consume things one could not in one's own local area. Emphasis has somehow become placed on the consumption of certain types of goods and experiences (often those with a classic European 'pedigree') in order to gain 'suzhi' (quality) as a person. Regardless, the reserve army of consumers intended to be drafted in from the rural provinces is proving harder to recruit than expected. This in itself is testament to the way in which, despite the State's repositioning of consumption as a duty (in China and elsewhere), consumers are not brainwashed into consuming more, or indeed into a new relationship with the State. Rather, messages have become part of a culture that posits individuals as losing their worth if they are unable to consume – as being a weight that others have to carry, and this eventually starts to have an impact. At the beginning of the welfare state in Britain, one was seen to 'weigh' upon society if one was unemployed and needed to receive benefits; now, in addition, one can also weigh on society if one is unable to be part of the nation's consumerist habits.

This is how the 'need' to consume has become so far removed from the kind of 'false needs' often talked about by Frankfurt School theorists. Today's 'needs' are almost entirely removed from the product itself (and certainly from its 'false promise' of happiness); they are, however, very much to do with the 'need' (duty) to be a consumer, even if that is in the cheapest of stores. This is not to underestimate the extent to which many regular bargain store consumers are simply trying to buy necessities at the lowest possible price rather than fulfilling a duty; rather, it is to recognize the extent to which the need to perpetuate the *idea* of the ability to buy (even as survival) has driven the growth of stores that enable buying for even the poorest.

iii) The Buddha, the Bonsai and the Chinoiserie Vase: Taste and Kitsch in a World of Bargains

I am desperate to escape the striplight world of the chain bargain stores with their clearly labelled shelves of life's mundanities. Their sheer functionality and their promotion of the myth that everything within them is cheaper than elsewhere are frustrating me, and frankly, boring me. I am craving the less well-ordered, darker, pokier spaces of the family-run stores with their often characterful and bizarre products. Even the idea that these products may be bad economic choices on the part of the store owners, or at the very least more risky choices, pleases me. I like the way they stack things right up to the ceiling. I like that you have to squeeze past other people or back out of certain aisles, enforcing interaction. And I like that things in these stores are often arranged with little conventional logic, rather than in the themed sections of the chain stores. Walter Benjamin's description fits well: 'the commodities are suspended and shoved together in such boundless confusion, that [they appear] like images out of the most incoherent dreams' (Benjamin 1999: 56). Inside one such store a pile of plastic rasta-men stare out at me. They are grotesquely exaggerated, with enlarged facial features and huge joints of rolled marijuana protruding from their mouths.

Figure 4.2 £1 Buddha.

Worse, they are submissive – on their knees, leaning forward, with their hands behind their backs in order that their bodies form a space that can be used to place a mobile phone as it sits on a desk. They are garishly painted in the colours of the Jamaican flag and hideously politically incorrect.

Further down the aisle, a two-metre stretch of shelf is devoted entirely to an array of buddhas – Sakyamuni sits cross-legged in his classic mudra, in amongst piles of tea-towels and plastic bowls, adorned with a bright yellow £1 price tag which peels up at the edges where it will not stick to the fake-aged gold spray underneath.

A woman eyes them carefully, and seeing me looking at them too smiles and says 'funny what you find in here isn't it. My mum will like this though. She loves things that make her imagine other places…. I think she likes to escape!' I smile – 'perhaps we all do', I say. 'Yeah … she's got this stuff everywhere though, little sculptures from Africa and Japan, models of this and that … none of them real of course. They drive me mad sometimes – there's so many everywhere in her place!' I laugh. 'Well, if they make her happy.' 'Yeah, that's what I think. This one's nice though – I like how it looks old. It looks better than the horrible plastic ones she sometimes gets – they just look like something out of a Christmas cracker!' She picks up one of the Buddhas and puts it in her basket. 'Pretty good for the price,' she says.

The appreciation of the 'old', or rather the 'fake aged', is often a factor that elevates certain bargain store products above others. There is something that feels 'good value for money' to bargain store shoppers about buying something for a low price that looks as if it has existed for a long while. It is perhaps the power of suggestion of the 'antique'; the embodiment of time in an object

Figure 4.3 Plastic Bonsai.

whose price reflects the fact that it is not an antique, but whose 'look' provides the connotations that come along with an antique. As Baudrillard says,

> The antique object no longer has any practical application, its role being merely to signify. It is astructural, it refuses structure, it is the extreme case of disavowal of the primary functions. Yet it is not afunctional, nor purely 'decorative', for it has a very specific function within the system, namely the signifying of time.' (Baudrillard 2005: 77–8)

The bargain store Buddha is proof that the signifying of time is a quality that can extract itself from the realm of antiques. In many ways, it speaks to Baudrillard's dislike of the way in which the (genuine) antique 'puts itself forward as authentic within a system whose basic principle is by no means authenticity, but, rather, the calculation of relationships and the abstractness of signs' (Baudrillard 2005: 78). For him, the antique object is a myth of origins and therefore encompasses the assumption that 'authenticity', of the type Walter Benjamin relied upon when theorizing upon the destruction of the 'aura', exists (Baudrillard 2005: 80). The bargain store Buddha on the other hand, pretends to no such origins, playing instead upon the qualities the realm of antiques contains, whilst declaring its mass-produced availability loudly and proudly. In other words, it can signify time, without the problematic claim of authenticity. It gives insta-history – an instantaneous sense of cultural knowledge, yearning or belonging. It *creates* time, time that the consumer never lived, time that is consciously enjoyed as phantasmagorical, imagined life experience. As Baudrillard says of antiques, 'they are a way of escaping everyday life, and no escape is more radical than escape in time' (Baudrillard 2005: 85).

Looking at what the Buddha gives the consumer in terms of time is helpful in putting Benjamin's concept of the 'aura' to use. It enables us to put to one side the issue of authenticity – the 'aura' that great original artworks had and that was 'smashed' in the 'age of mechanical reproduction' by the proliferation of copies (Benjamin 1997). Instead, we can concentrate on his description of the aura as 'a strange weave of space and time: the unique appearance or semblance of distance, no matter how close the object may be' (Benjamin 1997: 250). If we accept that the 'authentic' (or rather the appearance of what we think of as at least symbolizing 'authenticity') is connected to the *semblance of distance* through time, we can recognize the qualities attached to the bargain store Buddha without having to explain how such qualities can operate when we know we are buying one of millions of copies. The important feature for objects such as the £1 Buddhas is the way in which they embody a feeling of *distance* for the consumer; a feeling of being from *somewhere else*, somewhere with a substance 'deeper' than that of the place occupied by the consumer.

In the Buddhas, this is harnessed by their falsely aged appearance – artificially created patches and rubbings-away as if they have experienced the eons of time and the depths of religious significance. Such ageing attempts to provide the commodity with its own memories (faded jeans or scrubbed leather sofas are similar examples) and is now a potent weapon in the commodity's fight to get noticed. As Peter Stallybrass points out, gone are the days when 'from the perspective of commercial exchange, every wrinkle or "memory" was a devaluation of the commodity' (Stallybrass 1998: 196). The search for the authentic (or at least fake authentic) is now critical, in line with Susan Stewart's assertion that experience is mediated and abstracted and the lived relationship of the body to the world is replaced by 'a nostalgic myth of contact and presence' (Stewart 1993: 133). It is as if the aura has become hyper-real. Only its presence as a signifier matters to the consumer seeking a piece of fake distance – a quick-fix for the bargain store commodity's lack of 'real' experience. And buying fake-distance is not an issue, as long as it comes at a bargain price.

Passing further down the street, a shopfront is piled high with pillows and duvets, and sheets and tablecloths, and topped by a large fluorescent cardboard sign upon which is written in black marker pen, 'Duck-feather pillows only £2.99. Must end today.' From just inside the door, the owner shouts, 'Nice linen, natural fibres, very nice, you will sleep well.' Inside, an elderly man shuffles his way down the narrow aisle towards the gloves, his trolley behind him. A woman grabs cleaning fluid and bubble bath and beats a hasty path to the till. A child points up to a high shelf where two clocks sit side by side, identical apart from the image on their faces, and asks 'Can we get that Mickey Mouse clock Mum – next to the one with Jesus on?' Mickey and Jesus both command £3.99. Squeezing past huge buckets of dishcloths, jars of spices and flip-flops, a woman stops to examine the decorative plastic bonsai trees which sit in a line in front of some colouring pens. She looks intrigued as she peers at one in the form of a miniature fir tree, with an oversized white plastic bird perched in its branches and its scale further confused by a tiny blue plastic teddy bear at its trunk. She turns to ask the owner how much it is, referring to it as a 'plant', despite its being man-made and nonliving, as she curiously fingers its plastic-fringed branches. She explains to me that keeping houseplants is not her strong point, but she likes to have 'something green' around and goes on to say how she knows a bonsai takes years to grow normally and requires a lot of patience which she, she says, does not have.

The desire at play here is to have an object that immediately embodies age and time, without being required to put in any ingredient of one's own, whether that be physical (water, soil, nutrients) or non-physical (care, patience). The consumer may grow attached to the bonsai as an object, but she will not have invested material or time into it: despite being symbolically hinged upon taking time, it has come to her 'fully formed'. Similarly, on a different occasion, a woman is gingerly fingering a small wooden box painted in 'shabby-chic' style with faux-weathered white paint. 'They look like they're made from driftwood or something don't they,' she says, picking up the box and turning it over in her hands 'They make me think of summer … plus with this style you can't tell whether something was cheap or not can you,' she laughs. The object has satisfied the criteria of instant age, whilst also overcoming any remnants of reticence or stigma over price.

In many ways, it is often kitsch objects which have the unique ability to dispel issues of signification and connotation, almost acting as a crutch to lessen any embarrassment felt due to shopping for the cheap. It allows people to dismiss something as kitsch as and when it does not live up to any other category, but to do so in a knowing way making themselves part of a looking down on kitsch. Much of what characterizes things as kitsch has to do with the creation of the 'ancient-looking' from cheap, plentiful and immediately available materials. As Lefebvre says:

> These memory-objects, these palpable, immediate traces of the past, seem to say in daily life that the past is never past. Not explicitly but implicitly, it signifies the reversibility of time. In this fractured, fragmented time, we can

return to the past, since it is there. More so than others, the kitsch object possesses these strange properties: a blending of memory, recollection, the imaginary, the real. (Lefebvre 2008 [1981]: 133)

For Celeste Olalquiaga, this relationship between the 'ancient' and the readily available 'modern' is conceptualized by reading kitsch as the fragments of Benjamin's aura, that debris which survived the aura's shattering caused by the proliferation of the 'copy' under mechanical reproduction (Olalquiaga 2000: 19). In this way, Olalquiaga links the immediacy of kitsch to Benjaminian thinking on the ease of reproduction and its concomitant lack of aura. Whilst Olalquiaga does not suggest in any way that these pieces of debris from the aura are in any way lesser than the 'original' (and by original we must include manifestations of 'high art'), her theorizing does rely upon understanding kitsch *purely* as imitation – as the objects that can be quickly produced to copy and/or replace those original auratic objects (Olalquiaga 2000).

In contrast, Sam Binkley argues for 'the uniqueness of kitsch as a distinct style, one which celebrates repetition and conventionality as a value *in itself*' [my italics] (Binkley 2000: 133). His is a nuanced argument which, while it celebrates the toppling of old assumptions in regard to cultural hierarchies based on the supremacy of 'high culture' and agrees with those theorists within cultural studies who posited consumers as intrinsically creative and critical in their choices (Grossberg 1992; Fiske 1989; Hall 1996), wishes to assert kitsch as a distinct category which deflects creativity and innovation whilst celebrating routine, sentiment and banality. For Binkley, 'mass culture theorists had it right when they identified the repetitive conventionality of kitsch, but got it wrong when they failed to recognize the social meanings that a repetitive, derivative style might hold' (Binkley 2000: 134). They had correctly dismantled the hierarchy of taste which put kitsch at the bottom, but had created a regime in which 'creativity' now marked out a culture's worth. Kitsch, Binkley argues, spurns creativity per se, revelling in a repetition of the familiar and a resounding affirmation of the everyday.

For Binkley, this affirmation of the everyday is akin to Pierre Bourdieu's 'taste of necessity', in that it expresses the conventionality of everyday forms and their embeddedness in everyday life (Bourdieu 1984: 371). However, for Bourdieu, it is precisely kitsch's embeddedness in the everyday, this uniformity with past aesthetics, which categorizes its consumers as those whose economic lives are governed by scarcity: kitsch is aesthetics for those who cannot (financially) afford to make mistakes or experiment with their decorative choices. Meanwhile for Binkley, consumer choices in regard to kitsch are *knowingly* spurning creativity, rather than simply relying upon safe choices. Perhaps though, kitsch goes even further, not only affirming the everyday, but celebrating it. Furthermore, this celebration is done with a knowing nod to the past and to its reinterpretation in the present. Kitsch is self-referential. Therefore, whilst it does indeed spurn creativity as Binkley argues, it is, on a subtle psycho-social level, creative in itself as it exists to encourage enjoyment in re-creating the past in the present. With kitsch, whilst, of course, the market decides which pieces of 'high art' to copy, it cannot 'brand' them in the same way it would other objects as they must be presented as 'copies' of the 'original'.

Bargain kitsch, then, is at once destructive and creative – it destroys (or rather disallows) both old hierarchies of culture and the ability of marketeers to make the object define the person. Yet, it creates and strengthens connections to the everyday. It places high culture imagery within the most mundane of contexts – 'images socially marked as unique and exceptional … are subordinated to the practical everyday problems of the household' (Binkley 2000: 143). Yet, relations to kitsch have moved on since Bourdieu wrote *Distinction*, and it can no longer be argued that a taste for 'trinkets and knick-knacks' is altogether about a working-class attempt to gain 'maximum effects at minimum cost' (Bourdieu 1984: 379). As Richard Peterson (1992) argues, the terms 'elite' and 'mass' have been replaced by multiple usages and readings of objects which can no longer be simplistically placed along a class hierarchy as they have become 'omnivore' and 'univore' due to consumers mixing objects from all parts of the taste hierarchy. For example, Judith enjoyed mixing the good-quality furniture she had saved up for with kitsch ornaments in order to remain 'down to earth' and so that her lounge didn't 'look stuffy'. In an almost opposite logic, Sarah hoped that by buying 'one or two quality vases', her old, faded sofa would look 'chic' rather than 'clapped out'. For Tracey, having 'a few bits of kitsch around the place' gave it a slightly bohemian look, which reassured her that she had not completely given up on the lifestyle of her youth.

This playing around with the meanings of kitsch is perhaps most evident in the ship-in-a-bottle that I had first seen in the markets of Yiwu when shadowing Jay as he went about his business. On this occasion, I am witnessing it on Donald's windowsill – a classic sailing clipper, like those that would have sailed the oceans in colonial times. Yet, it has lost its colonial connotations and in its kitsch version becomes simply a piece of seaside regalia that reminds Donald of childhood holidays by the sea. In previous eras, it would have been an object that represented the majesty of the age of sail, negating the looming presence of colonial backlash such as the opium wars and the ever-brewing tensions in the South China seas – an object linked to a national sense of one's country's place in the world.

In Britain, the population of the late nineteenth century had lived in an age where the idea of overseas territories was still a source of pride and had not yet become a guilty embarrassment; an age in which the sheer scale of the journeys undertaken, the ships that made them and the weird and wonderful things they brought back had created a sense of wonderment. Ships-in-bottles captured the sense of adventure and danger felt by a nation which in many ways still felt itself to be on the crest of a wave of global pioneering. They would sit in the cabinets of wealthy Victorians alongside tropical butterflies pinned to velvet, taxidermic wonders and other exotic curios typical of the age. They were objects intricately embedded in the meanings of imperialistic relations. Indeed, James Bunn argues that such collections were linked to the mystifications produced by the imperialist economy throughout the seventeenth and eighteenth centuries (Bunn 1980: 319). To collect was to perceive oneself as a 'citizen of the world' who could not be tied to 'a single region' or 'the limited learning of one era' (Bunn 1980: 313). Similarly, in the essay, 'Unpacking my Library', in *Illuminations*, Walter Benjamin argues that the collector places objects in a kind of magical arrangement which enables a 'renewing of the world' as the collector comes to life in the objects. Using stamp collections as his example, he says collecting can also capture the power of great states (Benjamin 1999). Perhaps much of this mystification was precisely made possible due to the miniaturization of the colonial experience through the ship-in-a-bottle. As Susan Stewart argues, history is erased by the miniature – 'the function of the miniature is to bring historical events to life, to immediacy, and thereby to erase their history, to lose us within their present-ness' (Stewart 1993: 60).

This position of the ship-in-a-bottle as an object of colonial prowess was not to last, however. Something else was also happening during the era that the clippers had come to rule the waves – the idea of the 'great British seaside'. As John Walton (1983) writes, sea bathing emerged in the first half of the nineteenth century among the higher strata of English society as part of a fashionable concern with pursuing health and was capable of attracting substantial business development, transforming old towns and even creating new ones. In fact, the seaside town was the fastest-growing type of British town in the first half of the nineteenth century.[11] The growth of the railways from the 1840s onwards greatly aided the development of seaside towns and made it possible for middle and lower classes to afford a trip to the seaside. During this period, the seaside was a romantic image, much as the countryside was, in ways that counteracted the impact of the industrial revolution, but with the addition of 'pleasure' and 'luxury' as powerful connotations. Queen Victoria's love of the seaside aided its development too and the sea became very much about the 'seaside', the resort and holidaying, as opposed to something perceived solely as connected to trade and ships. It was through this process that the ship-in-a-bottle became first a souvenir, and then when mass produced, a kitsch souvenir. It no longer served to lessen the sense of the gargantuan nature of the oceans – these were now mapped and 'conquered' and understood, rendered acceptable, unthreatening; rather, it enabled a celebration of the 'seaside'. It was a comforting object that celebrated agreed-upon values of 'good, clean, family fun' by the sea, but maintained a small hint of darker histories. This description certainly rings true in

Donald's case. He recalls energetic days playing in the sand and then windswept evenings during which his grandfather would regale the children with stories of shipwrecks and pirates. His bargain store ship-in-a-bottle, then, is an object that harks back to a pre-1970s' Britain, before the 'traditional' family seaside holiday had fallen from favour due to changing social tastes and norms and the availability of affordable holidays abroad.

Importantly though, it also harks back to an age before the repercussions of empire had become fully part of life in Britain (and indeed other ex-colonial countries) – before new groups of ethnic minorities had become part of its history and fabric and its sense of self in the world had become specifically nuanced by being a former colonial power. Donald fully admits that it is about nostalgia for him and that is why he bought it. His attitudes are representative of a wider sentimentality about the seaside, the same sentimentality (and defiance) present when London duo Chaz and Dave sang, 'you can keep your Costa Brava, tell your mate I'd rather, have a day down in Margate with all the family' – although of course few people would rather 'have a day down in Margate' by this time. The seaside was becoming an object of communal nostalgia for simpler times – days when Victorian mores meant rules were rules and those who broke them were punished; when fun could be innocent and culture was (apparently) not yet sexualized and self-conscious; and when the grandiose stucco-fronted buildings of seaside towns (now crumbling facades) were stars of the unfolding drama of the times, rather than fading bit-part actresses. In addition, not for Donald as an individual but on a national level, the simpler times' pictures are undeniably days when Britain ruled the waves; days before the onset of pluralism, when values were more unified. Whether intended or not, Empire, as Eric Hobsbawm puts it, 'became part of the sentimentalised literary and cinematic memories of the former imperial states' (Hobsbawm 1995: 222).

Ironically, it was precisely the sentimentalizing of the seaside as part of a golden age, not only of Empire, but also of Britain's social history, that led to the market for mass-produced seaside trinkets such as ship-in-bottles. Ship-in-bottles became pieces of cheap frippery on the windowsills of seaside cottages, to be smiled at with nostalgic but knowing looks in which the looker recollected some vague and now mismatched ideas of trade, Empire, bathing carriages and lighthouses in a manner very much akin to what Lefebvre terms 'a blending of memory, recollection, the imaginary, the real' (2008 [1981]: 133).[12]

Now, the onset of mass production and containerization of global trade saw huge container ships traversing the same historic sea routes as their sail predecessors, bringing hundreds of factory-made ship-in-bottles to be sold as nostalgic tourist paraphernalia in tacky seaside souvenir shops. In fact, Chinese factories churn out bottled versions of the very tea clippers that brought misery to Chinese shores during the opium wars, kitsch-ing their own colonial experience to sell back to those who created the kitsch-ing of it in the first place.

It is worth noting, however, that the kitsch-ing of the ship-in-a-bottle has also enabled the subversion of its previous meanings, leaving it open to multiple interpretations and associations. So, it is, therefore, with the advent of the ship-in-a-bottle as a mass-produced kitsch object that it also becomes a contested object – one which, now carrying associations from various parts of its past, can be discussed precisely as its parts, rather than as a single object with a unified meaning.[13] This lack of unified meaning had its base not only in the postmodern nature of the images now associated with the ship-in-a-bottle, but also in the more tangible fact that in a post-colonial era, 'meaning' was no longer agreed upon. History itself was a contested realm – whose history, of what, where, when and defined by whose agenda? The post-colonial subjects of Britain's former empire, now citizens, could not entirely accept the trinketizing of their historical experience and their 'collective' memory of colonial times began to compete with the other 'collective' memory of the British seaside, making the ship-in-a-bottle a contested memory object, whose meaning was fought over and of which diverse readings were supplied.

Yet another way of dealing with contested identities and histories revealed by the ship-in-a-bottle is seen in twenty-first-century China, where ship-in-a-bottle makers have embraced the global competition of their craft and been determined to win medals for their depictions of the very same clipper ships that travelled to China at the height of the opium wars. They have specifically chosen to depict clippers, as these are seen by the ship-in-a-bottle craft community as the 'classic' ship-in-a-bottle and as the most difficult models to make. They have also, however, used them in their manufacturing revolution, reappropriated the role such vessels played in the British colonial exploitation of China and forged them as part of their own current-day production prowess. 1£/$/€ versions of these crafts are readily available on the business-to-business website alibaba.com and, as I saw, in the markets of Yiwu.

The bargain store commodity, then, often plays upon the ways in which kitsch operates as knowingly embedded within the everyday. In many ways, it is, therefore, also implicit in breaking down old hierarchies of taste – ornamental bargain store commodities are often objects which allow consumers to rely upon old categories of 'taste' in order to destroy and/or re-create them within the present context. So, we are left with a strange situation in which, whilst the bargain store shouts its single-price policy from every available wall and shelf, demanding us to see all its commodities as equal bargains, it cannot undo other social categories whose potency and embeddedness in our attitudes give us other criteria and other hierarchies upon which to judge its commodities. Bargain store commodities may often be equal in price, but they are far from equal psycho-socially. Class connotations still rule. I stumble upon an excellent example of this about three weeks after the opening of the new Catford bargain store (where I had stood in the queue talking to Jean and Sue), when I notice that the local Indian restaurant has bought a bulk load of Chinese-style vases that I had seen for sale in the new store. One of these now adorns each table in the restaurant and contains a single silk flower. I comment on the vases to the restaurant owner and he looks pleased when he confirms that he got them from the new bargain store – 'classy right?' he says.

It is interesting that the Chinese-style vase, despite being a bargain store product – an inexpensive version of a 'real' Chinese vase – holds enough connotations of luxury, style and 'good taste' to be a symbol of 'sophistication'. In fact, those connotations are so strong that it is perfectly rational to have a version of the vase that is very clearly an inexpensive 'fake' as a decorative object on a restaurant table – it still works as a way of connoting 'classyness'. As Baudrillard (2005) recognized in *The System of Objects*, the factors that differentiate commodities lie outside of a structural-technical analysis as this is insufficient for everyday objects whose safety and basic ability to work is easily satisfied. What emerges as important and defining are their cultural connotations: 'Each of our practical objects is related to one or more structural elements, but at the same time they are all in perpetual flight from technical structure towards their secondary meanings, from the technological system towards a cultural system' (Baudrillard 2005: 6).

The vase in the Indian restaurant in Catford is very much a copy of what became known as 'Chinoiserie' – Western-made furniture and ornamental goods that drew upon motifs from across the East and blended them together as a kind of homogenous 'Eastern-ness' as typified by furniture by Chippendale and ceramics by Minton. As collecting and display reached its epitome in the Victorian parlour of the late nineteenth century, Chinoiserie became symbolic of global exploration and domination and encapsulated Victorian ideals of luxury and craftsmanship, alongside middle-class respectability – knowledge, good-breeding and taste. It showed a well-rounded knowledge and a pride in 'progress'. In short, it provided 'class' (just as the owner of the Indian restaurant in Catford said).

The vase aims to mimic Satsuma ware, a Japanese style that was, on the whole, made for a Western market. Having its own rich traditions of ceramic making, China did not copy Satsuma ware until recent decades.[14] Here, in copying a style that itself played into the West's fondness for Chinoiserie and all things Eastern, the fake Satsuma vase provides the connotations of class and style that came along with that – and, in fact, still do. Minton's now ubiquitous willow-pattern tea sets are still objects that connote a certain level of what we might loosely call 'education' and what Bourdieu would certainly see as part of cultural capital. In fact, the association of 'respectability' with willow-pattern has recently been played upon by a Scottish design company who have created wallpapers and fabrics using willow-pattern motifs but with gritty, urban scenes when one takes a closer look. By playing upon the respectability, they are effectively also acknowledging it of course.

The Chinoiserie vase shows how bargain commodities tap into a logic still based on the kind of criteria identified by Baudrillard, whilst contemporaneously being part of very different logic of disposability. It draws upon cultural connotations linked to the 'exotic' (the 'far-East'), respectability, liberalism and worldliness, at the same time as being part of a system in which abundance increases under the constraints of calculated *scarcity* (Baudrillard 2005: 162). Despite the apparent abundance via stocky displays, one must 'snap up' a bargain. Despite being an entity that is attached to ubiquitous objects, it can become 'unavailable' at any moment and so must be searched out by the consumer who is faced with the possibility of finding that it has become obsolete. Class can be had for bargain price, but only if one is quick enough to spot the opportunity to gain it.

iv) Births, Deaths and Marriages: Bargains from Cradle to Grave

On a late-September afternoon, I meet up with Jackie, who has agreed to take me shopping with her on her local high street, where there are three different bargain stores, all of which she uses regularly. She relates to me how a few years back she had bought a £1 gravestone to put on the spot in her garden where she and her children had buried the family cat. When they had moved house two years ago, they decided to take the gravestone with them, partly as 'it felt strange to leave it there for the new people moving in' and partly to remind them of their departed pet. The gravestone was then later used to mark the spot of a goldfish her youngest child had won and which had not survived long in its tank. Although the children had become mature enough to respond very level-headedly to the death of the goldfish, they had liked the idea that any family pet (regardless of how loved or how substantial a part of their lives it had been) should be buried with the gravestone marking the spot. Thus, the £1 stone had become linked to a history of the family's pets, and indeed its future pets.

Similarly, on one occasion, market mavern Helen had explained to me how she feels bargain stores are a part of her because she has always shopped in them and cannot remember a time when she did not. This feeling has only grown stronger since one specific bargain store product became part of a very important day of her life:

> I got married last year and my mum made my dress and all that. She'd been
> working on it for months and had ordered some flowers that would go well

with it from the local florist. But they're so expensive, real flowers, and we were determined not to spend more on the flowers than the dress! So I said, well, just order a few real ones and we'll make-up the bouquet with plastic ones from the pound shop. My mum thought I was mad. I spent about two months collecting really nice plastic flowers – you know, subtle ones not the horrible big bright ones. Each time I went out shopping I'd scour the pound shops to see what they had in. And on the day it looked really fantastic. Everyone commented on how unusual and beautiful it was. I didn't want to throw it over my shoulder!... although I did, of course.... I wanted to keep it! I was so proud of it, and I was even more proud because I had made it out of nothing – I mean it had cost hardly anything. Also, I felt like it really represented me, because I love pound shops and also I suppose if I'm honest because I had gone through quite a few years of being quite poor and that's not much fun on your own, and now I was putting those years behind me. I was getting married and I wouldn't have to cope with being poor on my own any more – but it had become a part of me, and although I hadn't enjoyed being poor I had a kind of pride in how I'd survived it.

For Helen, bargain stores themselves and some of the items they typically stock, particularly, of course, the plastic flowers, hold special import due to the role they have played in her life – they have gained more meaning due to becoming imbued with emotion. The plastic flowers are no longer simply objects for her, but things that have meaning as part of her own life story; they were key players in what she considers to be the most important day of her life so far.

This type of affective relationship between subject and object is often held up as the solution to the impersonality of commercial transaction and therefore the extent to which market relations have come to govern all relations. However, in unpacking this notion, it quickly becomes clear that not only is it increasingly difficult to draw the line between having a deep connection to an object and simply fetishizing it, but also this 'appropriate' relationship of deep connection is in itself becoming marketed and fetishized, whilst at the same time fetish behaviour is becoming reappropriated in a self-aware postmodern way.

Being part of the object is also what Helen describes when she explains how she felt the plastic flowers had 'really represented me' and how they were symbolic of her poverty at the time and that poverty (and therefore the cheap pound store flowers) had become 'part of her'. Certainly, she has attached an idea and sentiment to the flowers – they have become a 'thing' for her, but she has not fetishized them; rather she has with them exactly the kind of entanglement with the everyday that Lefebvre describes. Similarly, Gell's (1998) notion of the 'distributed mind',[15] in which people act through objects by distributing parts of their personhood in them, is useful here, as is Strathern's (1999) similar notion of the 'partible person', divisible into things along certain exchange trajectories.

Both Gell's and Strathern's notions could be applied to the way in which Helen saw 'parts' of her old life and her old self as embodied in pound commodities. Her relationship with these commodities would also stand to disprove Edgar Morin's[16] (2001) distinction between the 'biographical object' and the 'protocol object' or standardized commodity. For Morin, the biographical object has unity with its user and the user's identity and the owner develops his or her personality through it, whereas the protocol object is not used as a self-definition and causes its owner to be decentred and fragmented by the acquisition of things. As Helen's case shows, it is absolutely possible for standardized commodities to become biographical objects, partly due to the manner in which they can become 'things' for that individual due to being imbued with personal ideas and partly due to the way in which individuals can find alternative uses for mass-produced commodities.

Therefore, along with the recognition that things can become part of a life story is a concurrent recognition which sees things as moving in and out of thing-hood. This acknowledgement challenges Bill Brown's (2001) argument which, despite citing the 'object/thing dialectic' (Brown 2001: 5), remains faithful to Derrida's notion that the thing is not an object and cannot become one, because it is a sign, whereas an object is not (Brown 2001: 126). For Brown, an object becomes a thing on the occasions it begins to have an idea attached to it as well as simply being tangible – 'things' are perhaps 'what is excessive in objects ... what exceeds their mere materialization as objects or their mere utilization as objects' (Brown 2001: 4–5). A thing is an object plus an idea, and those objects which assert themselves as things, constitute a 'changed relation to the human subject and thus the story of how the thing really names less an object than a particular subject-object relation' (Brown 2001: 4–5). However, Brown's 'things', whilst indicative of the subject having imbued the thing with sentiment, are perhaps not as indicative of a fundamentally changed relationship between subject and object (or 'thing') as he would like to think. As he goes on to say, the magic by which objects become 'things' is ultimately inextricably woven with their becoming values, fetishes, idols, and totems' (Brown 2001: 4–5). Brown, therefore, suggests that it is the thingness of an object, its status as sign or idea, which creates its fetishistic nature. For Brown, the thing is the fetish.

Mrs Lucas's garden gnome is a good example of the way in which the thing can be imbued with sentiment. His name is Gerald. He is just under a foot high, with a painted-on red pointed hat, green trousers and yellow shirt. He stands leaning on his own spade, eyes closed, with a knowing and somewhat impish smile upon his face. I recognize him as a brother of those other gnomes I saw so far away in Yiwu. Mrs Lucas saw Gerald one sunny afternoon in late June a few years ago and decided he would make a nice addition to her patio garden. 'It's quite a dull garden for lots of the day as it's north-facing, and I thought he'd cheer it up ... now, sometimes, you know, when I'm pottering around, I just start nattering to him about something that's happened or something that annoyed me. It's like, you know, he can just listen 'cos that's all he can do and even though I know he's just a gnome it doesn't really make any difference 'cos you still feel you've told someone – I mean, it could be anyone or anything really, it's just about getting it out of your system ... yeah, he knows a lot about me that gnome.'

For Brown, this imbuing of Gerald with sentiment means that he has become a thing and cannot move out of the thing state. In contrast, Igor Kopytoff's famous biographical approach shows that things move in and out of the *commodity* state and that these movements can be fast/slow, reversible/terminal, normative/deviant – the same is true of the *thing* state. Appadurai differentiates between Kopytoff's cultural biography and the social history of things, arguing that cultural biography is useful for specific things, but a social history of things is needed to look at classes or types of thing (Kopytoff 1986: 34). His explanation of 'regimes

Figure 4.4 'Gerald' the garden gnome.

of value' can be applied to 'value' in the sense of whether or not something is an object or a thing. Appadurai argues that 'value coherence may be highly variable from situation to situation' (Kopytoff 1986: 15). In other words, there may be a 'minimum fit' between cultural and social dimensions of commodity exchange. In the same way, we could argue that in certain settings along its trajectory, there is a minimum fit between object status and thing status in the life of any given object/thing. There are situations in which everyone would agree on the status of an object/thing and situations when the agreement would be minimal, leading to much confusion over its status. This is why moving from thing-hood back to object-hood, contrary to what Brown suggests, *is* possible on both an individual and a societal level. Indeed, many marketed 'things' failed the test of time and returned to object-hood; only 'classic' items still have thing-hood decades later. These 'classics' are somehow so representative of the time they were fashionable that their thing-hood remains intact.

We return, however, to the original conundrum – the question of how a subject–object relationship can exist without the object becoming fetishized. There are two syndromes to be on guard against: the fetishizing of a more knowing/thinking relationship with the object and the (re)appropriating of the fetish. An example of the former syndrome are the types of consumer campaigns which, in attempting to bring proximity between consumer and producer by making apparent the 'ethical conditions' under which a product was manufactured, end by creating a brand from that relationship itself – the fair trade movement unfortunately has the secondary result of fetishizing itself. The latter syndrome – (re)appropriating the fetish – involves a type of 'knowing' relationship with the fetishized object in which buying it or wearing it *in acknowledgement* of its fake/fetishized nature is deemed a form of anti-fetishism. It is a kind of self-referential relationship with the fetish, in which the consumer plays with his or her own identity as a consumer, but seems to be saying 'I am removed from all this though because I know the thing I have bought is fetishized.' This reaction from the consumer is rather like Žižek's (2002) example of the Hopi's masks. The unmasking ceremony of the Hopi tribe causes those being initiated to realize for the first time that what they thought was sacred and magic is actually their fathers and uncles behind masks. However, after the initial shock has worn off, the mask itself somehow becomes the holder of magical meaning, or, as Žižek puts it,

We know the mask is only a mask – the mask is only a signifier which expresses an internal, invisible spirit, a mystical preserve. However, we must not forget that this mystical spirit, invisible Beyond, *is not what is hidden behind the mask* – behind the mask is the everyday image in which there is nothing holy or magic. All the magic, all the invisible mystical spirit, *is in the mask as such*. (Žižek 2002: 247)

To apply this to the commodity thing – removing the mask is the equivalent of removing the fetishization from an object. It is the moment of knowing and potentially of defetishizing. However, if the mask itself, or the fetish itself (the branding, image, etc. of an object), is then deemed to contain the magic, this defetishization simply becomes a reappropriation of the fetish; a celebration of having understood the way it works, but a respect for it nonetheless. It allows the subject to feel in control of his or her relationship with the commodity, unaddicted as it were, and as Žižek points out, if individuals can feel that they are not addicted to the commodity thing, they can believe that they are not part of a totalitarian regime, yet knowing that they really are. Žižek refers to this syndrome as one in which the (il)logic is constantly one of 'I know it to be true, but nevertheless it's not true' – a pathological state of constant denial through agreement (Žižek 2002: 244). With certain types of knowing or 'unaddicted' enjoyment of the bargain store commodity, this amounts to a form of postmodernism which, in acknowledging the fetish, feels it is trampling upon it, when in actuality it is celebrating it, albeit in a nonchalant manner.

I did encounter one commodity upon my travels that can perhaps be said to deny the fetish – a $1 pregnancy test. I had been hearing about $1 pregnancy tests for a while and had found various factories that produced them in Zhejiang province, close to Yiwu. The introduction of $1 (I have also seen £1) pregnancy tests caused mixed reactions. Parenting forums had numerous comments posted about the tests, with many parents-to-be leaving derogatory remarks about not trusting them and expressing their disdain for the tests (and indeed, those who used them). As is often the case, it was not long before the backlash arrived, consisting largely of common-sense arguments surrounding the minimal costs involved in producing pregnancy tests, and the ways in which well-known brands played upon precisely such fears as those being displayed in order to overcharge for their products. One forum member expressed her bafflement when, after talking to a group of friends with children, it turned out that they had all used dollar store pregnancy tests to determine whether or not they were with child, but had not told anyone because they felt embarrassed and slightly ashamed. Another told me that now, whenever she is in a dollar store and hears other customers expressing disdain and asking who on earth would buy a pregnancy test from the dollar store, she always lets them know that the tests work perfectly well and are exactly the same as branded tests. She says, 'I always get my pregnancy tests from dollar stores now. I know it's stupid and doesn't make any logical sense, but I almost feel like it's a good omen for me because it worked the first time. I was so glad to be pregnant and it was the $1 test that showed me I was for the first time. Bargain pregnancy tests have definitely become a fact of life for me now that we're planning our second.'

What enables the $1 pregnancy test not to become fetishized, even though it is an extremely intimate part of one's life story, is the nature of its disposability.

It is an object that reveals a truth – that of there being a pregnancy (or not) – and once it has revealed that truth, its job is done. This means that although it is then jettisoned, it leaves (if positive of course) an impact bigger than itself; an impact that disenables the object itself to become the fetish. The foetus that it has revealed and the baby that foetus will become are the fetish. The discovery of life can be gained at a bargain price, but the object that reveals this life is, so far, removed from fetishism.

Conclusion ... and Back to the Dump?

The vast container ship sat in the dock at the port of Tianjin is not full of China-price products ready to be shipped to bargain stores of the West. It has come from the West carrying a rather different cargo – not new commodities, but rather the remains of old commodities. Every single one of its immense containers is full of waste; the waste of the West shipped back to China to be melted down and made into new commodities. This is a precious cargo indeed, secured at cost, each ton weighed and valued depending on the materials contained within it; a cargo that will provide the good-quality raw materials so important to China if it is to continue its steady growth. Steady growth is what concerns China now. It finds itself in the unusual position of trying to curtail its runaway growth of recent years in order to create something more sustainable, less prone to falls and therefore less likely to cause social unrest due to loss of jobs or inability of factories to pay their workers.

These containers will go to the outskirts of Tianjin where an army of workers will unload the packages from them in a vast field of bundled trash. This waste is often from local authorities in the West who, keen to find cheaper solutions to meeting their recycling criteria, have stopped the expensive process of setting up domestic recycling plants, and have instead sourced waste buyers in China who will actually *pay them* for the rubbish produced in their countries. Tianjin is like Shanghai's Baoshan district, times one hundred. Waste is not just part of the city's economy, it is its predominant industry. Its waste-processing quarters are never-ending. The percentage of its population involved in the waste industry is unmeasurable, but huge. It has a global reputation for collecting the world's waste, particularly that from the West as it tends to be better quality materials. What is disposable in the West is hugely valuable here in Tianjin. Journalists visiting Tianjin's sorting companies have found remnants of utility bills from customers as far away as Kent, United Kingdom, and Arizona, United States, amongst other household waste and commodities at the ends of their lives.

Tianjin is proof of the point to which the gap between consumption and re-consumption has come.

Waste is crucial to the narrowing of the gap, and this is, of course, precisely the story of China's current development policy. The securing of waste, either by buying it in from elsewhere or by creating it domestically is paramount. This has seen what could be called policy-aided consumption increase at unprecedented rates. Welfare 'safety nets' have been created to encourage people to part with their hard-earned savings. 'Golden week' holidays have been created specifically to provide time for rural residents to travel to cities and buy products they may not have access to in their home provinces. The rural masses have become a vast and as yet relatively untapped source of consumptive practices, now crucial if China is to survive the decrease in export orders from Western nations. When the United States and Europe stop buying as much, rural Chinese must spend to plug the gap. In this way, China's relation to waste becomes double-edged – on the one hand, waste must be created by consumption and on the other hand, consumption must be (re)created by waste. Things must be 'wasted', but they must also, in doing so, be put back into play as raw materials for the creation of new products. Lefebvre's assertion about being able to draw conclusions regarding a social group from their waste has never been more true:

> A social group is characterized just as much by what it rejects as by what it consumes and assimilates. The more economically developed a country is, the more gets thrown away, and *the faster it gets thrown away* … [my emphasis] In underdeveloped countries, nothing is thrown away. The smallest piece of paper or string, the smallest tin is of use. (Lefebvre 2008 [1962]: 43–4)

What is most crucial about this disposability is that it maintains movement within the commodity chain. The narrowing of the consumption–reconsumption gap so often seen as characterized by speed is actually characterized more by movement – and any movement enables survival, regardless of how fast it is. This is because continued movement allows small amounts of profit to plug up the holes in the economy just enough to keep it moving, and this is true on both local and international scales in both the East and the West. In the East, the immense import of the Yangtze River Delta to China as a whole means that it simply must maintain production levels and therefore growth levels – its success is China's success to a large extent. Despite the increase in large consumer goods and the desired move via these to service industries, China's economic survival still depends very much upon its bread-and-butter low-end manufacturing industries.

It is this dual concern with a 'progress' that moves away from basic manufacturing, but that acknowledges its importance, that has seen China portray itself to the world in a seemingly contradictory set of images ranging from the super-glossy international Shanghai Expo, to the pride in Yiwu as the world's factory, to the presentation of the traditional elements of Chinese culture at the Beijing Olympics opening ceremony. While the Expo concentrated on innovation and globalization, Yiwu focuses on sheer availability and production capacity, and the Olympics focused on the way in which 'modern' China is grounded in a rich history of ethnic and cultural belongings. These elements are picked up by the French Sinologist David Gosset who argues that the 'Chinese Dream'[1] is the intersection of 'Modern China', 'Civilizational China' and 'Global China'. He sees this as embodied in current leader Xi Jin Ping's wife – Peng Liyuan – a 'modern' woman, celebrated globally for her stylish and professional look, who is a famous singer of traditional Chinese folk songs. It could equally be argued that the Chinese Dream is also present in the marketing of Yiwu – a beautiful ancient village that was home to Confucian poets; a green yet efficient hotbed of efficiency and modernism; a provider of commodities for the world. In fact, it is this same combination that is apparent in ex-premier Hu Jintao's 'harmonious society',[2] a policy tagline that aimed to balance economic development with social equality and environmental care.

Meanwhile in the West, the narrowing of the consumption-reconsumption gap is enabled solely by the low price of the commodity. The consumer's willingness to jettison and re-buy denies the practice of 'make do and mend', bringing disposal closer to purchase and repurchase closer to disposal. The bargain store product's obsolescence is not only built in due to its simplicity and the inferior materials it is made from but is also a happy psychological by-product of these physical qualities. Low price and low specification provide a low price tag, which, in turn, confers upon the product the ability for its owner to jettison it without concern. Function is reduced to fad in the case of the bargain store commodity, but this could not be the case without the Chinese end of things creating an abundance of cheap products.

What feeds the narrowing of the gap is the idea of the bargain. The bargain store promotes itself as a cheap alternative to other stores, and most who shop in them do so due to a belief that this is the case, and, of course, out of necessity. However, the notion of the bargain itself contains other layers of meaning, layers that become most deeply attached to our societal norms and values. Perhaps surprisingly, what the bargain store promotes (by accident as much as intent) is not simply old-fashioned thrift, but morals. The postmodern acknowledgement of the shopping fetish, that is, the 'fun' of 'going wild' in a bargain store, is a current-day admission of the kind of 'wild' consumption that seemed to define the 1980s and is imbued with a guilt-ridding idea that buying lots, but cheaply, is in no way morally reprehensible (unlike those 'immoral'1980s' shoppers).

This is not to say that sometimes fads don't surprise us – things bought in the knowledge that they are disposable can find strange places in our lives and sentiments. In many ways, the objects followed in this book are, therefore, exceptions to the rule. The pet gravestone became an object that 'belonged' to a whole family, each of whom attached emotions they had for former pets to it; the plastic flowers took on parts of Helen's own past and identity, representing her on an important day of her life; the ship-in-a-bottle became a memory object for Donald, allowing him to think back with fondness about childhood holidays spent by the sea; the Chinoiserie vase allowed the restaurant owner to feel he was accessing some perhaps hard-to-reach connotations of class; and Mrs Lucas embedded her everyday woes within Gerald the garden gnome. These were bargain store commodities that would outlive their peers, that broke the cardinal rule of the bargain store chain – *do not last long.* They were mavericks.

Yet, despite these exceptions, the bargain store commodity more frequently enables, rather than dis-enables, the narrowing of the consumption–reconsumption gap, and, most crucially, this ties in to the legitimizing myth of the 'good consumer'. As the idea that all citizens must continue to consume becomes increasingly prevalent in the economic ideology of Western countries, the bargain becomes a salvation for the financially poor consumer and the bargain store a temple in which even they can fulfil their duty to capitalism. The bargain holds the promise of eternal abundance, provided we continue to shop and so create jobs, demand, growth and wealth. It subtly instils a pride in the ability to purchase for those usually unable to do so, causing them to remain participants in a capitalist ideal. The bargain store is a means of commodity worship for the economic underclass (even those who, aware of its religious pull, do not choose to shop there). Millions of debt-ridden consumers search for cheap products in bargain stores across the West, enabling the stores to become ideal vehicles for consumptive thrift.

This plugging of the gaps with the trickle of profits from the poorest manufacturers and shoppers sits in stark contrast to the purported economic aspirations and beliefs of both East and West, whose economies are built on the idea of trickle down. The bargain store places emphasis on those who should be receiving the benefits of trickle down to join the effort to keep us afloat. So, we see how spending has started to become a moral duty of those who can (just) afford to do so. Under the name of 'cheap', it has smuggled in the permanent necessity to spend. In providing 'spontaneity', it has created ever firmer enslavement to consumption and therefore to labour, changing our relationship with our own days, weeks and years of time in our lives. It has made 'freedom' the ability for all (even the poorest) to accept the logic of consumption, by representing an apparent great democracy of consumption – the very least, achievable by all, inclusion economics for the underclass. Consumptive thrift is a state and societal expectation – spending becomes saving (money), but also saving the nation. Danny Miller comments in a similar manner on the way in which spending has become confused with saving, arguing that looking for bargains is the modern form of ritual sacrifice, enacted daily in the high-street mini market:

> It is possible for shoppers to regard virtually the whole of the shopping expedition and the purchase of almost any specific item within that expedition, not as an act of spending at all, but as an act of saving. (Miller 1998b: 56)

This logic of 'spending our way out of trouble' has found its way into the economic logic of other nations now – China, finally, caved in to the promotion of consumption and still stoically clings to the notion that the trickle-down factor from the spending of the wealthiest will create an equal middle class acceptable to all. Being 'thrifty' to spend is fine; being thrifty to save is not – spending becomes saving, 'pure' saving is bad. This consumptive thrift has arisen from the new age of austerity – the austerity mentioned in the introduction as that in which the cheap functions not in its own right, but to facilitate the continuation of patterns from past eras –certain levels of consumption, at certain paces, maintaining a psychology of conspicuous consumption, but that now emphasizes quantity rather than quality, and the ability to waste without concern. Yet, this necessity for the chain to complete its cycle faster does not translate to a generalizable 'speed' of the chain in general. As we have seen, the chain is as beset by rupture and slow mechanisms, as it is by smoothness and efficiency. It is inherently short-term-ist. Its ability to think short term and leap on opportunities as they emerge is what has made the bargain store so resilient in the latest times of austerity. It is not simply that a store selling the cheapest of products is more likely to survive – the receivership of Woolworths just after the recession hit proves that it is not enough simply to be 'thrift store'. Rather, it is certain characteristics of the bargain store chain which allow it, and those involved in it, to survive – it is the logic of the bargain.

What are these characteristics? First, there is the ability of those on the manufacturing side of the chain to eke out small amounts of profit from minimal resources. We see this in the collection of small pieces of waste that become crucial to a national economy, in the ownership of basic means of production that enable a small business to survive and in the sharing of containers by many small companies in order to provide cost-effective distribution. This in itself enables a reactive spontaneity – the ability to collect, make and distribute that which is in demand as trends change. Secondly, there is the ability to foster alternative local networks of solidarity which enable the sidestepping of newly introduced legalities or processes – the continued existence of 'back-alley banking' is typical here as is the sharing of small bits of production work amongst aligned companies. Thirdly, there is the ability to transport commodities on a mass scale across the globe without the inventories becoming large, or more importantly, stagnant. Stuff is not actually piled up for very long – rather it is in a constant state of flux.

Fourthly, there is the responsive nature of the stores themselves which exhibit what is known in the retail business as 'opportunistic supply chains' and an 'unstable stocking model'. This lack of supply chain planning is often spoken of as a negative attribute, but in the current recession, it is precisely what has proved the stores' resilience – instability, it seems, is better adapted than stability to surviving in a context of instability. Immediacy, spontaneity, disposability, quantity, flexibility, surface-level speed (underpinned by slower mechanisms) and instant gratification that acknowledges the flaw inherent in the obsolescence-fuelled commodity – this is the logic of the bargain.

As mentioned in the introduction, these characteristics can be defined as tactics because they operate in ways which *wilfully* play upon the existing operations of the commodity chain they find themselves part of, sometimes smoothing its progress, sometimes creating stumbling blocks, but always playing with what is available. A tactical domain is the only one available to many of those along the low-end commodity chain for whom, in their daily activities, there remains only a small amount of choice to be made and tiny windows of opportunity. Therefore, those along the chain find ways of pursuing their own interests whilst *appearing* to comply with another agenda – they wear what Michel de Certeau (1984) describes as 'the wig' (la perruque) of disguise. They exhibit a conscious will to innovate, an ability to put imagination into action and a desire to avoid pitfalls and exploit availabilities. Furthermore, as the global recession puts a long-term squeeze on profits, new practices are forced by a certain kind of desperation and these practices have become increasingly tactical.

There are, of course, discrepancies between the tactics of individuals and the movements of larger systems. This is to juxtapose the survival mechanisms of individuals and groups of individuals with those of the global commodity chain and the supranational systems through which it operates. It is to understand that the tactics of people and places are constantly interacting with societal systems – usually with a certain degree of friction. This distinction often finds form in a differentiation between tactics and strategies; between day-to-day survival and a longer-term view; between the plans of individuals and those of large-scale structures and organizations. However, these neat delineations become more problematic when applied to the low-end commodity chain. At first glance, it seems obvious to suggest that the operations of individual waste pedlars, manufacturers or consumers along the chain should be defined as tactics, whilst the ways in which these are drawn out as characteristics of the chain should be seen as strategy. However, this makes a number of false assumptions.

First, the defining criteria of a tactic ought to be the extent to which those using it have power in the context of their actions, as well as the extent to which they are acting 'together' and 'consciously'. It cannot be argued that one person's struggle for survival disenables that person from working towards a joint outcome with others; the two are not mutually exclusive. The inherent suggestion that tacticians are lacking knowledge of the bigger picture quickly becomes patronizing; the issue is rather that they understand the bigger picture but are powerless to engage in anything other than tactics. Secondly, defining the characteristics I have drawn out of the chain as strategy suggests that the entire chain acts as one organism, always in agreement with what its next move ought to be. This would be to paint over the highly specialized and localized parts of the chain, and more importantly to fail to acknowledge the way in which it is precisely the ruptures between different tactics which give the chain its character and increase its strength. While it is certainly the case that the characteristics identified enable us to understand the nature of the chain *in general*, it is not the case that these characteristics are equally as powerful as one another at all times, or in all parts of the chain; rather they are constantly changing and coming to the fore or falling back. Finally, the characteristics identified are sometimes those of less powerful localized cultures (e.g. the agglomeration of Yiwu) and sometimes those of established, embedded cultures (e.g. the expectation of immediacy from consumers). In other words, they are sometimes operations of the weak(er) within the chain and sometimes those of the strong(er). Therefore, the question of power must be considered differently in the light of each characteristic.

Regardless of the ways in which the characteristics of the bargain chain can be said to be tactical or not, there is no doubt that they have enabled an expansion in the number of bargain stores in the West. Shopping centres in North America are witnessing an influx of bargain stores, with bargain retail brands such as Dollar General, Dollar Tree, and Family Dollar opening an average of 2,000 new stores each, per year, while big name retailers find themselves in a precarious situation.[3] And while Walmart got the lowest score on the 2013 American Customer Satisfaction Index, dollar stores all scored very highly. In Europe, Poundland[4] profits rose by 81 per cent in 2010 and in 2011 increased by another 27 per cent at a time when high streets everywhere were struggling.

Consumptive thrift is the defining syndrome of the new austerity. Contrary to British Prime Minister David Cameron's[5] claims that it was about committing to the end of years of, in his view, excessive government spending, the real character of this austerity is far more moralistic on a personal level. It is about reeling in personal debt whilst continuing to spend; about working harder than ever despite an increasing proportion of earnings being required for basic housing and utilities. On the public level, it may be about not spending, but on the personal level, it is very much about continuing to earn and then spend.

The 'Arcades Project for the working classes' that this book started life as has revealed in the end that the greatest outcome of the low-end commodity chain is to enable the continuation of Western economic growth via the consumption of those who are least able to consume with impunity. The bargain store commodity chain is the great survivor of capitalism. Its low-price commodities enable participation in consumer society for all – even the underclass can be part of the economic survival of a nation. And this essentially is what this new 'age of austerity' is about – the continuation of consumptive habits despite stagnant wages, rises in the cost of living and worryingly fast erosion of public services. It is not the fault of the manufacturers, or even the bargain stores themselves, and it is certainly not the fault of those who shop in them, but it is nonetheless an unignorable manifestation of the woes of the twenty-first-century age of austerity.

Notes

Introduction

1 Georges Perec's 1978 work *Life: A Users' Manual* used the inventory most effectively as a literary technique to describe the daily lives of various characters within a Parisian block of flats. Meanwhile, his *Things: A Story of the Sixties*, shows a nuanced understanding of the (false) promises of commodities.

2 This refers to a line in Deng Xiaoping's 1978 speech in which he said that socialism should not be equated with poverty and that 'to get rich is glorious', calling it 'socialism with Chinese characteristics'. The phrase 'to get rich is glorious' has become synonymous with Deng's general ethos and specific opening-up policies.

Chapter 1

1 Baichwal's film documents the work of the photographer Ed Burtynsky whose photographs feature landscapes of areas transformed by human activity.

2 *Wenming* has been a problematic word in Chinese culture as it has had connotations of 'civilisation' being 'Western civilisation'. After 1949, its meaning shifted to denote general 'manners'/'civilised behaviour' rather than 'Western' behaviour, although its contemporary usage has perhaps regained some of the old connotations.

3 Wang Jinglian is the founder and president of Jinsheng Copper – China's largest private copper company, worth billions. In an interview with Adam Minter, he explained how he was once a pedlar, saying 'I had a bicycle and I collected steel.' (See http://www.shanghaiscrap.com/2008/03/recycling-money-and-the-peddler-king/. Accessed 11/3/2014.

4 Schumpeter's belief, as outlined in his most famous work *Capitalism, Socialism and Democracy* (1954), is that the success of capitalism will lead to a form of corporatism and a fostering of values hostile to capitalism, especially among intellectuals. His primary concern was to point out the flawed project of socialism, but fearing that socialists would not read it and therefore not realize the futility of their aims if it appeared to favour capitalism, Schumpeter wrote it in a way that appears sympathetic to socialism.

5   Special Economic Zones allow for trade between China and other countries and
        offer more free market-oriented economic policies and flexible governmental
        measures than other parts of mainland China. Namely, they offer (1) special tax
        incentives for foreign investments, (2) greater independence on international
        trade activities, (3) economic principles based on attracting foreign capital for
        construction, enabling Sino-foreign joint ventures, producing export-oriented goods
        and allowing economic activities to be primarily driven by market forces. Since
        1980, the PRC has established special economic zones in Shenzhen, Zhuhai and
        Shantou in Guangdong Province and Xiamen in Fujian Province, and designated
        the entire province of Hainan a special economic zone. In addition, fifteen free trade
        zones, thirty-two state-level economic and technological development zones and
        fifty-three new and high-tech industrial development zones have been established in
        large and medium-sized cities.

6   The key reason for this emphasis on domestic consumption is in order to maintain
        demand and therefore growth levels despite the drop in demand for exports. The
        government believes eight percent growth to be the rate necessary for the Chinese
        economy to create enough jobs to absorb the workforce and therefore to avoid
        social unrest.

7   The paradox of thrift was a key component of Keynesian economics and has been
        considered a key part of mainstream economics since the late 1940s. There are
        a few key criticisms worth taking into consideration. First, applying 'Say's Law'
        provides a way out of the paradox, that is, if demand was to slacken (through thrift
        or anything else), prices would fall and this would (re)stimulate demand. Keynesians
        answered this criticism by saying that some prices are 'sticky' and do not fall
        regardless of demand or recession. Secondly, when individuals have more savings
        held in banks, banks are able to loan more to their customers, which, in turn, lowers
        interest rates and stimulates borrowing (and in the end spending therefore). (This is,
        of course, unless the bank either decides to retain its reserves or decides to lend
        regardless of lack of reserves. It also assumes that people will keep their savings in
        their own country, rather than holding them abroad.)

8   Mandeville's book, *The Fable of The Bees: or, Private Vices, Public Benefits*, was
        published in 1714. However, the poem *The Grumbling Hive: or, Knaves turn'd
        Honest* was published in 1705.

9   The Gini coefficient was developed by Italian statistician and sociologist Corrado
        Gini and was first published in his 1912 paper Variability and Mutability. It is a
        measure of the income distribution of a nation's residents. A Gini coefficient of
        zero would express perfect equality of income, (i.e. where everyone has the same
        income); a Gini coefficient of one would express maximal inequality (i.e. where one
        person has all the income).

10 Heraclitus wrote one single book – *On Nature* – which largely consisted of aphorisms,
        including the most famous 'everything flows', 'you cannot step into the same river
        twice' and 'the fairest cosmos is a rubbish heap piled up haphazardly'. These were
        typical of his view of existence as constant flux, in constant creation and constant
        decay, and earned him a reputation as the philosopher of 'becoming' rather than
        'being'. Heraclitus renounced the binary law of Milesian philosophy which posited
        objects as either in full existence or not existing at all, and proposed a state of
        existing that could be both 'on' and 'off'.

Chapter 2

1 2005 Chinese government figures.

2 The first Yiwu copycat opened in Warsaw, Poland, 1992, having been established by the local government of Guangdong, China. It occupies an area of 200,000 metres, upon which are built four two-storey halls containing 600 firms. In 2003, a joint venture between an Austrian and a Chinese businessman saw the opening of the AsiaCenter in Budapest, which comprised of 125,000 square metres. However, the Chinese partner was unable to fulfil his promises to the booth tenants within the centre, and the Austrian partner took 100 per cent control and changed the functioning of the centre to make it more of a retail outlet than a wholesale market. In 2004, a Chinese government agency – Chinamex – created the 'Dragon Mart' centre in Dubai, which contained 4,000 booths. Agreements for a further centre to be situated at Schiphol airport area in Amsterdam were signed in 2007. Most recently, Chinese company Fanerdun Ltd proposed a copycat market in Kalmar, Sweden. The Kalmar complex was due to be opened in September 2008, but was stalled due to ongoing issues with Chinese construction workers not being paid and safety regulations not being followed. Unlike the Warsaw market, which was initiated by the Chinese government, and the Budapest and Dubai markets which are joint investments, the Kalmar is completely owned by Fanerdun Ltd – a private Chinese company which bought the land outright from the Swedish authorities.

3 Binwang market is named after the poet Luo Binwang, whose tomb is nine miles east of Yiwu County. Born in the early Tang dynasty (618–907), he is famed for writing his first masterpiece at the age of seven. 'Ode to the Goose', as it is known, is learnt by Chinese children to this day. In adulthood, Luo Binwang joined a rebellion against Empress Wu Zetian. The rebellion failed, but Binwang evaded capture, disappearing from public altogether and was believed either to be dead or to have become a Buddhist monk in an isolated location.

4 Statistics from the Yiwu official website: http://en.yiwugou.com/purchaserservice/detail/43511.html (Accessed 28/3/2014).

5 'China Price' refers to the pricing pressure placed on developing economies by Western brands and companies seeking the lowest possible product unit price. It became the hallmark of China's low-end manufacturing sector and was explored by Alexandra Harney in *The China Price: The True Cost of Chinese Competitive Advantage*, 2008.

6 The *Cutty Sark* was a British clipper, built on the river Clyde in 1869 for the Jock Willis shipping line and one of the last clippers to ever be built. Today, the *Cutty Sark* can be visited on dry land in Greenwich, London.

7 *Thermopylae* was built in 1868 and designed especially for the tea trade. In 1872, *Thermopylae* raced the *Cutty Sark* from Shanghai back to London, winning by seven days after the *Cutty Sark* lost her rudder.

8 *The Flying Cloud* set the world's sailing record in 1854 for the fastest passage between New York and San Francisco – eighty-nine days eight hours. This record was not broken until 1989.

9 The opium wars saw Britain battle China from 1839 to 1842, and again from 1856 to 1860 as the Chinese authorities desperately tried to stop the British smuggling in

opium, in exchange for tea. It was in order to limit this trade to specific areas that China relinquished Hong Kong as a trading to Britain in 1841. By this time 90 percent of all Chinese men under the age of 40 in the coastal areas were addicted.

10   Arvatov was an art historian who saw the potential for objects made in socialist conditions to constitute a fundamentally changed relationship between object and subject in which possession would become an irrelevant concept. For Arvatov, this changed relationship would be nothing less than a complete psychological upheaval in how one interacts with and perceives the object. Whereas in capitalism, there is, according to Arvatov, a deep rupture between things and people due to the way in which people lack a sense of respect or responsibility for them and therefore fetishism of the object rules, under socialism, people feel more connected to them, and a new kind of rapprochement between subject and object replaces the fetishized relationship (See Arvatov 1977 and Kiaer 1997).

11   Technically neo-Confucianism began in the Tang dynasty (772–841) when Han Yu and Li Ao strove to empty it of its more mystical elements that had come from Buddhism and Daosim and place emphasis on the creation of rules for an ethical life. It became prominent during the Song and Ming dynasties.

12   According to Li Zhang (2001: 67–8), Zhejiangcun was created in stages. The first, 1980–4, saw 1,000 migrants arrive and live in local households without creating a community of their own. The second (1985–90) saw it expand rapidly due to the greater demand for clothing, new social networks and relaxed migration policies, attracting around 30,000 migrants. During this stage, and due largely to the events in Tiananmen Square in 1989 and the Asian Games in 1990, the government mobilized several 'clean-up' drives to force out migrants, but around two months after each drive, migrants would resume their former activities. The third stage, from 1990, saw the complete razing of Zhejiangcun in 1995 causing a mass exodus of around 40,000 migrants and its subsequent rebuilding as an enormous modern plaza – the realization of the authorities' plans and a 'suitable' representation of the new China.

13   Guanxi is often translated as 'relationship' or 'connection', but is best explained as a combination of 'ganqing' (depth of feeling within an interpersonal relationship) and 'renqing' (moral obligation and 'face' or social prestige). It describes personal relationships in which one is able and obliged to perform and receive favours – a long-term, obligated and heartfelt connection in which individuals have the right to demand fair return, benefits sharing and reciprocity (See Blau 1964; Homans 1958; Hwang 1987; Lin 1999; Luo 1997). It is generally accepted that the principles of guanxi come from Confucian thought. Guanxi's emphasis on interpersonal connections caused it to attract the interest of network analysts from the late 1970s onwards.

14   Celebrity businessman Jack Ma (who stars in China's version of the TV show 'The Apprentice') is the founder of the 'ali' group of companies, which includes the business-to-business website, alibaba.com. It is his belief that the future will be based on small to medium-sized enterprises (shrimps), rather than large corporations (whales), and this has informed his highly successful business models.

15   Gudeman is, of course, borrowing the terms 'embedded' and 'disembedded' here from Karl Polanyi's *The Great Transformation*. Polanyi's substantivism embraced a cultural approach to economics, which emphasized the way in which economies are embedded in society and culture.

16 The mass line (from the Chinese *qunzhong luxian*) is the political, organizational and leadership method developed by Mao and the CCP. It describes a method of leadership that seeks to learn from the peasants via a process which seeks to investigate the conditions of the people, learn about and participate in their struggles, gather ideas from them and create a plan of action on the basis of these ideas and concerns of the people. Because what was 'allowable' had, therefore (arguably), come from the people, the mass line was used as a form of 'law', that is, people had to stick to the rules of the mass line.

17 Deng made the political rhetoric of Mao less grandiose and was concerned with functionality and achievable goals. *In theory*, Deng-ism does not reject Marxism or Mao Tse-deng thought, but seeks to adapt them to the existing socio-economic conditions. One of his famous maxims, that well illustrates his pragmatism, was 'It doesn't matter whether a cat is black or white as long as it catches mice.'

18 See Wang Yanzhong's argument that Mao Tse-deng fever reflects a popular longing for the charismatic leader in an age of growing industrialization (In Zhanbing and Yifu, *Zhongguo: Mao Zedong.* Taiyuan: Beiyue Wenyi, 1991: 275–6 and 280–1).

19 Lotta is a Marxist writer, closely affiliated to Bob Avakian, the chairman of the Revolutionary Communist Party, USA. He has conducted extensive work in regard to the socialist revolutions of the twentieth century and what he describes as the restoration of capitalism in the former Soviet Union and China. Lotta has attempted to uncover Mao Zedong's actual thinking in guiding the Cultural Revolution, tackling what he sees as distortions of Mao's real views, in *And Mao Makes 5*(1978), a major collection of primary source documents and speeches from forces associated with Mao. His views on the extent to which capitalism has won out in China are most recently and best witnessed in his article, 'China's Rise in the World Economy', in *Economic and Political Weekly*, 21 February 2009.

20 The use of the word 'suzerain' is interesting in the context of Chinese communism, as previously in China's history it has been used to describe the relationship between the Emperor of China and all other world rulers. Chinese political theory recognized only one emperor and asserted that his authority was paramount throughout the entire world. This system broke down during the seventeenth century when the ethnically Manchu Qing dynasty justified its rule through theories different from traditional Han Chinese theories of the emperor as universal ruler. The system also broke down as China faced European powers whose theories of sovereignty were based on international law and relations between equal states.

Chapter 3

1 Cheung Kong (Holdings) Limited was founded in the 1950s as a plastics manufacturer and has become one of Hong Kong's leading multinational conglomerates. It is one of the largest developers of residential, office, retail, industrial and hotel properties in Hong Kong and has built many of Hong Kong's most notable landmark buildings and complexes.

2 The use of the word 'whizzy' in relation to capitalism can be attributed to John Hutnyk's work over a number of years, but most recently as mentioned in his 2004 book – *Bad Marxism.*

3 Dennis Burman was a dock worker who fell 115 feet from a crane on 17 June 2003 and died shortly afterwards in Ipswich hospital, aged fifty-one. He had only been working at the port for a few weeks and was undergoing training. Hutchinson Whampoa who operate Felixstowe port were fined £250,000 for breaching safety rules and failing to ensure that workers were not exposed to risks. His death is marked every year with a memorial service by Felixstowe dock workers.

4 Filippo Tommaso Marinetti announced the *Futurist Manifesto* in 1909, two years before Taylor's *Scientific Management*. The movement was very varied and often internally ruptured due to the differing takes on its aims by its various proponents. Most remembered, however, is Marinetti's proto-fascist prose which proclaimed the glorification of war and the fight against moralism, feminism and 'intellectualism' (in the form of libraries, museums, etc.) Surrealism in many ways was the exact opposite to Futurism. Lefebvre was immediately against the blind rationalism of the latter, and in time, deeply sceptical about the existentialism of the former.

5 In fact, Virilio applies this logic to China (way ahead of his time it must be said), arguing that 'it is enough to hear the speeches of today's Chinese leaders about "consumer goods" to know that the old thinker [Mao] did no more than delay the institution in China of the West's fearsome system of intensive growth' (Virilio 1977: 67).

6 The film *On The Waterfront* was based on the real-life story of Thomas Collentine, a hiring boss on North River Pier 92 at the New York docks. He worked for the John W. McGrath Stevedoring Company and was in charge of handing out work to a lucky few amongst the many who collected there. The writer Malcolm Johnson was later to win a Pulitzer prize for his dramatic series on the murder, which ran in the *New York Sun* in 1948, and which exposed the tangled web of organized crime and corruption in which Collentine worked.

7 The conceptual development of Lefebvre's rhythmanalysis is broadly as follows: A future project of rhythm analysis is first mentioned by Lefebvre in volume two of *Critique of Everyday Life* (1961). Then comes *The Production of Space* (1974), at the end of which Lefebvre notes that an analysis of rhythms would complete that of the production of space. The final volume of *Critique of Everyday Life* (1981) follows up on the promise of volume two and provides the beginnings of rhythmanalysis. Two short essays co-authored with his last wife Catherine Regulier follow this – 'The Rhythmanalytical Project' and 'Attempt at the Rhythmanalysis of Mediterranean Cities'. Then comes his book, *Elements of Rhythmanalysis*, which he considered to be the fourth volume of *Critique of Everyday Life* in many ways. It is these last three works together which now make-up the 'book' we call 'Rhythmanalysis' (1992).

8 Flamming in music is when two beats are so slightly out of sync that they create a kind of double beat which interrupts the rhythm and is experienced as unbearable to listen to. A DJ who has badly beat-matched will inevitably create a 'flam'.

9 Lefebvre seems to have connected his dislike for Bergson with that for the surrealists. Despite initially engaging with the surrealists, Lefebvre was to offer a vicious critique of their activities and philosophy as early as volume one of *Critique of Everyday Life*, describing the surrealist project as a 'game for aesthetes' and their idea of the 'modern marvellous' as 'a bit of metaphysics and a few myths in the last stages of decay … some psychoanalysis, some Bergson-izing … an eclecticism, an impenetrable doctrinal confusion, together with a remorseless Parisianism' (Lefebvre 1947: 119).

10 Lefebvre, in writing the theory of moments in volume two of *Critique of Everyday Life*, returned to the notion of the vecu (lived) which had impressed him so many years earlier. (See *La Pensée et l'Esprit*, 1926.)

11 This idea of lived-in space was to provide the inspiration for Yi Fu Tuan's appreciation of space and place (Tuan 2005). For him, the identity of a place only becomes vividly real through the dramatizing of aspirations, needs and functional rhythms of personal and group life (Tuan 2005: 178).

12 Benjamin's thinking stems famously from Klee's painting of the Angelus Novus which Benjamin sees as depicting the Angel of History, looking back to the past and seeing a growing pile of rubble. The Angel wants to mend what is broken, but cannot due to a 'storm' blowing in – the storm of progress.

13 In this sense, the expression remains far truer to his Marxist-Communist credentials and the idea of the potential for revolution than the English translation would have us believe. It reminds us that through Lefebvre's sometimes ponderous speculations, there remains a more revolutionary bent, and that whilst critiques of his inability to actually describe a plan for revolution are perhaps valid, his oeuvre has tended to be misjudged as a cynical commentary on commodity culture rather than an inspiration for action. For example, the Situationists described Lefebvre's relations with the New Left as 'Argumentist dung' (quoted in Michel Trebitsch's introduction to Volume 2 of *Critique of Everyday Life*), complaining that he gave no plan for a revolution himself, yet accused the Situationists of being little more than a youth movement.

Chapter 4

1 Georges-Eugene Haussmann was the Prefect of the Seine Department and was commissioned by Emperor Napoleon 111 to carry out a vast public works programme to renovate Paris between 1853 and 1870. It included the demolition of crowded and unhealthy medieval neighbourhoods (including the old shopping arcades Benjamin wrote of), the building of wide avenues, parks and squares, the annexation of the suburbs surrounding Paris, and the construction of new sewers, fountains and aqueducts. Haussmann's work met with fierce opposition and he was finally dismissed by Napoleon III in 1870, but work on his projects continued until 1927.

2 'Stocky' is a retail expression meaning full of stock, or leaving little room for artistic arrangement and display.

3 The concept of 'savoir vivre' was first developed by Stiegler in the three volumes of his *Mécréance et Discrédit* (Stiegler 2004, 2006). These volumes outlined the way in which the industrial organization of production and then consumption has had destructive consequences for the modes of life of human beings, in particular, the way in which the loss of *savoir faire* and *savoir vivre* (i.e. the loss of the knowledge of how to do and how to live) has resulted in what Stiegler calls 'generalised proletarianisation'.

4 What Stiegler posits as a replacement to this is a world in which rather than there being consumers on one side and producers on the other, there are simply 'contributors' who '*participate* in the creation of the world in which they live' – a world which could be described as 'open source' (Stiegler 2010: 162).

5   The concept of 'false needs' was at around this time picked up on by members
     of The Frankfurt School as indicative of the operations of the Culture Industries.
     However, it was, initially at least, used in reference to Herbert Marcuse's original
     differentiation of types of needs in *Eros and Civilization*. This was in itself, of course,
     a synopsis of Freud and Marx, and Marcuse's differentiation can be interpreted as
     largely springing from Marx's statements regarding the needs of the stomach vis-à-
     vis those of the imagination.

6   www.halesowennews.co.uk/news/4635382.Police_to_help_control_crowds_
     as_99p_store_opens/ (Accessed Nov. 2010).

7   Mavern is an old Yiddish word meaning 'collector of knowledge'.

8   Friedman asserts this argument in *Capitalism and Freedom* (1962), in which he
     discusses the role of economic capitalism in liberal society, saying that economic
     freedom is a precondition for political freedom.

9   Lefebvre defines mystification as a generalized social lie, expanding across the
     whole of society and finding new 'masks' as it unfolds (Lefebvre 1999: 78). The
     process is one of the real being substituted by an abstract representation and that
     representation then inverting the real and turning upside down ('bouleverse') the
     possible (Lefebvre 1999: 22). It is, therefore, that moment of the social conscience
     where its form hides its ancient contents; when it itself becomes a liar; when people
     begin perpetuating lies on behalf of the original lie (Lefebvre 1999:79). For Lefebvre,
     this meant that neither the private conscience nor the collective conscience
     could properly criticize the truth, as the conscience in all its forms is manipulated.
     Importantly, these ideologies are led by people who are not aware that they are
     lying; who do not intend necessarily to be part of mystification – the best liars are
     those who do not know they are lying (Lefebvre 1999: 132). Furthermore, their real
     destructive and totalizing nature lies in the fact that they do not simply mystify the
     present but give an image for the future, in doing so, disallowing alternative images
     and proving themselves to be 'doubly mystifying' (Lefebvre 1999: 120). Lefebvre's
     concept of mystification was born from his witnessing of the rise of Fascism and the
     events leading up to the Second World War; it was only later in his career that he
     began to employ it to describe the onset of consumer culture and its impact.

10   The thrust of the theory is that sustainable development can be created via proven
     methodologies of social and economic governance which minimize the potential for
     conflict amongst different groups in society whilst contemporaneously improving
     economic and cultural wealth.

11   According to Walton, the origins of the seaside town lay in the 'spa' but shared a
     belief system with much of Catholic Europe that saw the sea as having prophylactic
     powers at the August spring tides. The sea-bathing tradition began in the north
     of England in Whitby and Scarborough but even by the 1810s had extended to
     areas of south-east England closer to London, such as Margate, Weymouth and
     Brighton – where George IV created the archetypal resort on the basis of frivolity
     and hedonism (Walton 1983: 16).

12   Lefebvre, *Critique of Everyday Life,* volume 3 (London: Verso 2008 [1981]), 133.

13   A good example of this alternative reading is the work of British artist of African
     descent, Yinka Shonibare, who has reasserted the colonial nature of the ship-in-a-
     bottle by making a 1.30-metre replica ship-in-a-bottle of Nelson's HMS Victory. First
     displayed on the fourth plinth in Trafalgar Square (which in 1999 became a space

for a rotating display of contemporary art), the ship now sits permanently outside the Greenwich Maritime Museum in London. Shonibare, who was born of Nigerian parents, describes the inspiration for his work as his awareness of the part the colonial process (including the HMS Victory itself) played in the formation of his own identity. The sails of Shonibare's ship are made from Dutch wax fabric that in past eras was sold to West Africa as part of colonial trading. So, despite being associated with African dress and identity (at one time being worn by African nationalists as a sign of solidarity), the cloth has actually accrued many complex and often ambivalent associations, in addition – those of colonialism, industrialization, emigration, cultural appropriation and the invention (and reinvention) of tradition. See interview with Yinka Shonibare written up in *The Telegraph* newspaper: http://www.telegraph.co.uk/culture/art/art-features/7739981/ Fourth-Plinth-Yinka-Shonibare-interview.html

14 This lack of copies is unusual in the light of China's long tradition of shanzhai culture. Shanzhai is the art of copying or adding original twists to an existing style. It can be traced back to the Canton export art painters of the eighteenth to nineteenth centuries, such as Lam Qua, who became extremely skilled in George Chinnery's painting style. The Dafen Oil Painting Village in Shenzhen is a current-day version of this – essentially an area full of painting factories, in which each painter specializes in one aspect such as bodies, clothing, trees, etc. It can be seen in creative reappropriations such as China's 'Dolce and Banana' T-Shirts, or in the recreation tourist villages of Tianducheng near Hangzhou, and 'Thames Town' three hours from Shanghai, that re-create Paris and English village, respectively, complete with Eiffel towers and fountains in the case of the former and quaint pubs and red phone boxes in the case of the latter. (For more on Shanzhai, see Karen Tam's chapter in Hulme (Ed.) *The Changing Landscape of China's Consumerism* (2014). Chinoiserie was in many ways a reverse shanzhai – the West copying the East and reappropriating it by creating objects 'in the Chinese taste'.

15 In his celebrated work Art and Agency (1998), Gell replaces a purely aesthetic theory of art with one that emphasizes the effects art has achieved as a 'distributed agency'. Central to this is the theory of abduction, which states that things do not necessarily happen as a result of causal inference, but rather due to inferred intentionality. His is, therefore, a theory of the people behind objects and those peoples' intentionality. Thus, the creative products of a person become his 'distributed mind', which has agency as it influences the minds of others.

16 In many ways, Morin had much in common with Lefebvre. He too began a military career, leaving it in order to join the French Communist Party. He too fought for the Resistance during the Second World War. He too experienced a difficult relationship with the French communists and was eventually expelled from the party in 1951. Morin also founded and directed the magazine *Arguments* (1954–62). Appropriately perhaps, he replaced Lefebvre at the University of Nanterre, where he became involved in the student revolts of 1968.

Conclusion

1 The 'Chinese Dream' is a phrase Xi Jinping started promoting as a slogan from 2013 onwards, leading to its widespread use in the Chinese media. Xi describes the dream as 'national rejuvenation, improvement of people's livelihoods, prosperity, construction of a better society and military strengthening'. The idea stresses the importance of the entrepreneurial spirit, glorifies a generation of self-made men and women, and celebrates those who came from rural poverty and have made money in the urban centres. Its focus is less on the emergence of a political ideology based on egalitarianism (as Mao's was) and more on a liberal individualist approach. It is sometimes thought to have been triggered by Helen Wang's 2010 book *The Chinese Dream* which was based on over 100 interviews of members of the new middle class in China.

2 Harmonious Society plays upon Confucian thought and is in large part responsible for the notion of the *xiaokang* (functionally well-off middle class). It was first proposed by the Hu Jintai-Wen Jiabao administration during the 2005 National People's Congress. Essentially, it serves to change the focus from economic growth to overall societal balance and harmony.

3 Figures from Cassidy Turley research.

4 Poundland was founded in 1990 by a father and son combination, Steve Smith and his father Keith, opening their first shop in Burton on Trent. Today, it is the biggest single-price store in Europe.

5 The term 'Age of austerity' was popularized by British Conservative leader David Cameron in his keynote speech to the Conservative party forum in Cheltenham on 26 April 2009, in which he insisted upon the necessity of decreasing government spending.

References

Agger, Ben (1989), *Fast Capitalism: A Critical Theory of Significance*. Champaign: University of Illinois Press.

Agger, Ben (2004), *Speeding Up Fast Capitalism: Cultures, Jobs, Families, Schools, Bodies*. Boulder: Paradigm Publishers.

Alneng, Victor (2007), *The Right Price: Local Bargains for Global Players* (paper presented at *Thinking through Tourism*. London: Metropolitan University, UK.

Appadurai, Arjun (1986), *The Social Life of Things: Commodities in Cultural Perspective*. Cambridge: CUP.

Arendt, Hannah (1958), *The Human Condition*. Chicago: University of Chicago Press.

Aristotle (1962), *The Politics*. London: Penguin Books.

Arrighi, Giovanni (2007), *Adam Smith in Beijing: Lineages of the Twenty-First Century*. New York: Verso.

Arvatov, Boris (1997 [1925]), 'Everyday Life and the Culture of the Thing (Towards a Formulation of the Question)'. *October* 81: 119–28.

Auge, Marc (1995), *Non-Places: Introduction to an Anthropology of Supermodernity*. London: Verso.

Bachelard, Gaston (1969), *The Poetics of Space*. Boston: Beacon Press.

Bachelard, Gaston (1983), *Water and Dreams: An Essay on the Imagination of Matter*. Dallas: Pegasus Foundation.

Bachelard, Gaston (2000 [1936]), *The Dialectic of Duration*. Manchester: Clinamen Press Ltd.

Barthes, Roland (1973 [1957]), *Mythologies*. London: Granada.

Bataille, Georges (1985), *Visions of Excess: Selected Writing 1927–1939*. Manchester: Manchester University Press.

Bataille, Georges (1991), *The Accursed Share*. New York: Zone Books.

Bataille, Georges (1997 [1934]), 'The Notion of Expenditure', in Fred Botting and Scott Wilson (eds), *The Bataille Reader*. London: Blackwell.

Baudrillard, Jean (1998), *The Consumer Society*. London: Sage.

Baudrillard, Jean (2005), *The System of Objects*. London: Verso.

Bauman, Zygmunt (2001), 'Excess: An Obituary'. *Parallax* 7(1): 85–91.

Bauman, Zygmunt (2005), *Liquid Life*. Cambridge: Polity Press.

Bauman, Zygmunt (2007a), *Liquid Modernity*. London: Polity Press, 216.

Bauman, Zygmunt (2007b), 'Collateral Casualties of Consumerism'. *Journal of Consumer Culture* 7(25): 25–57.

Benjamin, Walter (1997a), *One-way Street and Other Writings*. London: Verso.

Benjamin, Walter (1997b), *Charles Baudelaire: A Lyric Poet in the Era of High Capitalism*. London: Verso.

Benjamin, Walter (1999), *Illuminations*. London: Pimlico.

Benjamin, Walter (1999), *The Arcades Project.* Cambridge, MA: Harvard University Press.

Benjamin, Walter (2009), *Thesis on the Philosophy of History.* Charleston: CreateSpace Independent Publishing Platform.

Bennett, Jane (2001), *The Enchantment of Modern Life: Attachments, Crossings, and Ethics*. New York: Princeton University Press.

Bergson, Henri (1913), *Creative Evolution*. London: MacMillan.

Bergson, Henri (1950), *Time and Free Will.* London: George Allen and Unwin.

Bergson, Henri (1991), *Matter and Memory.* New York: Zone Books.

Berman, Marshall (1988), *All That is Solid Melts into Air*. New York: Viking Penguin.

Binkley, Sam (2000), 'Kitsch as a Repetitive System: A Problem for the Theory of Taste Hierarchy'. *Journal of Material Culture* 5: 131–52.

Blau, P. (1964), *Exchange and Power in Social Life.* New York: Whiley.

Bloch, Maurice and Parry, Jonathan (1989), *Money and the Morality of Exchange.* Cambridge: Cambridge University Press.

Bourdieu, Pierre (1984), *Distinction: A Social Critique of the Judgement of Taste.* London: Routledge and Kegan Paul.

Bowlby, Rachel (2000), *Carried Away: The Invention of Modern Shopping.* London: Faber and Faber.

Bray, David (2005), *Social Space and Governance in Urban China.* Stanford, CA: Stanford University Press.

Brown, Bill (2001), 'Thing Theory'. *Critical Inquiry* 28(1): 1–22.

Brown, Bill (2004), *Things.* Chicago: University of Chicago Press.

Bunn, James (1980), 'The Aesthetics of British Mercantilism'. *New Literary History* 11(2): 303–21.

Callon, Michel (1998), 'Introduction: The Embeddedness of Economic Markets in Economics', in M. Callon (ed.), *The Laws of the Markets*. Oxford: Blackwell, 1–57.

Callon, Michel (2007), 'An Essay on the Growing Contribution of Economic Markets to the Proliferation of the Social'. *Theory, Culture and Society* 24: 7–8, 139–63.

Campbell, Colin (1983), 'Romanticism and the Consumer Ethic: Intimations of a Weber-style Thesis'. *Sociological Analysis* 44(4): 217.

Campbell, Colin (1987), *The Romantic Ethic and the Spirit of Modern Consumerism*. Oxford: Basil Blackwell.

Cao, Jinqing (1993), 'From the danwei system to the individual subject: The market economy and human socialization'. *Probing and Contending* 5: 32–6.

Cao, Jinqing and Chen, Zhongya (1997), *Leaving the Ideal Castle: Research on China's Danwei Phenomenon.* Shenzhen: Haitian Press.

Castells, Manuel (2000), *The Rise of the Network Society.* Oxford; Malden, MA: Blackwell Publishers.

Clausewitz, Carl Von (1976), *On War*. Princeton: Princeton University Press.

Clausewitz, Carl Von (1992), *Historical and Political Writings*. Princeton: Princeton University Press.

Confucious (1993), *The Analects.* Oxford: Oxford University Press.

Cook, Ian and Harrison, Michelle (2007), 'Follow the Thing: West Indian Hot Pepper Sauce'. *Space and Culture,* 10(1): 40–63.

Crogan, Patrick (2010), 'Knowledge, care and Trans-Individuation: An interview with Bernard Stiegler'. *Cultural Politics* 6(2): 157–70.

Cudahy, Brian (2007), *Box Boats: How Container Ships Changed the World*. New York: Fordham University Press.

Davis, Mike (1992), *City of Quartz: Excavating the Future in Los Angeles*. New York: Vintage Books.

Debord, Guy (1995 [1967]), *Society of the Spectacle.* New York: Zone Books.

De Certeau, Michel (1984), *The Practice of Everyday Life.* Berkeley: University of California Press.

Dicks, Bella (2003), *Culture on Display.* Maidenhead: Open University Press.

Du Gay, Paul and The Open University. (1997), *Doing Cultural Studies: The Story of the Sony Walkman.* Milton Keynes: Open University Press.

Dutton, Michael (2005), *Policing Chinese Politics: A History.* London: Duke University Press.

Eriksen, Thomas Hylland (2001), *Tyranny of the Moment.* London: Pluto.

Fiske, John (1989), *Reading the Popular.* Boston: Unwin Hyman.

Freud, Sigmund (1976 [1900]), *The Interpretation of Dreams.* Harmondsworth: Penguin.

Friedberg, Anne (1993), *Window Shopping: Cinema and the Post-Modern*. Berkeley: University of California Press.

Friedman, Milton (1962), *Capitalism and Freedom*. Chicago: University of Chicago Press.

Friedman, Thomas, L. (2006), *The World is Flat: The Globalized World in the Twenty-First Century*. London: Penguin.

Frow, John (1997), *Time and Commodity Culture: Essays on Cultural Theory and Postmodernity.* Oxford: Clarendon Press.

Frow, John (2001), 'A Pebble, a Camera, a Man who turns into a Telegraph Pole'. *Critical Inquiry* 28(1): 270–85.

Frow, John (2003), 'Invidious Distinction: Waste, Difference, and Classy Stuff', in Gay Hawkins and Stephen Muecke (eds), *Culture and Waste: The Creation and Destruction of Value.* London: Rowman & Littlefield.

Game, Ann (1995), 'Time, Space, Memory, with Reference to Bachelard', in Featherstone, Lash and Robertson (eds), *Global Modernities.* London: Sage.

Garon, Sheldon (2013), *Beyond Our Means: Why America Spends While the World Saves*. New York: Princeton University Press.

Gell, Alfred (1998), *Art and Agency: An Anthropological Theory.* Oxford: Clarendon Press.

Gereffi, Gary and Korzeniewicz, Miguel (1994), *Commodity Chains and Global Capitalism.* Westport, CT: Greenwood Press.

Gleick, James (1999), *Faster: The Acceleration of Just About Everything.* London: Vintage.

Goldstein, Joshua (2006), 'The Remains of the Everyday: One Hundred Years of Recycling in Beijing', in Madeleine Dong and Joshua Goldstein (eds), *Everyday Modernity in China.* Seattle; London: University of Washington Press.

Gottdiener, Mark (1985), *Social Production of Urban Space.* Texas: University of Texas Press.

Graeber, David (2001), *Toward an Anthropological Theory of Value.* New York: Palgrave.

Granovetter, Mark (1973), 'The Strength of Weak Ties'. *American Journal of Sociology* 78(6): 1360–80.

Grass, Gunter (1989), *Show Your Tongue.* San Diego, CA: Harcourt Brace Javonovich.

Grossberg, Lawrence Nelson, Carey and Treichler, Paula, (1992), 'Cultural Studies: An Introduction', *Cultural Studies Reader*, New York: Routledge.

Gudeman, Stephen (2001), *The Anthropology of Economy.* Malden, MA: Blackwell, 219.

Hall, Stuart (1996), *Critical Dialogues in Cultural Studies*. London; New York: Routledge.

Harvey, David (1973), *Social Justice and the City.* London: Edward Arnold.

Harvey, David (1989), *The Urban Experience.* Baltimore: John Hopkins University Press.

Harvey, David (1990), *The Condition of Postmodernity: An Enquiry into the Origins of Cultural Change.* Oxford: Basil Blackwell.

Harvey, David (1992), 'Afterword', in Henri Lefebvre (ed.), *The Production of Space.* Oxford: Basil Blackwell.

Harvey, David (1999), *The Limits to Capital.* London: Verso.

Hawkins, Gay and Muecke, Stephen (2003), *Culture and Waste: The Creation and Destruction of Value.* Oxford: Rowman and Littlefield.

Heidegger, Martin (1962), *Being and Time.* Oxford: Blackwell.

Heidegger, Martin (1967), *What is a Thing?* Indianapolis: Regnery/Gateway.

Heidegger, Martin (1977), *The Question Concerning Technology and Other Essays.* New York, London: Harper and Row.

Hess, Remi (1988), *L'Aventure du Siecle.* Paris: Editions A. M. Metailie.

Highmore, Ben (2002), *Everyday Life and Cultural Theory.* London: Routledge.

Hirschman, Albert (1977), *The Passions and the Interests: Political Arguments for Capitalism Before its Triumph.* Princeton; Guildford: Princeton University Press.

Hobsbawm, Eric (1995), *The Age of Extremes.* London: Abacus.

Hohn, Donovan (2011), *Moby-Duck: The True Story of 28,800 Bath Toys Lost at Sea.* New York: Viking.

Homans, George Casper (1958), 'Social behavior as exchange', in *American Journal of Sociology* 63(6): 597–606.

Hopfl, Heather (1997), 'The Melancholy of the Black Widow', in Kevin Hetherington and Rolland Munro (eds), *Ideas of Difference.* Cambridge, MA: Blackwell.

Huang, Yasheng (2008), *Capitalism with Chinese Characteristics.* Cambridge, MA: CUP.

Hulme, Alison (2014), *The Changing Landscape of China's Consumerism.* Oxford: Chandos/Elsevier.

Hutnyk, John (2004), *Bad Marxism: Capitalism and Cultural Studies.* London: Pluto Press.

Hwang, Kwang-kuo (1987), 'Face and Favor: The Chinese Power Game'. *American Journal of Sociology* 92: 944–74.

Hylland Eriksen, Thomas (2001), *Tyranny of the Moment.* London: Pluto Press.

Kern, Stephen (2003), *The Culture of Time and Space 1800–1918.* Cambridge, MA: Harvard University Press.

Keynes, John Maynard (1964 [reprint of 1936 edition]), *The General Theory of Employment, Interest and Money.* London: Macmillan & Co. Ltd.

Kiaer, Christine (1997), 'Boris Arvatov's Socialist Objects', *October* 81: 105–18.

Knowles, Caroline (2009), *Hong Kong: Migrant Lives, Landscapes, and Journeys.* Chicago, London: University of Chicago Press.

Kopytoff, Igor (1986), 'The Cultural Biography of Things: Commoditization as Process', in Arjun Appadurai (ed.), *The Social Life of Things: Commodities in a Cultural Perspective.* Cambridge: CUP.

Laporte, Dominique (1993), *The History of Shit.* Cambridge, Mass and London: MIT Press.

Lasch, Christopher (1979), *The Culture of Narcissism: American Life in an Age of Diminishing Expectations.* New York: Norton.

Lefebvre, Henri (1947), *Critique de la Vie Quotidienne: Introduction.* Paris: L'Arche Editeur (in French).

Lefebvre, Henri (1961), *Critique de la Vie Quotidienne: Fondements d'une Sociologie de la Quotidiennete.* Paris: L'Arche Editeur (in French).

Lefebvre, Henri (1971), *Everyday Life and the Modern World.* London: Continuum.

Lefebvre, Henri (1972), *The Sociology of Marx.* London: Harmondsworth/Penguin.

Lefebvre, Henri (1976), *The Survival of Capitalism.* London: Allison and Busby Limited.

Lefebvre, Henri (1981), *Critique de la Vie Quotidienne: De Modernite a Modernisme.* Paris: L'Arche Editeur (in French).

Lefebvre, Henri (1988), 'Towards a Leftist Cultural Politics: Remarks Occasioned by the Centenary of Marx's Death', in Cary Nelson and Lawrence Grossberg (eds), *Marxism and the Interpretation of Culture.* London: MacMillan.

Lefebvre, Henri (1989), *La Somme et le Reste.* Paris: Meridiens Klincksieck.

Lefebvre, Henri (1991), *The Production of Space.* Oxford: Blackwell.

Lefebvre, Henri (1992), *Rhythmanalysis.* London: Continuum.

Lefebvre, Henri (1995), *An Introduction to Modernity: Twelve Preludes.* New York: Verso.

Lefebvre, Henri (1999 [1936]), *La Conscience Mystifiée.* Paris: Editions Syllepse.

Lefebvre, Henri (2008 [1947, 1961, 1981]), *Critique of Everyday Life, volumes 1, 2 and 3.* London: Verso (in English).

Lefebvre, Henri (2009 [1989]), *La Somme et le Reste.* Bélibaste, 4° éd. Paris, Anthropos.

Levinson, Mark (2006), *The Box: How the Shipping Container made the World Smaller and the World Economy Bigger.* New York: Princeton University Press.

Levi-Strauss, Claude (1966), *The Savage Mind.* London: Weidenfeld and Nicolson.

Lin, Nan (1999), 'Social Networks and Status Attainment', in *Annual Review of Sociology* 25: 467–87.

Lipovetsky, Gilles (2005), *Hypermodern Times.* London: Polity Press.

Lotta, Raymond (ed.) (1978), *And Mao Makes Five*. Chicago: Banner Press.

Lotta, Raymond (21 February 2009), 'China's Rise in the World Economy'. *Economic and Political Weekly* 44(08). http://www.epw.in/perspectives/chinas-rise-world-economy.html.

Luo, Y (1997), 'Guanxi: principles, philosophies, and implications'. *Human Systems Management* 16(1): 43.

Mandeville, Bernard (1997), *The Fable of the Bees.* London: Hackett.

Marcus, George (1995), 'Ethnography in/of the World System: The emergence of multi-sited Ethnography'. *Annual Review of Anthropology* 24: 95–117.

Marcuse, Herbert (1964), *One Dimensional Man: Studies in the Ideology of Advanced Industrial Society*. London: Routledge & Kegan Paul.

Marinetti, Filippo Tommasso (1973 [1909]), 'The Founding and Manifesto of Futurism', in Umbro Apollonio (ed.), *Futurist Manifestos*. London: Thames and Hudson.

Marx, Karl (1973), *La Grundisse.* London: Penguin.

Marx, Karl (1974 [1867]), *Capital* (vols. 1, 2 and 3). London: Lawrence and Wishart.

Marx, Karl (1988), *The Economic and Philosophical Manuscripts of 1844.* London: Prometheus.

Marx, Karl (1998), *The German ideology: Including Theses on Feuerbach and Introduction to The Critique of Political Economy.* Amherst, NY: Prometheus Books.

Marx, Karl and Engels, Fredrich (1969), 'Manifesto of the Communist Party', in Lewis S Feuer (ed.), *Marx and Engels: Basic Writings on Politics and Philosophy*. London: Fontana.

Mauss, Marcel (1990 [1950]), *The Gift: The Form and Reason for Exchange in Archaic Societies.* London: Routledge.

Miller, Daniel (1987), *Material Culture and Mass Consumption*. Oxford: Basil Blackwell.

Miller, Daniel (1995), *Acknowledging Consumption.* London: Routledge.

Miller, Daniel (1997), 'Consumption and its Consequences', in Hugh Mackay (ed.), *Consumption and Everyday Life.* London: Sage.

Miller, Daniel (1998a), *Material Cultures: Why Some Things Matter.* Chicago: University of Chicago Press.

Miller, Daniel (1998b), *A Theory of Shopping.* Oxford: Polity.

Miller, Daniel (2006), 'Consumption', in Christopher Tilley Webb Keane, Susanne Kuechler, Mike Rowlands and Patricia Spyer (eds), *Handbook of Material Culture.* London: Sage.

Miller, Daniel (2008), *The Comfort of Things.* Cambridge: Polity.

Mintz, Sidney Wilfred (1986), *Sweetness and Power: The Place of Sugar in Modern History.* New York: Harmondsworth/Penguin.

Montesquieu (2002), *The Spirit of the Laws.* London: Prometheus Books.

Morin, Edgar (2001), *La Méthode* (Volume 5). Paris: Broche.

Mukhopadhyay, Bhaskar (2010), 'Taking Callon to Calcutta: Did Economist-Administrators make Markets in the Colony?' (working paper)

Nacey, Susan (2015), 'Blurring fiction with reality: American television and consumerism in the 1950s', in Alison Hulme (ed.), Consumerism on TV. Farnham: Ashgate [forthcoming mid-2015].

Olalquiaga, Celeste (2002), *The Artificial Kingdom: on the Kitsch Experience.* Minneapolis: University of Minnesota Press.

Packard, Vance (1960), *The Waste Makers.* London: Penguin.

Perec, George (1999), *Things: A Story of the Sixties.* London: Harvill.

Perec, George (2003 [1978]), *Life: A Users' Manual.* London: Vintage.

Peterson, Richard (1992), 'Understanding Audience Segmentation: from Elite and Mass to Omnivore and Univore'. *Poetics* 21: 243–58.

Podgorecki, Adam (1986), *Law and Society.* London: Routledge and Kegan Paul.

Polanyi, Karl (2001), *The Great Transformation: The Political and Economic Origins of Our Time.* Boston, MA: Beacon Press.

Prentice, Rebecca (2008), 'Looping the Value Chain: Designer Copies in a Brand-Name Garment Factory'. *Research in Economic Anthropology* 28: 97–121.

Rivoli, Pietra (2006), *The Travels of a T-Shirt in the Global Economy: An Economist Examines the Markets, Power, and Politics of World Trade.* London: John Wiley and Sons.

Robertson, Roland (1992), *Globalization: Social Theory and Global Culture.* London: Sage.

Sahlins, Marshall (1976), *Culture and Practical Reason.* Chicago: University of Chicago Press.

Scanlon, John (2005), *On Garbage.* London: Reaktion Books Ltd.

Scott, James (1985), *Weapons of the Weak.* New Haven; London: Yale University Press.

Schumpeter, Joseph A. (1954), *Capitalism, Socialism and Democracy.* London: Allen & Unwin.

Shields, Rob (1999), *Lefebvre, Love and Struggle.* London: Routledge.

Simmel, Georg (1991), 'The Berlin Trade Exhibition'. *Theory, Culture and Society* 8(3): 119–23.

Simmel, Georg (2004), *The Philosophy of Money.* London, New York: Routledge.

Smiles, Samuel (1875), *Thrift.* London: John Murray.

Smith, Adam (1991 [1776]), *The Wealth of Nations.* London: Everyman's Library.

Smith, Neil (2008), *Uneven Development: Nature, Capital, and the Production of Space.* Athens: University of Georgia Press.

Soja, E. W. (1989), *Postmodern Geographies: The Reassertion of Space in Critical Social Theory.* London: Verso.

Stallybrass, Peter (1998), 'Marx's Coat', in Spyger, Patricia (ed.), *Border Fetishisms: Material Objects in Unstable Places.* London: Routledge.

Stewart, Susan (1993), *On Longing: Narratives of the Miniature, the Gigantic, the Souvenir, the Collection.* Durham and London: Duke University Press.

Stiegler, Bernard (2004), *Mécréance et Discrédit: Tome 1, La décadence des démocraties industrielles*. Paris: Editions Galilée.

Stiegler, Bernard (2006), *Mécréance et Discrédit: Tome 2, Les sociétés incontrolables d'individus désaffectés*. Paris: Editions Galilée.

Stiegler, Bernard (2006), *Mécréance et Discrédit: Tome 3, L'esprit perdu du capitalisme*. Paris: Editions Galilée.

Strathern, Marilyn (1999), *Property, Substance, and Effect: Anthropological Essays on Persons and Things*. New Brunswick, NJ: Athlone Press, 224.

Tang, Xiaobing (2002), 'The Anxiety of Everyday life in Post-Revolutionary China', in Ben Highmore (ed.), *The Everyday Life Reader*. London/New York: Routledge.

Thomas, Nick (1991), *Entangled Objects: Exchange, Material Culture and Colonialism in the Pacific*. Cambridge, MA: Harvard University Press.

Thompson, M. (1979), *Rubbish Theory: The Creation and Destruction of Value*. Oxford: OUP.

Tomlinson, John (2007), *The Culture of Speed: The Coming of Immediacy*. London: Sage.

Trentmann, Frank (2009), 'Crossing Divides: Consumption and globalization in history'. *Journal of Consumer Culture* 9(2): 187–220.

Tsai, Kellee S. (2002), *Back-Alley Banking: Private Entrepreneurs in China*. London: Cornell.

Tuan, Yi-Fu (2005), *Space and Place*. Minneapolis: University of Minnesota.

Urry, John (2000), *Sociology Beyond Societies: Mobilities for the Twenty-First Century*. London: Routledge.

Urry, John (2003), *Global Complexity*. Cambridge: Polity Press/Blackwell.

Veblen, Thorstein (1994 [1899]), *The Theory of the Leisure Class*. New York: Penguin.

Virilio, Paul (1977), *Speed and Politics*. New York: Semiotext(e).

Wallerstein, Immanuel (1974), *The Modern World-System: Capitalist Agriculture and the Origins of the European World-economy in the Sixteenth Century*. London: Academic Press.

Wallerstein, Immanuel (1993), *The World System: Five Hundred Years or Five Thousand?* London: Routledge.

Walton, John (1983), *The English Seaside Resort: A Social History 1750–1914*. Leicester: Leicester University Press.

Wang, Hui (2009), *The End of the Revolution*. London: Verso.

Xiang, Biao (2005), *Transcending Boundaries: Zhejiangcun: The Story of a Migrant Village in Beijing*. Leiden: Brill, 225.

Zhang, Li (2001), *Strangers in the City: Reconfigurations of Space, Power, and Social Networks within China's Floating Population*. Stanford, CA: Stanford University Press.

Zhang Zhanbing and Song Yifu (1991), *Zhongguo: Mao Zedong*. Taiyuan: Beiyue Wenyi.

Žižek, Slavoj (2002), *Did Somebody Say Totalitarianism: Five Interventions in the (Mis)use of a Notion*. London: Verso.

Web sources

China Economic Net, http://en.ce.cn/Business/Macro-economic/200410/19/t20041019_2023881.shtml (Accessed 16/6/2014).

www.time.com/time/asia/magazine/2000/0228/cover.ma.html (Accessed 1/8/2014)
    'Crazy man Jack Ma goes for the Shrimps not the Whales'

Visual sources

Baichwal, Jennifer (2007), *Manufactured Landscapes* (FILM).

INDEX